MW00452831

THE FIRST MAYA CIVILIZATION

The First Maya Civilization illustrates the latest archaeological finds that force a revision of old theories on the beginnings of Maya civilization. As we know today, the Lowland Maya developed and sustained state societies centuries prior to the Classic period. The period archaeologists refer to as the Preclassic (2000 BC–AD 200) represents the first of a series of complete cycles of Maya civilization. Thanks to new data, the massive Preclassic temple pyramids of El Mirador are no longer seen as an unprecedented phenomenon but as the outcome of a gradual process begun several centuries earlier by Lowland farmers.

Francisco Estrada-Belli focuses largely on two newly discovered early cities in the eastern part of the Petén, Cival and Holmul, the location of spectacular and early finds by the author, as well as recent discoveries by other Mayanists at San Bartolo, Nakbe, El Mirador and Tikal. Spectacular finds that have forced a revision of old theories include writing, monumental art and architecture, as well as dense settlements, some of which are among the earliest in the New World. The ceremonial center of Cival, among the oldest recorded to date, was founded circa 900 BC. By 500 BC the Lowland Maya had developed a sophisticated civilization. It reached its peak around AD 100, after which time it underwent a political reorganization, and some centers were abandoned.

In the periods that followed, the Classic and Postclassic periods, Lowland Maya kings steadily maintained the tradition of ritual, art and architecture as well as trade and warfare established by their Preclassic ancestors. The art, ritual and power institutions created by the Preclassic Maya comprise one of the richest and most long-lived legacies of the Americas' ancient civilizations.

Francisco Estrada-Belli is Visiting Assistant Professor at Boston University. He specializes in Mesoamerican archaeology, the emergence of Maya civilization, and GIS and remote sensing. His publications include *The Archaeology of Southeastern Pacific Coastal Guatemala: A regional GIS approach* (1999).

THE FIRST MAYA CIVILIZATION

Ritual and Power before the Classic Period

Francisco Estrada-Belli

Routledge
Taylor & Francis Group

LONDON AND NEW YORK

First published 2011
by Routledge
2 Park Square, Milton Park, Abingdon, Oxon OX14 4RN

Simultaneously published in the USA and Canada
by Routledge
270 Madison Ave, New York, NY 10016

Routledge is an imprint of the Taylor & Francis Group, an informa business

© 2011 Francisco Estrada-Belli

The right of Francisco Estrada-Belli to be identified as author
of this work has been asserted by him in accordance with sections
77 and 78 of the Copyright, Designs and Patents Act 1988.

Typeset in Garamond by Keystroke, Station Road, Codsall, Wolverhampton
Printed and bound in Great Britain by
TJ International Ltd, Padstow, Cornwall

British Library Cataloguing in Publication Data
A catalogue record for this book is available from the British Library

Library of Congress Cataloguing in Publication Data
Estrada-Belli, Francisco.
The first Maya civilization : ritual and power before the classic period /
Francisco Estrada-Belli.
p. cm.
Includes bibliographical references.
1. Mayas–Guatemala–Petén (Dept.)–Antiquities. 2. Excavations (Archaeology)–
Guatemala–Petén (Dept.) 3. Maya architecture–Guatemala–Petén (Dept.)
4. Petén (Guatemala : Dept.)–Antiquities. I. Title.
F1435.1.P47E77 2010
972.81'2–dc22
2010019911

ISBN 13: 978–0–415–42993–1 (hbk)
ISBN 13: 978–0–415–42994–8 (pbk)
ISBN 13: 978–0–203–83913–3 (ebk)

FOR NIÑA

CONTENTS

FIGURES

PREFACE

My fascination with the Maya began at age seven. It was during my second trip to visit family in Guatemala that, luckily for me, my parents decided take me on a one-day excursion to Tikal. This was in 1970. The Pennsylvania Museum project had just ended. There was no road to Tikal and the daily flight into Tikal was on what must have been a Second World War surplus airplane. The landing on the site's dirt airstrip was a memorable experience in and of itself. Looking out from the small airplane window as the plane almost touched the treetops, I had no idea where we were going to land. At the last minute, the white landing strip appeared below us. The experience only grew more astonishing for me from that moment on. The view of temples of the Great Plaza left the biggest impression on me. The sounds and sights of Tikal's wildlife were also something I never forgot. Because the restorations had just been finished, the pyramids were blindingly white and stood in contrast to the dark green of the tropical trees around them. During the tour, I remember asking many questions. The answers were rather disappointing. There were too many "we don't know"s. I distinctly remember that the most pressing question I and everyone else was asking was "How did the Maya build such an impressive civilization in this fearsome jungle with stone tools?"

I probably did not spend the next thirty-something years of my life constantly thinking about this question, but it was certainly in the back of my mind as I set out to become an archaeologist. I was fortunate enough to be admitted into a graduate program that was most closely focused on the early periods of Maya civilization (Boston University). By then, much progress had been made in Maya archaeology since my first visit to Tikal. But most of the new information had come from the decipherment of hieroglyphic inscriptions and therefore it dealt primarily with the lives of Classic Maya kings. It said little about the time before kings. So there was still plenty for me to contribute on the subject of how the Maya had built their civilization. The answers were obviously to be found in the obscure eras prior to the Classic period. When it came to choosing a dissertation project, I wanted to take up a site in the unexplored Peten district of Guatemala. Norman Hammond, my advisor, suggested Holmul because ever since 1911 it had been known to have some of the earliest polychrome ceramics, which in turn everyone believed were indicators of the beginning of Classic Maya culture. But after a brief and difficult one-day trip to this remote site in March 1992, I convinced myself that as a poor graduate student I could not find the resources to work there. Holmul was not a huge "lost" city, but it had some very beautiful standing architecture that surely needed consolidation. Any archaeologist working there would have to foot the bill for centuries of neglect. So I turned to the Pacific Coast of Guatemala for my dissertation, where I documented many sites, some very early but easy to work at, as the jungle had long since been removed by farming. I returned to Holmul in 2000 with a Ph.D. degree, sufficient money and friends who were experts in various specialties and willing to join the adventure in this new area.

What ensued in the next ten years of explorations at and around Holmul was a series of discoveries that would affect my thinking regarding how the Maya built their civilization and how archaeologists before me have been approaching this subject perhaps erroneously. Many of these thoughts and facts are summarized in this book. The first major discovery came in 2001, when we located Cival. This site was astonishingly beautiful in terms of its pristine and serene wetland jungle environment. It was even more beautiful than Holmul because it was, incredibly, a completely Preclassic city. Until that time, Maya cities that had not been inhabited in the Classic period were known only in the Mirador Basin. Our various findings at Cival may have sent a few ripples if not shockwaves into the archaeological community. I wondered: if Cival was as early, if not earlier, than El Mirador and Nakbe, could this area be regarded as a cradle of Maya civilization, alongside the Mirador Basin? I hoped so.

During that same year (2001) came the discovery (or relocation) of a much smaller site, La Sufricaya, a stone's throw from Holmul. From this site we learned much about the onset of the Classic period and the so-called Maya–Teotihuacan *entrada*. While significantly later than Cival, La Sufricaya had a lot of information about an important old theory about the "origins" of Maya civilization, the one that focused on the role played by the influential central Mexican state of Teotihuacan. Because of the fine-grained nature of our data (including readable texts) we were able to put the Maya–Teotihuacan connection within a historical context. Much of this history was simply not known in the 1960s when that theory was formulated (see Chapters 2 and 6).

A third significant finding of my collaborative research at Holmul came from the center of Holmul itself, within the very building that had attracted me to the site, Building B of Group II. This was a small pyramid that had produced some of the most spectacular funerary offerings ever excavated by Maya archaeologists. This material had been stored at Harvard's Peabody Museum since Raymond E. Merwin's work at the site in 1909. Deep within the core of the pyramid, in layers untouched by Harvard's excavators, we recovered a large sample of ceramics that did not fit into any of the common

Preclassic or Classic typologies we expected. They are part of a ware that was used at the beginning of the first millennium BC at only a handful of places. Until then the Lowlands were thought to have been completely deserted by humans prior to 800 BC. Instead, we were uncovering fine ceramics, in many respects finer than those of much later epochs of Maya history, from 1000 BC. Obviously, I thought, our assumptions must be wrong. Now we have come to regard these ceramics as much more than just traces of an incoming population. They reveal the very seed of Maya civilization in the Lowlands.

Finally, as I was exploring the need for and the difficulties of writing a book about the beginnings of Maya civilization, or whether I should focus on other important subjects for which I had more copious data, I visited El Mirador. This two-day visit was a turning point in my thinking about the Maya. It was in many ways an experience like my first visit to Tikal. There, I realized the true grandiosity of what the Preclassic Maya had accomplished. Everything I had seen before, even Tikal, paled in comparison. I found myself in agreement with many of Richard Hansen's claims about the site. But what was even more shocking to me was that El Mirador, although earlier than any Classic Maya city, had begun significantly later than Cival. Therefore, Cival and possibly many other sites like it had an important story to tell and I was its primary witness. I realized that not all the answers can be found at one site, no matter how great and important it may be. Moreover, even though we are far from having excavated a representative portion of El Mirador and Cival, or even found most of the Preclassic cities that are out there, the research on the Early Maya seems to have reached a critical mass that requires and sustains a redefinition of our paradigms.

With these thoughts in mind, I solidified my determination to take up the challenging subject of this book. Indeed, the field will progress tremendously in the next few years as a new wave of archaeologists and funding pour into the region. In my opinion research on the Preclassic Maya is the new frontier and cutting edge of Mesoamerican archaeology today. Ten years from now we will surely know much more about the early Maya, but it is my hope that the core ideas and data contained in this book will still be relevant and thought provoking by then.

ACKNOWLEDGEMENTS

The field research of the Holmul Archaeological Project that I summarize in this book has been possible thanks to grants and generous contributions from various institutions and private individuals to whom I am deeply grateful. The seed-grants for the first campaign were given by Peter Harrison, Boston University, FAMSI and the National Geographic Society in 2000. The 2001–2009 campaigns were funded by Vanderbilt University, the National Geographic Society, the National Science Foundation, the Ahau Foundation, FAMSI, the Reinhart Foundation, the New World Archaeological Foundation and the Alphawood Foundation. Generous donations were received from ARB-USA, Toyota Motors, Yamaha Motors, PIAA lights, Interco Tires Co., Optima Batteries, Garmin, American Racing, Traimaster, Bushwacker, Borla, Rhino Linings, Leer, Procomp Tires, Warn Industries, Holley, Flowmaster, K&N, ITP, Eureka and several private individuals, beginning with the Neivens, Estrada and Belli families. Over the years, it has been especially helpful to have the continued support of my friends Marco Gross and Inma Salcines, owners of the Rio Mopan Lodge in Peten. It was Marco who first led me to Holmul in his vintage Land Rover in 1992. Inma has kept the food coming to our camp.

I am also indebted to many dedicated officials with the Ministry of Culture and Sports and with the Directorate of Patrimonio Cultural in Guatemala who facilitated the necessary permits. Various scholars contributed their expertise in research and conservation. Magaly Koch (Boston University) helped acquire and analyzed multi-spectral and terrain data to understand the geology of the region and helped me detect sites. Gene Ware (Brigham Young University) brought his multi-spectral imaging for three consecutive seasons to document invisible pigments on mural paintings at La Sufricaya and Cival. Nikolai Grube (University of Bonn) documented the epigraphy and iconography of stelae at La Sufricaya and Cival. Alex Tokovinine (Harvard University) compiled the epigraphic texts on all portable objects from Holmul and La Sufricaya. David Wahl (US Geological Survey) contributed a paleo-environmental study of the region using data collected from lake sediments. Alberto Semeraro (Accademia di Carrara) curated the murals and carvings to ensure their survival after the trauma they had received from looters and years of exposure. Laura Kosakowsky (University of Arizona) analyzed the first season's ceramics. Michael Callaghan (University of Texas-Arlington) compiled a new complete ceramic typology of Holmul incorporating material from all existing collections. Bernard Hermes (University of San Carlos) helped us keep our ceramic analysis up to date with nearby typologies. Many young scholars made contributions by developing Ph.D. theses at and around Holmul: Michael Callaghan (Preclassic ceramic technology and exchange, Ph.D., Vanderbilt University, 2008), Alexandre Tokovinine (ritual space and performance, Ph.D., Harvard University, 2008), John Tomasic (Preclassic political economy, Ph.D., Vanderbilt University, 2009), Jason Paling (Preclassic lithic production at Hamontun, Ph.D., SUNY Albany), Heather Hurst (mural painting style and technique, Ph.D., Yale University, 2009) and Niña Neivens Estrada (Pre-Mamom ceramic production and exchange Ph.D., Tulane University). In addition, many graduate and under-graduate students from Guatemala, the US and other countries contributed their hard work every year. I owe all of them a huge debt of gratitude. Finally, hundreds of men and women from the town of Melchor have worked with me in the jungle to study and protect archaeological sites. I thank them for all their careful efforts and I hope one day these cultural resources will help them secure a more prosperous living for their children.

Among those who have shared their thoughts and helped me in creating this book over the last few years, I would like to thank Norman Hammond, Clemency Coggins, Niña Neivens Estrada, Karl Taube, Vera Kutzinsky, Pierre Colas, Nikolai Grube, E. Wyllys Andrews, George Stuart, Kathy Reese-Taylor, Stuart Miller, John Janusek and David Stuart. Finally, I would like to thank the many scholars who generously shared their data and images which I reproduce with their permission in this book: Robert Sharer, William Saturno, David Freidel, Donald Thompson, Nikolai Grube, Simon Martin, Stephen Houston, Richard Hansen, David Grove, Michael Coe, Christopher Jones, Merle Greene-Robertson, Marion Popenoe Hatch and Pat Culbert.

1

MAYA CIVILIZATION
IN PERSPECTIVE

The ancient Maya inspire awe and fascination in each of us today as they did to the first explorers more than two centuries ago, because of their cities buried in the tropical jungle and because so much about them is unknown. Two basic questions about them are: Where did they come from? And why did they disappear? The answers remain shrouded in an aura of mystery. This book explores their earliest beginnings with the hope that knowledge of how they built their civilization will also give us clues to what caused them to decline.

Contrary to common perception, we know quite a bit about the great Classic Maya civilization, thanks to over 100 years of archaeological excavations and more recent hieroglyphic decipherments. We refer to the "Classic Maya" as the people who built Tikal and many other great cities deep in the jungles of Mexico, Guatemala, Belize and Honduras during the first millennium AD. We use the term "Classic" to distinguish them from their predecessors, the Formative or Preclassic Maya of the first millennium BC, and from their successors, the Postclassic Maya who thrived until the arrival of Europeans in the 15th century.

But these ancestors are, of course, one and the same people as the present-day Maya who still inhabit the Yucatan Peninsula, and walk the streets of Guatemala City, Chichicastenango, San Cristobal de Las Casas, Merida and countless villages. The Maya are at a fundamental level a people united by one culture that underwent various transformations through time. Though now fragmented by more than 31 Maya languages[1] (Sergio Romero, personal communication, 2010), all share the worldview and agrarian way of life of their ancestors while becoming increasingly integrated in western culture.

Today, researchers no longer consider the terms Preclassic, Classic and Postclassic as stages of cultural evolution or devolution, but simply as arbitrary time divisions that are too engrained in our scholarly literature to be changed. As this book will demonstrate, far from being a primitive ancestor of the more evolved Classic period, the Preclassic period produced the first amalgamation of complex social norms, interactions, and production of material representations of the sort we normally associate with the greatest civilizations in world

1

history. The Preclassic period also witnessed the demise of this first incarnation of Maya civilization.

In the same way that ancient and modern Maya conceived of their own lives as existing in one of several cycles of creation, so many archaeologists today are replacing a linear evolutionary perspective of ancient culture—one that privileged progress, complex institutions and hierarchy—with another that focuses on cycles of aggregation and fragmentation of communities. From this new point of view, the making of culture is no longer seen as a process of emerging governmental institutions which can be reconstructed through their material correlates, but as a process of place-making, as the emergence of traditions of specific people tied to specific places (Pauketat 2007). In this perspective, communities were created in the process of place-making, including the construction of monumental buildings. Forms of government developed from this process, not vice versa.

To explore the period before the Classic most meaningfully, however, we should briefly review the Classic Maya themselves, and recent scholarship which has revised our knowledge. Thanks mainly to the decipherment of epigraphic inscriptions, we know much more today than even 20 years ago about Classic Maya civilization. We have gone from discussing abstract processes of cultural interaction (trade, migration, warfare) to delving into the history of kingdoms and the deeds of their rulers. But the general public still associates the Maya mainly with the towering pyramids of a mysterious culture. One ruined city, Tikal, figures prominently in western pop culture as the Rebel Alliance's spaceship base in the *Star Wars IV* film. With Chichén Itzá, the great city of the north, Tulum, the stunning coastal center and the beautifully sculpted Copan in Honduras, Tikal is one of the archaeological sites that today receive the greatest number of visitors from every corner of the globe. The images and narratives promoted everywhere by tour guides, brochures and scholarly books are typically the same:

- The Maya as great astronomers.
- The Maya as mathematicians and architects.
- The mysterious calendar and its prophecies—2012 and the end of the world recently the most popular.
- The mysterious Maya collapse.
- Their formidably complex hieroglyphic writing, which was baffling until deciphered by some of the most ingenious scholars of our time.
- Most of all, the Classic Maya fascinate us for having tamed the inhospitable jungle and built a thriving civilization with what today we consider very limited resources.

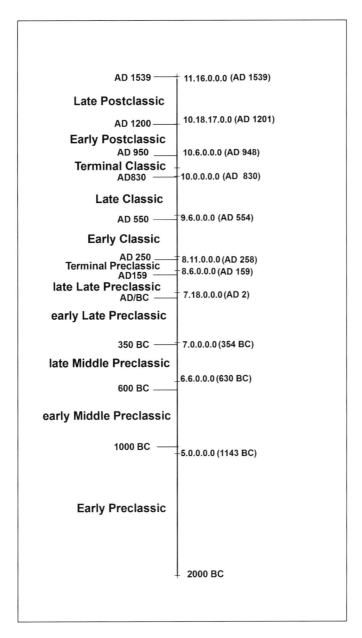

AD 1539 ——— 11.16.0.0.0 (AD 1539)

Late Postclassic

AD 1200 ——— 10.18.17.0.0 (AD 1201)

Early Postclassic

AD 950 ——— 10.6.0.0.0 (AD 948)

Terminal Classic

AD830 ——— 10.0.0.0.0 (AD 830)

Late Classic

AD 550 ——— 9.6.0.0.0 (AD 554)

Early Classic

AD 250 ——— 8.11.0.0.0 (AD 258)

Terminal Preclassic

AD159 ——— 8.6.0.0.0 (AD 159)

late Late Preclassic

AD/BC ——— 7.18.0.0.0 (AD 2)

early Late Preclassic

350 BC ——— 7.0.0.0.0 (354 BC)

late Middle Preclassic

6.6.0.0.0 (630 BC)

600 BC ———

early Middle Preclassic

1000 BC ——— 5.0.0.0.0 (1143 BC)

Early Preclassic

2000 BC

Figure 1.1 Time divisions used by Maya archaeologists and important, period-ending Maya calendar dates commemorated in Classic period inscription

Source: © F. Estrada-Belli

Note: Some of the Maya calendar dates correspond to archaeological division by coincidence or are deliberate attempts by archaeologists to fit their chronology to Maya cycles of time

An overview of Classic Maya research

An overview of what we know about the Classic Maya includes the two main sources of evidence: archaeology and epigraphy. The year 2009 marked an important milestone in Maya archaeology—the hundredth anniversary of the first archaeological excavation of a Maya site. This was the Péabody Museum of Harvard University's expedition to Holmul, Peten, Guatemala, led by a young graduate student, Raymond E. Merwin (Merwin and Vaillant 1932). In the following expedition, Merwin and his mentor, Alfred Tozzer, completed the work begun at Tikal by two earlier European explorers, Alfred Maudslay (Maudslay 1889–1902) and Teobert Maler (Maler 1911; Tozzer 1911). Following these pioneering efforts, each generation of Maya archaeologists excavated new sites in the harsh jungles of Guatemala, Mexico, Belize and Honduras. With each generation, the database increased by orders of magnitude allowing more complex research questions to be posed.

When seen in historical perspective, the older archaeological sample appears to be biased towards certain kinds of site. Typically, the largest sites in the Lowlands were targeted, neglecting medium-sized and small settlements. Also, many more centers with inscriptions were excavated than those without, leaving a whole section of ancient Maya society and its geography unexplored. Much of the research conducted since the 1960s has attempted to correct this imbalance, but more sites with inscriptions than not continue to be targeted by archaeologists. At the same time, the deciphering of hieroglyphs spurred a wave of new excavations at royal capitals rich in inscriptions. Filling gaps in Maya history became a major priority.

The history of Maya archaeology deserves a more detailed look, beginning with the sponsoring by the Carnegie Institution of Washington (CIW) of large-scale digs at Maya sites between 1915 and 1958.[2] The first large-scale Lowland excavation project at Chichén Itzá was led by Sylvanus G. Morley from 1923 to 1940. Chichén Itzá was chosen because of its accessibility, wonderful art and architecture, and also because of the wealth of artifacts dredged from its *cenote*[3] in 1904 by an amateur American archaeologist, Edward H. Thompson. The second great Lowland Maya dig was led by A. Ledyard Smith at Uaxactun from 1926 to 1937. Compared to Chichén Itzá, this was an infinitely more difficult site to work. In the heart of the remote Peten forest, it could be reached only by several days' mule-train travel. It was selected because the earliest carved inscription was found there in 1916 (Stela 9). The goal was to explore the beginnings of Maya civilization "in its purest state" (Morley 1943: 205). A Guatemalan archaeologist, Juan Antonio Valdés, resumed excavations at Uaxactun in 1983–1985. The Highlands of Guatemala and Honduras were the focus of CIW excavations in the 1930s and 1940s at Kaminaljuyú and Copan (Kidder *et al.* 1946; Morley 1943; Stromsvik 1946). The CIW's final project investigated the last phase of Maya civilization, just prior to the Spanish conquest, at Mayapan in the Mexican state of Yucatan (Pollock *et al.* 1962).

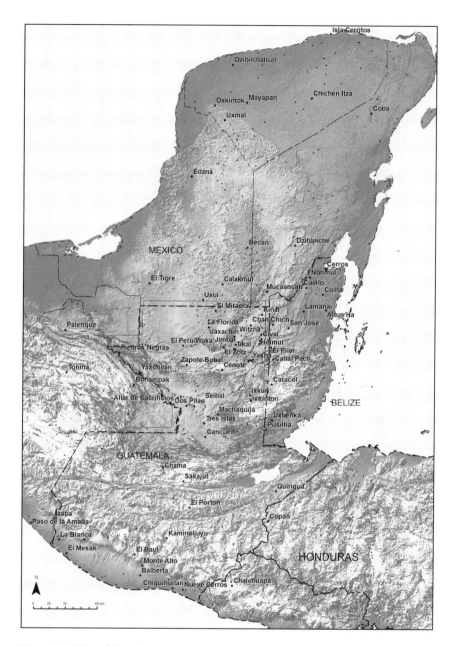

Figure 1.2 Map of the Maya region and sites mentioned in the text

Source: © F. Estrada-Belli, Topographic data courtesy of NASA SRTM mission

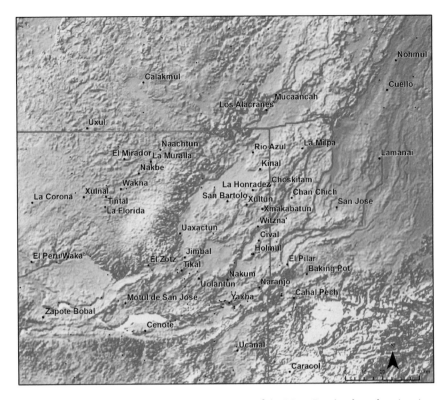

Figure 1.3 Map of the central and eastern region of the Maya Lowlands and major sites mentioned in the text

Source: © F. Estrada-Belli, Topographic data courtesy of NASA SRTM mission

Following the CIW model, the University of Pennsylvania carried out excavations and restorations at Tikal from 1955 to 1970, first under Ed Shook, then under William R. Coe (Hammond 1982). In the 1980s Guatemala sponsored its own excavations, led by Juan Pedro Laporte. Presently, Guatemalan-led excavations at Tikal are uncovering its greatest pyramid, Temple IV. On invitation by the Honduran government, Harvard planned a long-term project at Copan (Willey *et al.* 1975) that lasted until 1996. In Mexico, large-scale projects were carried out at Dzibilchaltun (Andrews and Andrews 1980), Palenque (Ruz Lhuillier 1955), Cobá (Folan *et al.* 1983) and more recently at Calakmul (Willey *et al.* 1975; Folan *et al.* 2001; Carrasco 1996), Oxkintok (Rivera Dorado 1987) and Ek Balam (Bey *et al.* 1998), to name just a few.

As is evident from this summary, Maya archaeology in the southern Lowlands, at least, was until recently site-based. That is, ceremonial centers, along with their temples, palaces, plazas and tombs, have been the focus of investigation more than other aspects of Maya landscape and society. This historically understandable bias of Maya archaeology has not gone unremarked

6

Figure 1.4 Sylvanus Morley and Eric Thompson with their consorts at Chichén Itzá
during the CIW excavations

Source: Donald Thompson

by the many researchers who have tried to gather a more complete picture of
the ancient Maya and their cultural trajectory. As early as 1953, Gordon
Willey introduced "total-coverage survey" as one method to document settlement and human–environment relations (Willey 1953). Such an approach,
however, was suited to the open landscapes of northern Yucatan, the Belize
River Valley and Highland Mexico but could find little application deep in
the jungles of the southern Lowlands. A more suitable method, the transect
survey, was first introduced by CIW's Ricketson at Uaxactun (Ricketson and
Ricketson 1937) and was later perfected by Dennis Puleston (Puleston 1983)
at Tikal for the Penn project. Narrow bands of forest were mapped in each
cardinal direction in order to get a measure of housing density from the site's
center to the periphery. But even this was a single-site-centered approach.
Later Anabel Ford (1986) carried out the first "inter-site transect mapping" of
a 30-kilometer strip of settlement between Tikal and Yaxha.

Today, with the help of Global Positioning System technology, we can
expand our surveys from charting sites and linear transects to mapping entire
regions. The complexity and diversity of Maya settlements through time
become more evident with each survey campaign (Estrada-Belli and Koch
2007; Saturno *et al.* 2007; Golden *et al.* 2008; Hansen *et al.* 2008b). Even so,

large tracts of the southern Lowlands remain unexplored and Maya cities and villages of all periods still await discovery. Principally, Preclassic sites have been added to our sample of Maya archaeology. Having been unoccupied in the Classic period, these lack carved monuments and standing architecture, at least on the surface. Ironically, these sites have been shunned by most researchers and looters, and consequently have seldom been reported. Even when reported, not much attention has been paid to them. Such was the case of the largest Maya site ever found, El Mirador, which was noted by airplane pilots in the 1930s but believed to be a natural hill until it was visited and mapped in the 1960s by explorer Ian Graham. Because of its remoteness, among other reasons, it was not further investigated for another 25 years. Only in the last decade, following many site-based excavations at El Mirador and nearby Nakbe, mostly thanks to the efforts of the Mirador Project (Hansen *et al.* 2008b), has the mapping of sites in northernmost Guatemala begun in earnest. These sites, with their extensive Preclassic populations, are giving us a new understanding of the Classic Maya and the locales which played important roles in shaping ancient Maya culture.

Parallel to these developments in the archaeological database have been new trends in archaeological theory. We have shifted our focus away from discussing cultural evolution patterns, which are typically seen in linear perspective and through the lens of fixed social types. Those discussions often led to dead-end arguments about whether the Maya were a tribe, chiefdom or state at one or another period. We should no longer emphasize abstract sociopolitical institutions with a goal of understanding general behavioral "laws" behind cultural development (Pauketat 2007; Yoffee 2005). Following newer directions in archaeological theory, in this book I focus instead on the history of people and places. With a long-term historical perspective, so akin to an archaeologist's dataset, we can learn about how the history and culture of a people are linked to places as well as interactions. Cities as built places are loci of religious, political and social gathering—providing a sense of community beyond the confines of their architectural layout. The making and remaking of places then become the making of a people's collective memory, identity and worldview. While we cannot tell the history of all places, some centers are more significant to us archaeologists because of their size, long or short life-spans, or simply, because of their state of preservation, there is more to be found there. Each site has an important story to tell and can give us clues to understand how that great aggregate of cultural achievements we associate with "Maya civilization" was created and changed through time.

Classic Maya people, places and history

Tikal

To some, Tikal is in many ways the most important among Classic Maya cities. Indeed, for a long time the ancient Tikaleños rightly thought of themselves as the greatest of all Maya. Inscriptions indicate that other cities and their kings were subordinate to Tikal's. Today, as it did 1200 years ago, the city boasts the largest number of towering pyramid temples and palaces. Its great plaza is littered with beautifully carved stelae—depicting its kings and recording their accomplishments, religious rites, and celebrations of calendar cycles. Though the modern restorations of its architecture are impressive, the sample they give hardly does justice to the dramatic viewscapes and vivid sounds that we know characterized the city's urban core. Much of it is now blanketed by tropical forest and, except for the occasional cries of wild animals, is silent. Buried beneath the temples, however, researchers have found rich tombs of kings and queens whose reigns spanned some 1000 years.[4] In the site's museum is a reconstruction of the tomb [Tomb 116] of perhaps the greatest Tikal king, *Jasaw Chan K'awiil*, who in the 7th century AD defeated his long-time rival Yich'aak K'ahk', king of Calakmul, bringing his city to its maximum expansion. One of the richest ever found by Maya archaeologists, the tomb was discovered in a small room cut into the soft limestone bedrock layer under the stairway of Temple 1 in the Great Plaza (Coe 1990). There, the king lay on a jaguar skin on a stone platform dressed in royal garments and covered with thousands of jade jewels. Around him were obsidian and stingray perforators, together with dozens of precious red *Spondylus* oyster shells, sacred receptacles for his bloodletting rituals, intended to connect with ancestors and gods. Among the most striking artifacts are several inscribed and carved bones. One in particular is from a human limb and depicts a captive. A finely carved column of hieroglyphs next to him identifies him as a lord from the Snake kingdom (Calakmul, see below). Another beautifully carved human bone depicts a canoe occupied by a young maize god ferried into the underworld by the paddler gods. Dozens of the finest painted ceramics sat beside him, along with food and beverages for his afterlife journey (Trik 1963). His chocolate-drink vases are painted with scenes from such well-known myths as the Old God conversing with his faithful messenger. Others depict the ruler in his palace, sitting behind curtains on a bench-throne while being visited by dignitaries. In addition, musicians, dwarfs and other courtiers provide the king with amusement. Some of these scenes may recall day-to-day interactions with lords of the kingdom or important diplomatic visits by powerful lords from elsewhere. In one of the most elaborately painted vases the king, sitting high on his throne, receives gifts—a bowl of delicacies and a feathered fan. The two donors—one kneeling, the other walking up a hieroglyphic stairway—wear elaborate loincloths and headdresses appropriate to their rank. On the right,

9

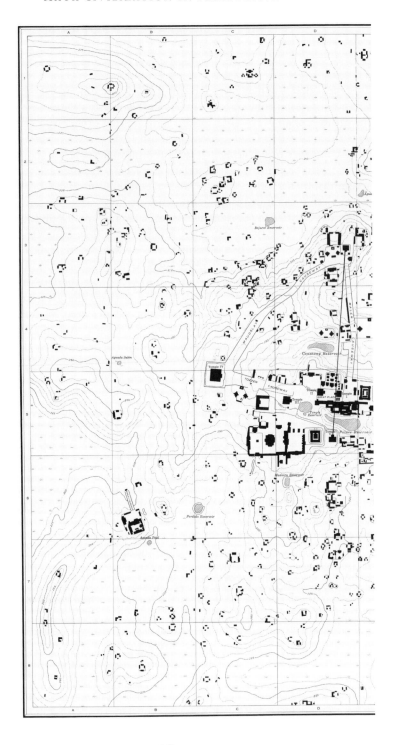

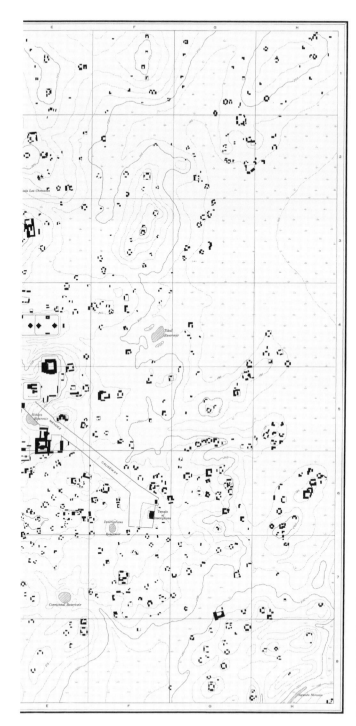

Figure 1.5 Map of
Tikal's central area

Source: After Carr
and Hazard 1961,
courtesy of the
University of
Pennsylvania
Museum of
Archaeology and
Anthropology

Figure 1.6 Rooftops of Tikal Temples I, II and III (foreground), seen from the top of
Temple IV

Source: © F. Estrada-Belli

four other lords stand witness to this ritual, each having a different headdress
but all wearing similar capes and shell necklaces. They appear to be lords of
the highest rank and their names are spelled in short columns of glyphs before
their faces. Finally, on the left, three kneeling lords observe the scene while
gazing at the king (Culbert 1993: Figure 68A). A great sense of vibrant pomp
permeates these palace images, underscoring the marked hierarchical nature
of this society.

As mentioned, other inscriptions from Tikal and elsewhere tell us that *Jasaw
Chan K'awiil* was the architect of a major comeback of the Tikal kingdom after
some 130 years of military defeats and failed political alliances. Since its first
defeat in the year 562 AD at the hands of a king from the Snake kingdom (later
associated with the city of Calakmul, see below), Tikal kings had struggled to
survive. Few monuments were erected during those years. At the same time,
scores of Tikal-allied kings were first defeated, then shamefully paraded and
sacrificed. Others broke ranks and offered allegiance to the Snake kings, later
waging war on their former Tikal ally. In one extraordinarily cruel case, a
sibling of the Tikal king went to establish a new kingdom for himself at Dos
Pilas, in the southern Petexbatun lakes region (Houston 1993). Within a short
time he was a Calakmul ally and sworn enemy of his own brother. Sibling
rivalry for succession is suspected here (Martin and Grube 2008).

Caracol

The kingdom of Caracol in Belize (known as *Uxwitzá'*—"three mountain-
water"; Stuart 2007b), may also have started as a close Tikal ally only to finish
among its most persistent enemies in concert with Calakmul. Caracol center
was located on a high plateau next to the Maya Mountains (see Figure 1.2,

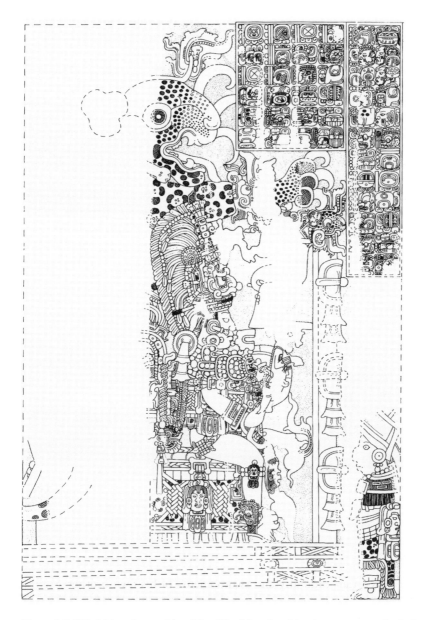

Figure 1.7 Tikal king *Jasaw Chan K'awiil* celebrating his victory over arch-rival *Chak Tok Ichaak* of the Snake kingdom (Calakmul) on September 14, 695 carved on doorway Lintel 3 of *Jasaw*'s funerary shrine, Temple I

Source: After Jones and Satterthwaite 1982, courtesy of the University of Pennsylvania Museum of Archaeology and Anthropology

13

above). From there, one of the most dominating locations in Maya geography, Caracol kings could control the river routes connecting the center and south-east of the Lowlands to the Highlands. In the Late Classic period, Caracol underwent a population boom, gathering close to 100,000 inhabitants within its sprawling, hilly landscape. Various elite complexes lay at the edges of this vast community, some as far as 7 kilometers from the center. A set of radiating causeways connected these ritual sites to Caracol's center (Chase and Chase 2001). Within this vast semi-urbanized landscape, the Caracoleños built thousands of agricultural terraces to optimize production in support of their large population (Chase *et al.* 1998). In the center, the royal palace perched atop a lofty pyramid called Kaana', once a massive Preclassic temple platform. The king's vassals' palaces strung along the front terraces of the platform shield these kingly quarters from the rest of the world. On one of the site's monu-ments (Altar 21), King *Yahaw Te' Kinich* records his accession "under the supervision" (*ukabiiy*) of King *Wak Chan K'awiil* of Tikal in the year 553. And in a dramatic turn of events, he also relates a first attack (*ch'ak*—"axe event") by Tikal on its former vassal king only three years later. Then, in 562, the defeat of Tikal at the hands of a Calakmul king, Sky Witness, is noted (Martin and Grube 2008).

Figure 1.8 Façade of the Kaana' pyramid at Caracol with its stairway leading up to the royal palace through rows of elite rooms looking towards the plaza

Source: © F. Estrada-Belli

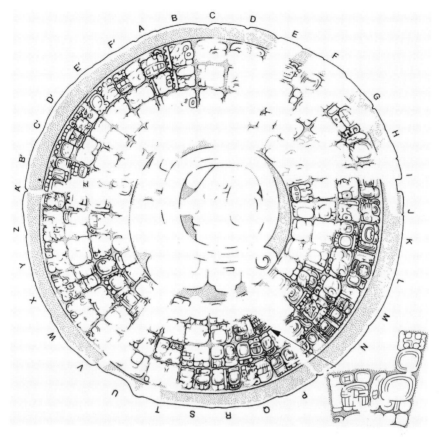

Figure 1.9 Caracol Altar 21 (drawn by Stephen Houston) and passage relating the Tikal war (text block insert drawn by Simon Martin)

Source: Courtesy of Stephen D. Houston and Simon Martin

Calakmul

Calakmul was located far to the north of all this, in the present state of Campeche, some 100 kilometers from Tikal (see Figure 1.3, above). Even so, its environment was in many ways similar to the tropical marshy and hilly forest of the southern Lowland cities and its history was similar, too. Its kings boasted the Snake kingdom emblem as royal symbol whenever and wherever they intervened in the affairs of other kingdoms. According to recent epigraphic evidence (Hansen and Guenter 2005), the Snake kingdom may be traced back to a great Preclassic city somewhere in the vicinity, perhaps even El Mirador, which was the seat of the greatest potentates of the Preclassic Maya. Another possibility is the recently discovered Preclassic site of Xcabal, located near Dzibanché and the Bay of Bacalar, on the east of the Yucatan

15

Peninsula. The Early Classic history of the Snake dynasty, new decipherments show, appears to focus on Dzibanché, some 130 kilometers northwest of Calakmul. Here, recent excavations by Mexican archaeologist Enrique Nalda may have unearthed the possible tomb of the Sky Witness Snake king known to have defeated Tikal in the year 562 (Nalda 2003; see below). According to the most recent study, only the last three kings of the Snake kingdom, each named Yuknoom, used Calakmul as their royal seat (Martin 2005).

It is easy to see why this place was chosen for the Late Classic capital of the powerful Snake kingdom. It is a hilly outcrop surrounded by immense marshes and high forest. Near the site were large manmade and natural water reservoirs. The place itself was known as *Chiik Nahb*, "watery place," a sacred locale of world creation and abundance. Calakmul had been a great ceremonial site in the earlier Preclassic era and had two high pyramids (Structures 1 and 2), together with a great plaza. Structure 2 was initially a tall truncated pyramid supporting an elevated plaza and as many as nine highly decorated buildings. By 350 BC, its front temple was adorned with intricately carved representations of rain deities (Carrasco and Colon 2005). Though clearly a place of ritual importance, Preclassic Calakmul likely existed in the shadow of powerful El Mirador, located a mere 40 kilometers to the south. On a clear day, it is still possible to see the great Danta pyramid complex from the top of Calakmul's

Figure 1.10 Structure 2 pyramid at Calakmul with Late Classic stelae erected on the plaza floor and pyramid's terraces

Source: © F. Estrada-Belli

16

Structure 2. The Late Classic period Snake kings took the city to new heights, constructing huge ritual plazas and erecting the largest number of inscribed monuments (117) at any Maya site (compare to Tikal's 40). Unfortunately, the quality of the local stone has not permitted us to recover many of those inscriptions, or we would have an astonishingly complete record of its history.

Calakmul's population rivaled those of Tikal and Caracol in numbers. Its kings were buried with some of the finest objects. Among the most remarkable artifacts are large jade masks and beautifully inscribed and painted codex-style vases. The vases themselves were created by elites residing nearby, probably at Calakmul itself and at Nakbe, one of the ruined capitals of Preclassic kings near El Mirador where codex-style ceramics have been recovered in large numbers (Hansen *et al.* 1991). The master painters of Calakmul were some of the finest in all of the Maya Lowlands. They decorated the outer platform of a north complex with watery symbols and glyphs spelling "*Chiik Nahb*," telling us this complex is the place mentioned in the inscriptions. Its central building was painted with images of elites drinking, eating, and receiving goods— probably as gifts or tributes, during a ritual of unknown nature. However, as the inscriptions from many other sites also tell us, the *Chiik Nahb* location was the plaza where kings were hailed in office—not just Calakmul's but those of its client kingdoms. The painted scenes of celebration may refer to one such ceremony (Carrasco and Colon 2005). At the site of La Corona (formerly known as Site Q), a panel by King *Chak Ak'aach Yuk*, a vassal of Calamul's *Yichaak K'ahk'*, records the rituals associated with the Long Count date 9.12. 15.0.0 (AD 687) as being performed at *Uxtetun Chiik Nahb*, or Calakmul itself. It was probably common for the vassal kings of the great Snake kingdom to travel to Calakmul on important occasions, thus strengthening their relations with the patron king (Martin and Grube 2008). On this and other monuments, the La Corona lords displayed the Snake emblem glyph, acknowledging Calakmul kings' power over them. The apparent lack of a La Corona emblem glyph suggests that it was not a separate client kingdom of the Snake kings, but instead formed an integral part of the Snake kingdom's greater territorial domain. The territory directly controlled by the Late Classic Snake kings will then have extended for a remarkable distance of nearly 80 kilometers to the southwest of their capital, Calakmul. To the east, the reach of the Snake kings may have extended for about 80 kilometers to Los Alacranes, another site that did not posses its own emblem glyph but displayed the Snake kingdom's. Far beyond these outposts, the Snake kings oversaw the activities of scores of allies as far south as Cancuen and Quirigua, on the very southern limits of the Lowlands.

Palenque

Palenque is another well-known city of the Classic period. Its ancient name was *Lakamha*, while its emblem glyph called it the *Baak* (Bone) kingdom.

Located in the west, where the Maya Lowland limestone hills merge into the lower plains of the Gulf of Mexico, its dynasty was established by a ruler named *K'uk Balam,* probably originating from another place. Later, in the 7th century, the Palenque kings made numerous references to Tikal, so it would seem that the Palenque kingdom was also established as a friend of the Tikal kings. In the 7th century, Palenque was ruled by *Kinich Janaab Pakal,* or *Pakal* the Great. During his seven-decade reign, he led the city into its golden age. Today the Palace and the Temple of the Inscriptions, containing his tomb, are his most evident legacies. Many today consider this the most beautiful among the surviving Maya temples. He built the central throne-room of the palace, House E (appropriately named the *Sak nuuk naah,* "White Skin House"). Its simple initial floor-plan was greatly expanded by his successors and turned into a labyrinth of well-lit rooms around secluded courtyards, all set atop underground hallways. The temple was decorated with an inscription constituting Palenque's longest text, recounting *Pakal's* accomplishments and linking the origins of his dynasty to the birth of gods some 1.2 million years ago (Schele and Mathews 1998).

Pakal's tomb, the most elaborate so far discovered in the Maya world, was built during his lifetime and finished by his son, *Kan Bahlam.* Situated below the base of the pyramid, it connects to the temple above by means of an internal zig-zag stairway. Inside a stone sarcophagus, *Pakal's* body lay wrapped

Figure 1.11 Temple of the Inscriptions, Palenque, resting place of King *Pakal*
Source: © F. Estrada-Belli

Figure 1.12 The Palenque palace after many additions

Source: © F. Estrada-Belli

Note: *Pakal*'s building, House E, can be seen on the left of the tower

in a cloth, with jade jewels in his hands and by his feet and groin, in cosmic arrangement. The sarcophagus was covered by a stone lid in which *Pakal* is depicted as a young lord in apotheosis, rising as a god after death. He had assumed the personae of the young maize god and that of a death god, the lightning god. He is shown reborn, emerging from the maw of an earth monster, as all things did at creation. A world-tree emerges from his body, as though it were the seed for sustenance itself. On the side of the stone slab are portraits of six generations of royal ancestors as fruit trees (Schele and Mathews 1998). To sanctify his interment, his son and successor had six people sacrificed outside the tomb chamber.

While *Pakal*'s reign (AD 615–683) was the period of greatest prosperity for his kingdom, it was not free from trouble. On one occasion a vassal lord fell captive to the kings of Piedras Negras, a large city on the lower course of the Usumacinta River. According to the inscriptions, in 654 *Lakamha* was subjected to an "axe event," one of the more violent forms of defeat, at the hands of a Calakmul king (Sharer and Traxler 2006). By the time of *Pakal*'s death, though, his kingdom had long recovered from this downturn and was a regional power in the western Lowlands.

Figure 1.13 Carving from the stone sarcophagous lid of King *Pakal*, who
died August 28, 683

Source: Courtsey of Merle Green-Robertson

Kaminaljuyú

As they are today, in ancient times the Highland regions of today's Chiapas, Mexico, Guatemala, Honduras and eastern El Salvador were populated by Maya speakers. Kaminaljuyú was probably the greatest highland Maya center in all of Maya history. At its zenith, the ceremonial core stretched over some

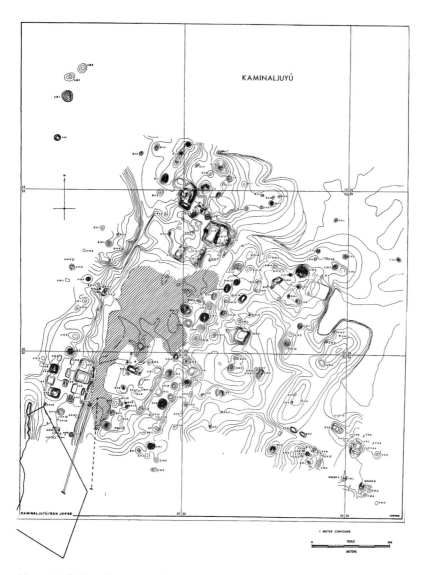

Figure 1.14 The CIW map of Kaminaljuyú

Source: After Popenoe Hatch 1997; courtesy M. Popenoe Hatch

14 square kilometers of the plateau now occupied by Guatemala City. This apogee was reached in the first and second centuries AD, prior to the Classic period. Dozens of plaza–pyramid complexes were built in different parts of a sprawling urbanized landscape. Score of basalt stone monuments stood in those plazas. Some depicted deities and mythological scenes; others were historical in nature, such as Monument 65. In it pairs of bound captives kneel to three lords seated on thrones. Each figure is identified by his headdress (Sharer and Traxler 2006: Figure 5.8). The water from a lake in its center was channeled to agricultural fields to support its population with sustainable farming (Popenoe Hatch 1997). The 5-kilometer-long effigy mound that weaved its way from the center towards the mountain ridges to the east was one of the largest structures ever built by the Late Preclassic Maya. Sections of it still stand 6–8 meters high today among Guatemala City's urban lots and throughways. The Preclassic rulers of Kaminaljuyú no doubt also received tribute from large sections of the Guatemala Highlands and Pacific slope. Judging from ceramic imports and from the similarities in ceramic and architectural styles in this region, Kaminaljuyú exerted hegemonic influence on coastal sites as far west as the Guatemala–Mexico boarder and as far east as the Guatemala–El Salvador border. Further in each direction were other great centers with their own regions of influence—Chiapa De Corzo in Chiapas, Mexico, and Chalchuapa in El Salvador. According to the data we have today, the rulers of all these centers shared most cultural traits and were responsible for the great innovations in monument carving and Long Count dating, prior to their Lowland neighbors. During the Classic period each of these important Highland centers experienced a contraction in population and eventually was eclipsed by new centers. In the fifth century AD Kaminaljuyú maintained a relatively modest population and was occupied by elite groups from Teotihuacan as well as from the Maya Lowlands (Sanders and Michels 1977). The foreigners built temples in their own style and were buried with lavish offerings. But this was a short-lived phase and the site slowly fell into oblivion during the Late Classic period.

Copan

The brightest star among Highland centers in the Classic period was undoubtedly Copan, in the Honduran Highlands. Its center was founded by a lord named *Yax K'uk' Mo'* who appeared in Teotihuacan garb in later Copan art, but was actually born and raised somewhere in the east-central Maya Lowlands, according to his bone chemistry (Sharer 2004; Stuart 2007b). One of his titles was *Wite' Naah Ajaw*—an epithet apparently reserved for Maya rulers of this epoch who claimed to have received their power from a place or temple called *Wite' Naah*, which may have been at Teotihuacan. Comparing references in the Maya Lowlands with the iconography of the Pyramid of the Sun at Teotihuacan, Fash *et al.* (2009) have suggested that *Yax*

Figure 1.15 Copan's Altar Q, dedicated by *Yax Pasac* to commemorate his 15
predecessors and the dynasty's founder, *Yax K'uk' Mo'*

Source: © F. Estrada-Belli

Note: Yax K'uk Mo' is depicted here (center left) passing *Yax Pasac* a lit torch, symbol of royal
office

K'uk' Mo' and a small number of Early Classic rulers, including Tikal's *Yax Nuun Ayiin*, may have traveled to Teotihuacan to receive the insignia of power at the Pyramid of the Sun, which included in its front a sanctuary of the new fire ceremony (also known as the Adosada structure). At Copan, *Yax K'uk' Mo'* built a ritual space for his newly founded dynasty in a style that was foreign to the Copan Valley and incorporated Maya Lowland and Teotihuacan elements (Hunal structure). After his death, his son and later successors continued to acknowledge the founder's foreign/Teotihuacan heritage while at the same time asserting a strong sense of Maya-ness in art and architecture.

The Copan kings not only maintained strong links with Tikal and the Lowlands but controlled the all-important Highland–Lowland route of the Motagua River, where jade and obsidian sources are found. Late Classic Copan kings continued to expand the ceremonial center by building over the founder's temple and tombs and turning its broad plaza into a massive acropolis complex. Their temples were beautifully decorated with intricate high-relief sculptures and hieroglyphs.

One of the greatest Copan kings, *Uaxaclajuun Ubah K'awiil*, erected some of the most spectacular carved monuments in the plaza. Perhaps the most impressive of Copan's buildings is Temple 26, with its hieroglyphic stairway,

Figure 1.16 Copan's King *Uaxaclajuun Ubah K'awiil*'s architectural legacy: the Great
Plaza at Copan with the ball court (foreground) and the hieroglyphic
stairway (under its protective canopy)

Source: © F. Estrada-Belli

commissioned by *Uaxaclajuun* himself and finished by his successor (Stuart
2004). In this spectacular monument, completed in spite of a shameful defeat
by a neighboring former vassal kingdom, Quirigua, the rulers celebrated the
greatness of their dynasty. Inside the temple, a strange inscription bore both
Maya and pseudo-Teotihuacan signs, recalling the foreign affiliations of the
dynasty's founder.

The long-term history of the Copan Valley shows that after the dynasty
ended in the 9th century, Lowland Maya culture there was quickly replaced by
a local ethnic culture with ties to the Honduran interior which had remained
"dormant" during the Classic period (Canuto 2004; Manahan 2004). This
transformation underscores the multi-ethnic nature of certain Maya kingdoms,
and suggests that foreign elite enclaves, such as at Copan, can remain largely
distinct from their host populations, even after 500 years of occupation.

A crucial turning point around AD 760

The web of interactions and hostile confrontations among Maya kings of the
Classic period led to a crucial turning point around the year 760, when something changed in the conduct of alliances and war. For the first time, from
what archaeology and epigraphy allow us to discern, dynasties began to end.

This did not occur everywhere at the same time; even defeat by rivals was not always final. Copan, for example, had been defeated and its ruler *Uaxaclajuun Ubah K'awiil* executed in the year 738 by his former subordinate, the King of Quirigua. But these events did not cause irreparable damage to Copan, for the dynasty eventually regrouped and continued to rule for another eighty years (Martin and Grube 2008). However, at places like Dos Pilas and Aguateca, something different was happening. In AD 761 the Dos Pilas ruling elite dismantled temples and their palace to build defenses barricading themselves inside their hilltop center. When the end was near, they fled, probably to nearby Aguateca (Demarest 1993), finding refuge there for some time. Then, four decades later, Aguateca itself was besieged and taken by an unknown enemy (Inomata *et al.* 2002). This marked the end of the Petexbatun dynasty. Slowly, a new kingdom emerged at Seibal, where a new lord from the distinguished dynasty of Ucanal installed himself as king. Seibal kings prospered until the end of the ninth century, erecting the last stela in the year 889, after which it too was slowly abandoned (Martin and Grube 2008).

Other cities and kingdoms were experiencing similar political crises. Calakmul kings were defeated by Tikal's *Jasaw Chan K'awiil* and his successor several times, until a final capitulation in 731. At that point, its dynasty entered a hiatus, slowly ceasing to erect monuments. The Snake dynastic emblem was not used again, but some of Calakmul's neighbors and former vassals, like Oxpemul, erected monuments until the year 899, displaying the Bat emblem from an earlier local tradition instead (Martin 2005). In the Usumacinta region, Yaxchilan had finally gained the upper hand over Piedras Negras, and Tonina had prevailed one last time over Palenque, until the bitter end came for all in the 9th century (Martin and Grube 2008; Sharer and Traxler 2006).

Rethinking the Maya collapse

Much effort has been put into trying to explain the Classic Maya collapse (Demarest 1997; Webster 2002; Demarest *et al.* 2004; Hodell *et al.* 1995; Haug *et al.* 2003; Culbert 1973). Some scholars challenge the concept of collapse, basing their objections on the evident continuity of vibrant civilizations not only in the Maya region but those elsewhere in the world that have followed so-called "Classic" periods (McAnany and Yoffee 2008). Generally speaking, there is little doubt that Maya civilization continued with little change into the Postclassic period. The most dramatic changes certainly occurred with the arrival of the Spanish conquistadors. The Terminal Classic and Early Postclassic cities of Uxmal, Cobá and Chichén Itzá in Yucatan ruled over large populations and produced some of the most exuberant art and architecture in Maya history. Chichén Itzá in particular was the capital of a large regional state, almost an empire, which ruled over much of the north and had political and trade connections even with the remaining cities of the south, such as Seibal and Lamanai (Robles Castellanos and Andrews 1986; Cobos 2003, 2004; Schele and Freidel 1990). This was perhaps the largest hegemonic state the Maya Lowlands had ever seen. Albeit with reduced power and resources, the Maya continued to erect temples and were ruled by kings up to the arrival of the Europeans. Since then, despite population losses caused by new diseases and the oppression they suffered at the hands of their conquerors, the Maya continue to exist. Today, an estimated ten million Maya-speaking people live in semi-autonomous communities in the Highlands of Guatemala, Chiapas and Yucatan. They have incorporated Catholicism into their pre-Columbian belief system, exchanging their traditional gods for saints and human sacrifices for more mundane offerings. Superficial western cultural influences aside, in many regards their ancestral culture and ways of living continue to be as original and vibrant as they were a thousand years ago.

If what we perceive as collapse was not a wholesale cultural downfall (as it seldom is), what was it? For some, it was the end of a system of dynastic rule centered on the person of a divine king and an exclusionary political strategy, typical of the southern Lowland states (Blanton *et al*. 1996). But others point out that dynastic rule persisted with some adjustments and greater inclusiveness until the Spanish conquest. What may have disappeared was the erection of portrait stelae, but not royal rule, hieroglyphic writing or calendrical

Figure 1.17 Kiche' Maya procession in the main plaza of Chichicastenango, Guatemala, amid market stands. Led by priests, four young men carry the image of Santo Tomas on a litter decorated with colorful feathers and flowers

Source: © F. Estrada-Belli

knowledge, for the Postclassic Maya continued to reckon time and tell their history using the count of *katuns*,[5] based on the Long Count system. The armies of Kiche' Highland Maya kings and the Lowland Maya of Yucatan and Tayasal, Peten, fought fiercely against the Spanish invaders and resisted conquest longer than any other Mesoamerican people (Fuentes y Guzmán *et al.* 1932; Jones 1998; Roys 1952). If we had not lost countless Maya books to the iconoclastic destruction of overzealous bishops in the 16th century, we would know much more about the religion, history and political systems of the Maya before the conquest (Thompson 1954).

What remains to be explained, then, is the death of the southern cities, and the final flight of their kings and populations, presumably towards better pastures. There is great variability in the timing and circumstances of the abandonment. Probably each case should be treated separately. When we look at the whole southern Lowlands, the process of abandonment is spread over the 9th and 10th centuries AD. And if we broaden the perspective even further to include the cities of northern Yucatan, the rise and fall of Maya kingdoms continued until the last great kings of Mayapan lost their hegemony over a number of smaller kingdoms in the 15th century.

There is no doubt that warfare, escalating to new levels in the Late Classic period, accounts for some of the specific site collapses, though scholars rarely agree on the causes of such confrontations and their deadly consequences for their kings and people. Some have looked at the burden placed by more, larger and more densely populated Maya cities on the environment, as well as episodes of drought during the 9th century (Beach *et al.* 2008; Gill 2000; Haug *et al.* 2003; Hodell *et al.* 1995). These factors alone may have brought Maya dynasties as a "system" to the brink of collapse. In this scenario, warfare would be a symptom of overall economic and political crises within each kingdom, further compounding these underlying problems. Environment-based explanations have many fans, but in such areas as Petexbatun, which had a short-lived and thin occupation in the Classic Period, soil and water studies have shown no great pressure on the environment and no evidence of drought (Demarest 1997). Other areas may have been affected by drought, but not the Petexbatun and not in the 8th century. According to Arthur Demarest (1997), the failing kingdoms of Petexbatun—Dos Pilas and Aguateca would have generated migrating refugee populations that could have put severe pressure on other parts of the Lowlands. And if other areas were at the limit of their land sustainability, the results could have been disastrous.

Some scholars (Freidel 1985; Webb 1973) have held that the rise of trading centers and a shift in trading networks outside of the southern Lowlands bypassed the old kingdoms of the south and took away their resources. But it is unclear how much support the economies of Maya kingdoms drew from long-distance trade. Indeed, as the cities of the southern Lowlands declined, cities in the north, such as Uxmal and Chichén Itzá, were quickly becoming great urban centers. Seen from the vantage point of Chichén Itzá, the Postclassic was a new era of greatness and political cohesion in the Maya Lowlands. The center of gravity had just shifted to the north.

In the end, the environmental/drought theories' greatest weakness lies in their failure to explain how the generally drier and more thin-soiled north could prosper during the droughts of the 10th century. As many others have pointed out, the final explanation for the Maya collapse may be out of reach at the moment, but hopefully not for ever. If we think in terms of several contributing factors and in terms of variability of sites' histories rather than single-cause, catch-all explanations, we will likely soon have a better under-standing.

The beginnings of Maya civilization

This book focuses on the beginnings of Maya civilization, itself the subject of many heated debates. Because of new data and new ideas, we may now be in our best ever position to understand it. While scholarly interest in the Preclassic Maya began in the 1920s with the Uaxactun excavation, it was soon superseded by the race to document sites with inscriptions. After a long pause, a new wave of focused studies began in the 1970s with surveys and excavations in northern Belize (Hammond 1973, 1974), and in the Highland regions of Verapaz (Sedat and Sharer 1972), Chalchuapa (Sharer and Gifford 1970), Kaminaljuyú (Sanders and Michels 1969) and in northern Yucatan (Andrews and Ringle 1992; Andrews 1981b). In the central part of the Maya Lowlands (northern Peten and southern Campeche) only in the last 20 years has this problem been addressed by targeted long-term excavation and survey projects in the heart of the southern Maya Lowlands (i.e. the north and eastern Peten region). Previously, Preclassic remains were found only as fortuitous by-products at the bottom of excavations designed to address questions regarding Late Classic Maya culture. With the expansion of excavations at sites such as El Mirador and Nakbe, as well as spectacular discoveries at centers such as San Bartolo and Cival, a new understanding of the Preclassic Maya is emerging. The first building blocks of this civilization were its ceremonial centers, symbols of new regional identities in the making. The substantial database we have accu-mulated is forcing us to reconsider old theories and to change our perspective; otherwise, great cities like El Mirador will continue to remain a mystery.

In essence, we have discovered that the Maya people created their first civilization in the Preclassic period. When seen in the perspective of 3000 years of constant refinement, the cultural peak we call the "Classic" civilization was a second, and even less dazzling, manifestation of cultural elaboration. Chapter 2 outlines older theories now at odds with available evidence about the earliest Maya. These theories envisioned a huge, empty landscape into which waves of migrants came as colonizers, building a new civilization with tools developed elsewhere, either in the Highlands of Guatemala or in the Olmec region. Old theories also stressed the simplicity of the Maya farming way of life during much of the Preclassic period. According to them, the explosive growth of El Mirador after 300 BC seemed unlikely without substantial input from outside the Maya world.

Chapter 3 looks at the issue of kingship, often regarded as a key ingredient of early civilizations. Here the epigraphic sources and archaeological evidence tell different narratives. In the material record, "royal" tombs and associated symbols of power clearly predate the earliest kings recorded by Maya scribes as well as the accepted beginning date of the Classic Maya period. The search for the founder of the Tikal dynasty, one of the longest-lived in the Lowlands, is a case in point. The "founding" of a dynasty may not mark the origin of kingship at Tikal, or anywhere else. Instead, the epigraphic evidence may indicate only the start of a line of rulers and a new era of prosperity. In short, Maya civilization needs to be understood in a broader context, beyond the written data purporting to show the beginning of dynastic lines.

Chapter 4 explores the nature of this broader context through an analysis of Preclassic centers as places of gathering, their planned nature, cosmological significance and ritual functions. The process of place-making is the key to understanding the making of a civilization, when the ideas, interests and aspirations of a people converge to form a new identity and community. Ceremonial plazas represent the catalysts for the integration and growth of large constituencies around a common heritage, a memory of place, of ancestors and supernatural forces (Ashmore and Knapp 1999).

The meaning of sacred landscapes carved in the façades of pyramids and temples is the subject of Chapter 5. The many different images in Preclassic Maya monumental art are symbols of a supernatural order which this world mimics. As in other cultures, the Preclassic Maya elite claimed a special place for themselves within this worldview, one of intermediaries and managers in the human–human and human–supernatural interactions. This is evident not only in the imagery but in the materiality of plazas, temples and elite residences on great platforms.

Having presented an overview of early manifestations of civilization, Chapter 6 reviews several important issues regarding the end of the Preclassic and the beginning of the Classic periods. Long thought to be an obscure but creative period in Maya history, this is a transition from a world of great homogeneity and possibly hegemonic power across the Lowlands to one of fragmentation and new competitors. It was clearly a period of restructuring of relations and expressions of new ideals. The key to understanding this transition might lie in the historical circumstances of such sites as El Mirador and Cival, on one hand, and Tikal and the Snake kingdom, on the other. The latter are the leading protagonists of Classic Maya history. The Classic period may be seen as a 500-year attempt to establish a political hegemony in the Lowlands by these two kingdoms.

Finally, Chapter 7 reviews the progress made in understanding the processes and historical circumstances by which the Maya created an original civilization.

Even though we might not have all the answers, we have come a long way since the publication of *The Origins of Maya Civilization* (Adams 1977), the last major book on this subject. Even though the past may forever remain an elusive target for archaeologists, social scientists and historians, through the accumulation of knowledge and the shifting of our perspectives we can ask ever more meaningful questions about this great civilization.

2

TRAJECTORIES
OF EVOLUTION

Maya archaeology and the Preclassic Maya

Theories of the origins of Maya civilization:
the first part of the 20th century

The archaeologists of the early part of the 20th century had to contend with a frustrating dearth of solid archaeological data regarding the emergence of Classic Maya civilization in the Maya Lowlands. Until the Carnegie Institution's excavations at Uaxactun in the 1930s there was little or no actual archaeological evidence for anything that preceded the Classic period—or the Old Empire, as it was then called. One of the most authoritative views on the antecedents to the Old Empire was by Herbert Spinden (1928). This was largely based on the scanty Paleoindian evidence pointing to the Highland regions of Mexico and Guatemala as having the longest history and accordingly being the places where complexity might be expected to have emerged first. The few Paleoindian remains in Highland Guatemala dating to 11,000 years ago were believed to be of a culture of hunters ancestral to the first farmers. The latter were identified with a style of "Archaic" figurines found throughout the Highlands. Only much later in this long Archaic period would the Highland farmers colonize the Lowlands. The similarities in style of the Archaic figurines in both regions were taken to indicate the ethnic identity of Highland and Lowland Maya populations, thus lending support to a migration theory.

After being adopted by such authoritative figures in Maya archaeology as Alfred Tozzer (1957), the Highland–Lowland migratory theory gained momentum in the post–Second World War period. It seemed especially convincing because archaeological progress at such Preclassic centers as Kaminaljuyú and Chalchuapa had shown the greater antiquity of Highland pyramids, tombs and inscriptions. According to another major figure of the time, Alfred Kidder (1950), the Highlanders had the advantage of more productive lands and a more manageable landscape, contrasting with the Lowlanders, who had to contend with taming the rainforest. This, he wrote, "would have been an almost prohibitively difficult environment for pulling oneself up, so to speak, by the bootstraps" (1950: 6). Thus, the Highland

Maya, with their longer history of sedentary living, were thought to have had the opportunity to acquaint themselves with agriculture, tame the hostile Lowland environment, and make a living in it.

By contrast, Sylvanus G. Morley (1946) argued that the earliest dated inscriptions and monuments at Tikal and Uaxactun could not be explained by Highland migrations but rather must have resulted from a long accumulation of knowledge in the same area. Kidder (1950) added that this could have been accomplished only by a class of individuals long removed from labors of subsistence and free to specialize without interruptions. According to this view, the invention of the Maya hieroglyphic script and, by extension, its civilization was a purely Lowland phenomenon. Morley (1946) also wisely predicted that as archaeological investigations made progress in the Peten, the developmental stages of Lowland Maya culture would become apparent, as had been increasingly obvious from the extraordinary pre-Classic temple (E-VII-sub structure) that was being unearthed at Uaxactun.

The Carnegie Institution's excavations at Uaxactun (Smith 1950a) brought to light not only an impressive temple but an extensive series of stratigraphic levels predating it. Due to its elaborate iconography that closely presaged Classic period art, the temple itself was assigned to the later part of the Late Preclassic Chicanel ceramic phase (400 BC–AD 200). Under the temples were ceramics of the Mamom phase (800–400 BC) that were interpreted as remains of the first Archaic Lowlanders. Because of their similarity with ceramic styles in Oaxaca, Veracruz and Highland Guatemala they were thought to be imports from the Highlands (Kidder 1950: 7).

In his 1954 book *The Rise and Fall of Maya Civilization*, J. Eric Thompson rejected his own earlier conviction that the Lowland Maya owed their innovations to their Highland neighbors. His first-hand observation of the impressive complexity of stucco masks on Uaxactun's Temple E-VII-sub persuaded him that the Maya people of the Highland and Lowland regions had developed closely related but distinct cultural traditions. In addition, he noted that the then-recently discovered Olmec sculptures and architecture at La Venta, Tabasco, also had much in common with Maya art, and were probably another case of parallel development.

In fact, after the excavations of the Olmec center of La Venta by Matthew Stirling in the early 1950s, the site was thought to have been built by a Maya-speaking people. The work at La Venta followed earlier finds, also made by Stirling (1940), at Tres Zapotes that included carved inscriptions, inserting new energy into a theory that had been propounded long before: the origins of Mesoamerican civilization had to be researched in the tropical Lowlands of the Gulf Coast of Mexico. The early proponents of this theory, George Vaillant (1947) and Miguel Covarrubias (1946), had been influenced by the finding of early sculpture, ceramics and calendar inscriptions in the region at that time (Stirling 1940). Later, the monumentality of La Venta and its complex iconography became better known, and its antiquity with respect to any known monumentality in the Maya region became more widely accepted as a result. Alfonso Caso (1947) and Michael Coe (1966) became the staunchest proponents of the theory that much, if not all, that was civilized in Mesoamerican cultures could somehow be traced back to the Olmec. Others soon imagined waves of Olmec farmers migrating east from Gulf Coast, towards the Maya Lowlands, during the Preclassic period (e.g. Borhegyi 1965; Jiménez Moreno 1966). This idea was later known as "Olmec as the Mother Culture of Mesoamerica" (Coe 1966), and it is still supported by some scholars today (Clark and Pye 2000; Coe 2005; Diehl 2004).

Advances in the archaeology of the Highland and the Pacific Coast of Chiapas and Guatemala in the mid-20th century increasingly showed that these were areas of great artistic and cultural innovation during the centuries prior to the Classic Maya florescence. Kidder's work at Kaminaljuyú had demonstrated the great wealth and monumentality of Highland chiefly lineages expressed in their lavish tomb furnishings, which overshadowed anything then known from the Lowlands, including the rich Early Classic tombs from Uaxactun (Kidder *et al.* 1946). Also, excavations at the site of Izapa produced the largest corpus of carved stelae south of the Maya Lowlands and in a style that was clearly similar to those of Kaminaljuyú's Maya sculpture and Lowland Classic Maya. Because the Izapa cultural style was placed in the Late Preclassic period, it represented the chronological as well as the geographical middle ground between the Gulf Coast Olmec and the Lowland Maya florescence (Coe 1966). Based on these perceived relationships, the Highland–Lowland theory of earlier decades was strengthened. Coe and others proposed that the Izapan and Kaminaljuyú Maya were largely responsible for transmitting the sculptural style, hieroglyphic writing and iconographic motifs from the Olmec, who came before them, to the Maya of the Lowlands, thereby stimulating the emergence of Classic Maya civilization (Coe 1966; Parsons 1986). Finally, as archaeological reconnaissance progressed at the Highland sites of Chiapas (Chiapa de Corzo; Lowe 1977, 1981), it pointed to that region as a natural intermediary between the Olmec and the Lowland Maya and also to a chronologically intermediate florescence there and a possible source of migrations into the Lowlands. The "colonization of the Lowlands by Highland farmers" theory gained increased momentum through the second half of the century when agricultural and urban expansion in the Highlands and Pacific Coast opened new areas for archaeological investigation and many new sites became known. Comparatively speaking, however, little was known about much of the Maya Lowlands during the Preclassic period.

Theories of the origins of Maya civilization: the second part of the 20th century

The discussion on the "origins" of Maya civilization in the second part of the 20th century centered on the two main subjects debated by an earlier generation of archaeologists: the arrival of the first farmers in the Lowlands, and the sudden appearance of the trappings of civilization at the end of the Preclassic period. However, the archaeological discoveries in the Lowlands over the last 20 years do not fit prior assumptions and have brought earlier theories under closer scrutiny. This has produced heated debate among proponents of different theories of the rise of Maya civilization that have continued into the present.

Until recently, the prevailing view has been that the Lowlands were unoccupied until farming migrants arrived there from the west, east and south following the main rivers towards the interior (Puleston and Puleston 1971). This was all based on scanty ceramic remains, dating no earlier than 1000 BC. The earliest Lowland ceramics are significantly later than the earliest known ceramic-producing villages along the Gulf Coast, and in the southern Highlands of Chiapas, Guatemala, Honduras and El Salvador. Because of the similarity among the ceramics to styles of neighboring regions, it was believed that the earliest Lowland ceramics had been brought into the region by migrant farmers from one or more neighboring regions.

By the 1970s, the theory that developed farming societies migrated into the Maya Lowlands from the south or the west had long been accepted, being treated as a corollary to other theories. In many respects, though, these theories would turn out to have feet of clay. They dealt with later developments in the Lowlands and stressed ecological conditions, as well as processes of adaptation and competition. One of the most influential models was that of Olga and Dennis Puleston (Puleston and Puleston 1971), who suggested that migrant farmers spread into the Lowlands' interior along rivers because of a village-splitting and multiplying process, thanks, at least initially, not to maize agriculture but to bread-nut tree nuts (*ramon*) being their main staple. This model much resembled the well-known model of the colonization of central Europe through the Danube river system during the late Neolithic by the culture known as the Linearbandkeramik (Childe 1929; Bellwood 2005). It presupposed an egalitarian society, exponential population growth, and vast empty spaces to be filled by communities moving increasingly away from the rivers as time went by. Other models pointed our attention to processes such as population pressure and competition over increasingly scarce land and water resources leading to consolidation into areas of greater productivity and therefore greater population density (the Central Zone) and areas of lesser productivity and lower population density which were also geographically marginal (the Belize, Pasion and Northern zones). This led to the Central Zone, the area of Tikal, Uaxactun and some of the largest sites known at the time in the Lowlands being identified as the more dynamic core within a core–periphery interaction region (Rathje 1971; Sanders 1977). Warfare and trade were thought to be the most important mechanisms of a process leading to increasing Lowland social complexity. Both mechanisms were understood to have been stimulated by population pressure amid scarce resources (Rathje 1971; Webster 1977).

The second issue about "origins" was related to the first. Because they were thought to have arrived relatively late in the Lowlands, the Maya were believed to have had a late start in the process of civilization when compared with their neighbors along the Gulf Coast and in the southern Highlands. The apparent lack of archaeological evidence for any sort of complexity prior to 300 BC seemed to support this view. It was believed that most, if not all, of the trappings of civilization had originated elsewhere and were transferred into the Maya Lowlands when conditions were ripe for their adoption. Those conditions, it was believed, were not in place prior to the Protoclassic period (circa AD 50–250). Excavations in the Olmec region, however, had documented much earlier art and architecture at such sites as San Lorenzo and, again, La Venta. The Olmecs of San Lorenzo, a great site in a water-rich area of southern Veracruz, flourished between 1100 and 900 BC, while La Venta, perhaps the largest Olmec site, flourished between 900 and 400 BC.

Impressive new data from the Gulf Coast led an increasing number of scholars to embrace the Mother Culture theory. The Olmec of San Lorenzo and La Venta, with their monumental sculptures, pyramids, earthworks, caches and complex imagery (partly related to kings), appeared to predate any other civilization in Mesoamerica. How the trappings of civilization were exported from the Olmec heartland of the Gulf Coast into the Maya Lowlands was less clear. Indeed, if the Classic Maya had adopted the attributes of civilization from the Olmecs, this transformation would necessarily have happened centuries after La Venta was abandoned and the Olmecs as a culture had disappeared. The latter proposition was discussed as a possibility in the 1970s. Some hypothesized that after the break-up of the advanced Olmec political systems, agriculturalists fleeing from the Gulf Coast moved into the Maya Lowlands bringing remnant "institutions of authority" along with them (Webster 1977: 358). This hypothesis was made more plausible by the belief that the Olmec of the Gulf Coast were Maya speakers (Coe 1966).

As noted earlier, the problem of the non-contemporaneity of Olmec and Maya was resolved by identifying a culture and a geographic zone in which civilization flourished in an intermediate time, during the Late Preclassic period. This intermediate culture corresponded with the Izapan culture of the Pacific Coast and the nearby Highland Maya culture. These cultures had a florescence of monumental architecture, sculpture and writing prior to the Classic Maya, and bore much resemblance to Late Preclassic and Classic Maya art, as well as to earlier Olmec "prototypes." Until the end of the 20th century, both cultures were viewed as direct sources of much of the iconography and the political institutions of the Lowland Classic Maya, notwithstanding the fact that those features had originally been formulated by the Gulf Coast Olmec (Parsons 1986). The Late Preclassic period was viewed as a time of rapid growth in the Lowlands and the most likely period of cross-fertilization with the Izapan and Highland Maya cultures.

Peasant pioneers

As noted, the timing of the first colonization of the Maya Lowlands was largely tied to the earliest known ceramics. These ceramics are best referred to as Pre-Mamom, because they predate the first homogeneous style of pan-Lowland Maya ceramics. The Mamom ceramic complex had first been identified by the Carnegie Institution's excavations at Uaxactun and were later recognized in little-modified form at most Lowland sites dating to the later part of the Middle Preclassic period, from 800 to 400 BC (Smith 1950b). Pre-Mamom

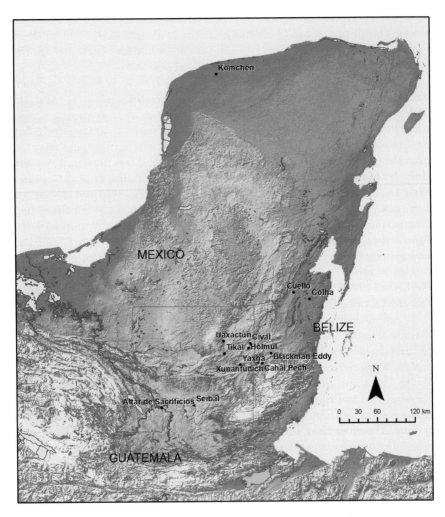

Figure 2.1 Lowland sites with Pre-Mamom ceramics (1100–850 BC)

Source: © F. Estrada-Belli, Topographic data courtesy of NASA SRTM mission

ceramics, on the other hand, were known only from a few sparse locations. They were first identified in the Pasion River region, at Altar de Sacrificios and Seibal, in the Belize River Valley and at Tikal. Subsequently, Pre-Mamom ceramics were also found in northern Belize, the Mirador Basin and at Holmul.

What is most striking about all the different sets of Pre-Mamom ceramics is that there is a high degree of stylistic divergence among them from region to region (Cheetham 2005). Similarities are strongest among neighboring sites. The Pre-Mamom ceramics of Altar de Sacrificios and Seibal appear to share enough similarities to suggest a homogeneous style. The ceramics of Holmul also share many similarities with the Belize River Valley (Cunil complex) and the Tikal/Uaxactun area (early Eb complex). The similarities across areas can be seen in the forms and decorations of serving vessels, while utilitarian vessels suggest greater local diversity. Clark and Cheetham (2002) have interpreted similarities among these early ceramic complexes to represent four major stylistic and interaction groups. These include a western Pasion group represented by the Xe ceramic complex of Seibal and Altar de Sacrificios (Adams 1971; Sabloff 1975). The central Peten group is represented by the Eb ceramic complex of Tikal, Uaxactun (Culbert 1977; Laporte and Valdés 1993), the Yaxha-Sacnab lake area's Ah Pam complex (Rice 1979) and the early Ox complex of Nakbe (Hansen 2005). In the third group is the Cunil ceramic complex of the Belize River Valley, with the possible inclusion of Holmul's Pre-Mamom types in it or in the Eb group (Awe 1992; Healy et al. 2004a; Strelow and LeCount 2001; Estrada-Belli 2006; Cheetham 2005; Callaghan 2006). Finally, the fourth group is represented by the Swasey/Bladen complex of northern Belize (Hammond 1973; Pring 1979; Kosakowsky 1987; Kosakowsky and Pring 1991, 1998). This ceramic complex is stylistically more dissimilar than similar to any other Pre-Mamom group. It lacks some of the incised decorations and has strong resemblances to the forms of the subsequent monochrome Mamom ceramic complex. Hypothetical migrations from various sources aside, it may be considered a regional variant more directly ancestral to the Mamom ceramic style than the other early complexes (Andrews and Hammond 1990; Cheetham 2005).

According to a recent reassessment (Clark and Cheetham 2002), the few scanty radiocarbon dates available for the Xe, Eb and Cunil ceramic complexes seem to cluster around the 1100–850 BC period. The same survey of early complexes proposes to place the beginning of Swasey/Bladen ceramics near 900 BC, therefore close to the end of the Pre-Mamom ceramic and cultural phenomenon, even though earlier published dates pushed its beginnings to as early as 2400 BC and subsequently to 1200 BC (Andrews and Hammond 1990; Andrews 1990).

At present there are no ceramics that predate 1100 BC in the Maya Lowlands. The set of known early ceramics is, to a large extent, the same as that examined by earlier generations of archaeologists. The same data or lack of any earlier data led them to hypothesize that Pre-Mamom ceramics reflected the colonization of the Maya Lowlands by groups of farming pioneers. The dates for the earliest ceramics gave the consistent indication that no farming villages were present in the Lowlands prior to 1100 BC and that the influx of pioneers and the spread of villagers into the interior were rapid processes. So strong was the belief in the validity of this model that many scholars failed to acknowledge another set of data that suggested a drastically different scenario.

The earliest Lowland farmers

In the late 1960s pollen data from the Peten lakes began to show signs of widespread deforestation and maize agriculture early in the Preclassic period, beginning at least as early as 2000 BC (Cowgill *et al.* 1966; Rice 1976). Interestingly, the lowest archaeological levels at the Belizean village site of Cuello have been dated by radiocarbon technique to 2600 BC (Hammond *et al.* 1976; but see below for corrected dates). These early dates remained controversial for some time. Later, more sediment data from Belize and the Peten lakes began to show consistently that deforestation and maize agriculture predated the advent of ceramics in the Lowlands. Most sediment cores provide dates for the beginning of deforestation and maize agriculture in the Lowlands clustering near 2500 BC, almost 1500 years prior to the earliest known ceramics (Neff *et al.* 2006; Pohl *et al.* 1996; Wahl *et al.* 2006b).

Although scarce, the sediment data come from geographically widespread Lowland locations and outline a consistent pattern of early or incipient agricultural societies throughout the interior, long before the postulated farmers' migrations.

Who were these early farmers? Some suggest that they were the direct descendants of late Archaic hunters and gatherers who left scanty remains of their stone tools, some of which have been recovered in the Belize coastal Lowlands (Clark and Cheetham 2002; Lohse *et al.* 2006). Here, two types of stone tool—the stemmed bifacial point or Lowe point and a heavier axe known as the constricted uniface—appear in Pre-Ceramic and Early Ceramic period levels, between 3000 and 850 BC. These stone tools are believed to be the only remaining evidence, besides pollen data, for the early inhabitants of the Pre-Ceramic period. They are known exclusively from northern Belize and their distribution largely overlaps with the distribution of Swasey and Cunil ceramics styles. The spatial correlation and continuity between the earlier stone tools and later ceramics suggest a cultural and ethnic continuity between the Pre-Ceramic and Ceramic inhabitants of the coastal Lowlands. Elsewhere in the interior of the Lowlands Pre-Ceramic stone tools are remarkably absent, perhaps due to accidents of discovery or because Pre-Ceramic farmers chose to live in very different locations than Early Ceramic villages and later settlements we archaeologists typically target for excavation.

Therefore, the northern Belizean stone tool data support the increasingly accepted proposition that there were widespread communities of Pre-Ceramic agriculturalists in the Lowlands as early as 2400 BC. The wide distribution of pollen core data and the ephemeral nature of these farmers' archaeological remains suggest that these early inhabitants were living in small, semi-permanent communities. In the rich wetlands, where early maize pollen has been found, extending into the adjacent upland areas, their subsistence was based on maize agriculture supplemented by hunting and gathering. Their residences have not been found, however, perhaps because they were ephemeral, semi-permanent settlements and the population relied on low-investment, slash-and-burn farming practices. On the other hand, their residences may not have been entirely ephemeral and their farming practices may not have required any shifts in settlement location. Instead, they may have been tied to wetland field cultivation, as in later periods, requiring limited investment. Given that few such areas have been the focus of intensive excavation, their fields and residences may simply not yet have turned up in archaeological samples.

Early villages and social ranking

At the moment, Pre-Mamom ceramics constitute the best archaeological evidence we have for the inhabitants of the Maya Lowlands circa 1000 BC. These ceramics are typically found in deeply buried contexts at the base of plazas, or directly on the modified natural rock surface below the most sacred and central part of a site. These spots invariably represent the highest and most prominent ground of an archaeological site and may have been selected by early farmers because they gave the advantage of visually controlling nearby resources. They also represent, in later periods, the most sacred space of a large ceremonial center and may therefore have been related to ritual since the beginning. Very few structures have been found in association with Pre-Mamom ceramics outside of northern Belize. At Cahal Pech, a few simple house platforms have been excavated in connection with Pre-Mamom (Cunil) ceramics at the bottom of Plaza B. One was more elaborate than the others and has been interpreted as a higher-status or ritual structure. This structure (B-IV 10c-sub) was a lime-plastered pole and thatch building resting on a 20-centimeter-high stone-and-plaster platform. Inside, against the back wall, was a lime-plastered bench. Its exterior plastered walls were painted red (Awe 1992; Cheetham 1998). A similar high-quality structure (B-1 10th–13th) was found below a Late Preclassic temple building at Blackman Eddy, a few miles downstream along the Belize River from Cahal Pech. This was an apsidal-plan pole-and-thatch structure whose exterior walls were also decorated with dull red painted plaster (Garber *et al.* 2004), as were ritual buildings of later Preclassic phases. At other sites, while no clear architectural remains have been found for this period, Pre-Mamom ceramics are found in bedrock pits or construction fill deposits below temple buildings and plazas, such as the North Acropolis and Mundo Perdido complexes at Tikal (Culbert 1977; Laporte and

Fialko 1993; Hermes 1993), the E-Group plaza at Cival and the Group II temple platform at Holmul (Estrada-Belli 2006). The latter location has produced the largest sample of Pre-Mamom ceramics in the Lowlands available today. In a few other cases, Pre-Mamom ceramics have been found in actual ritual contexts, such as the *k'an*-cross-pattern cache of Seibal, with four jade axes and a "bloodletter" effigy in the central location forming, like the Cival cache, the *k'an* symbol of Maya cosmic portals (Willey 1970) and a jade cache at Uolantun (Puleston 1973). In addition, a shell cache at Pacbitun, Belize, was dated to this period by C-14, although it included no ceramics (Healy *et al.* 2004b). All these finds present a consistent pattern of association of Pre-Mamom ceramics with ritual spaces, ritual activity and high-status structures, suggesting that early ceramics were possibly used primarily in elite or ritual contexts. This pattern is especially significant at large sites such as Tikal (and now also at Cival), where excavations have been extensive and yet failed to encounter Pre-Mamom ceramics away from the center.

All known samples of Pre-Mamom ceramics include a majority of serving vessels and jars. The most typical forms include spherical jars (*tecomates*) for liquids and round-sided or outcurving-side bowls, and flat-bottomed dishes with outsloping sides and everted rims, as well as vertical-side and outcurving-side dishes and plates to hold food. In addition to these, the Pre-Mamom ceramic inventory also includes censers, effigy bowls and mushroom stands. Differences among Pre-Mamom regional groups include certain unique vessel forms and jar handles. Surface finish is largely shared across groups. This is generally an orange-brown or buff dull finish, and red, black and more rarely white slips. Vessel forms are also largely shared among stylistic groups. Among these are peculiar wide-everted-rim dishes. The most notably recurring form is the globular *tecomate* jar, with or without short vertical neck. This form is also frequent in the southern Maya Highlands and Pacific Coast, as well as along the Gulf Coast of Highland Mexico in Early to Middle Preclassic contexts, indicating wide-ranging interactions among neighboring regions. White-slipped ceramic types are only known in limited percentages in the western Peten Pre-Mamom samples and may also indicate interaction with the west, primarily the Chiapas Highlands, where this surface color is more frequent.

The similarities among the earliest Maya ceramics and those of neighboring regions led many to assume that the farmers migrating into the Lowlands brought such ceramic technology and styles from their places of origin. According to Lowe (1977, 1981), these "donor areas" could be identified with Highland Chiapas; while Sharer and Gifford (1970) traced them to the Guatemalan and Salvadoran Highlands. The fact that a new, interrelated ceramic style was found in the area between the Highlands and the Lowlands, at Sakajut in the Alta Verapaz, strengthened the migration theory (Sedat and Sharer 1972). According to this same model, later innovations in Maya culture were also believed to have originated in the Highlands and transmitted to

Figure 2.2 Artist's reconstruction of the Pre-Mamom *K'awiil* ceramic complex from the Holmul region

Source: Drawing by Fernando Alvarez; © Holmul Archaeological Project

the Lowlands through migration. The existence of large Late Preclassic centers in the Highlands and the clear antiquity of hieroglyphic writing in that region supported the view that the Guatemala and Salvadoran Highlands and the Pacific Coast were the areas of greatest cultural dynamism during the Preclassic Maya. Because of their greater dynamism and the fact that they occupied the middle ground in time and space between the Olmec and the Lowland Maya, these areas were also more apt to have received influxes of complexity from the Gulf Coast (Coe 1966) and thus mediate contacts between the Olmec and the Maya.

However, similarities are greater among the Peten Pre-Mamom stylistic groups than between any of them and other styles outside of the Maya Lowlands. For example, the greatest similarities between two groups exist between the Holmul and Cunil. Similarities between Holmul and Seibal and Tikal or Cunil and Seibal are fewer. Seibal and Altar de Sacrificios, however, share the majority of ties. Each of these groups has a small set of similarities in color, forms and decorations with certain types in the Highlands and Pacific Coast. When compared to more distant styles, such as those of Oaxaca, for example, similarities are limited to incised decorative motifs. This pattern suggests the unlikelihood of these styles having been introduced to the Lowlands by a more developed group of migrants. Rather, these stylistic forms were a combination of locally developed forms (from the Pre-Ceramic) and symbolic expressions developed at similar times through inter-regional peer interactions.

The greatest similarity among the four Pre-Mamom stylistic groups of the Maya Lowlands is found in motifs incised on the vessels' surfaces. These typically include the flamed-eyebrow, the *k'an*-cross, the cleft-head, the

41

double-line break, the music brackets, the shark-tooth or bloodletter and the avian-serpent motifs. The *k'an*-cross and shark-tooth/bloodletter occur primarily on everted-rim dishes or on round-sided or vertical-sided bowls. The latest discovered Pre-Mamom ceramics from Holmul and Cival display the woven-mat, crossed-bands and U-shaped motifs in addition those noted above.

Outside of the Maya region, these motifs are found on ceramics of the late Early Preclassic and early Middle Preclassic periods in Highland Mexico, Oaxaca, the Gulf Coast, Highland and coastal Chiapas, and the Highlands and Pacific Coast of Guatemala and El Salvador. The vessels on which these signs occur are also generally similar to some of the forms of flat-based bowls and dishes from the Maya region.

The other common form across Mesoamerica, between 1200 and 900 BC, is the *tecomate*, the neckless globular jar. Flannery and Marcus (1994) suggest that the distribution of motifs on specific ceramic types (Gray and Yellow-white) within the Formative site of San Jose Mogote reflect clan divisions. Such divisions were clearly marked by the distribution of two sets of signs which these authors group under the headings "sky-monster," which includes the flamed-eyebrow, music-brackets and crossed-bands motifs as variants, and "were-jaguar" (a jaguar-faced human creature), which includes the double-line break and cleft-head motifs as variants (Flannery and Marcus 1994). During the San Jose phase the first set of signs was common on Leandro Gray ware while the second set occurred almost exclusively on Atoyac Yellow-white ware. It is interesting, however, that the distribution of such symbols on ceramics also marked a separation between low-status and high-status households. The high-status household had access not only to greater quantities of clan-symbol-decorated fine pottery but to several fine types imported from other regions, such as Tehuacan, Morelos/Valley of Mexico and the Gulf Coast. Similar varieties of incised motifs occur on pottery in those areas as well (Flannery and Marcus 1994: 339). These associations would indicate not only a preference for certain symbols among some clans/lineages within the Oaxacan commu-nity of San Jose but their ties through ritual and gift exchange with other emerging elites in far-distant regions of Mesoamerica.

Aside from the relatively higher-status structures of Cahal Pech, Blackman Eddy and some of the ritual caches from this period (Uolantun [Puleston 1973] and Seibal [Willey 1970]) noted earlier, the evidence for status dif-ferentiation during the Pre-Mamom phases is slim in the Maya Lowlands. The high quality of the ceramics and the meaning of the symbols they bear might be indications of the social context in which they were used. The fine quality of the ceramics can be seen in the lack of coarse paste among them and also in an abundance of fine paste and thin-walled forms with slipped surface finish and mostly post-fire incised decoration. The latter appears to have been applied after the ceramic was produced and possibly by someone other than the potter—a person of higher status who understood the meaning of abstract symbols.

The meaning of the symbols on Pre-Mamom ceramics can often be reconstructed using examples derived from the Late Preclassic and Classic periods as guides. The flamed eyebrow and crossed bands often occur together on the same vessel. Crossed bands often appear as representing the eyes of the sky-monster or the interior of its mouth. Music brackets are a variant of this avian symbol and apparently relate to the sky-monster, avian-serpent or principal bird deity of later Mesoamerican iconography. In Preclassic contexts, the celestial deity is depicted as a primordial god of creation. It is associated with a set of rain-evoking symbols, such as lightning, and the shark-tooth/bloodletter. The *k'an*-cross, cleft-head and double-line break motifs, and related variants of the were-jaguar, may be associated with the idea of the place of creation (cleft in the earth/mountain), the maize sprouting from a cleft in the earth, and ultimately the maize god. Finally, the mat motif is associated with the idea of rulership as well as with the maize and sun gods. With minor stylistic modification, both sets of motifs (sky and earth/maize) appear prominently in Late Preclassic and Classic period iconography (Estrada-Belli 2006). The media in which they appear in early Maya contexts are cache offerings such as the *k'an*-cross-shaped pits of Seibal and Cival, which are rich in jades as maize symbols, water symbols, and posts like the maize stalk and world-tree symbol (see Chapter 3). Other examples of avian maize god images are found on carved monuments such as the Cival Stela 2, where the figure wears a principal bird deity (PBD) mask pectoral identifying him as the personification of the maize god bearing the headdress of the avian god, as also depicted on Kaminaljuyú Stela 11. Recently, Lowland examples close in time to these have been discovered in Cival Mural 1 and in the West Wall of the San Bartolo mural (Hurst 2005; Saturno *et al.* 2005a). The avian-serpent imagery is also prevalent on temple pyramid sculptures at Nakbe, Cerros, Uaxactun and other sites where giant masks frame temple rooms in which the birth of the maize god is re-enacted (Freidel and Schele 1988; Hansen 1992). This theme is repeated on the friezes of Classic period temple buildings in the form of monstrous masks as well as on carved stelae as the rulers' headdress (Andrews 1995).

In light of the above observations, I think the motifs depicted on Pre-Mamom ceramics at various sites in the Maya Lowlands are consistent with rituals of evocation of sky deities, rain gods and the birth of the maize god, all of which are related aspects of the Maya (and Mesoamerican) story of creation. These symbols overlap in meaning with the accoutrements of Maya rulers of subsequent Preclassic periods, such as the avian aspects of the sun god, the maize god and various attributes of their costume. Rather than through migrations or colonization, these symbols are widely distributed across Mesoamerica because of intense inter-regional interaction and emulation across cultural and ethnic boundaries. Because the similarities in form and decoration are greater among groups within the Maya Lowlands than with groups in other regions, these similarities cannot be due to a flow of foreign populations into the area. Their meaning and context suggest that these symbols were used for semi-public displays during feasting rituals and other semi-public functions related to social ranking within farming communities in the Lowlands as in other parts of Mesoamerica. The wide distribution of these symbols and consistent association with high-status structures are further reinforced by the known disposition of emerging elites to engage in long-distance exchange to increase their status. This evidence supports a scenario in which the earliest ceramics known from the Maya Lowlands were adopted as elite objects within sedentary communities as status distinctions began to develop. Thus, the adoption of ceramics in the Maya Lowlands can be seen not as the first sign of farmer migrants entering the region but as the first sign of social ranking and the first step on the path towards state organization around 1000 BC. As a corollary to this, the evidence for egalitarian farming communities lies in the still-unrehearsed pre-1000 BC archaeological record of the Maya Lowlands as it is in neighboring parts of Mesoamerica.

Suddenly civilization?
Highland–Lowland migrations, again

After the work of the Carnegie Institution at Uaxactun, the large-scale excavations of the University of Pennsylvania at Tikal from 1957 to 1970 (Shook 1957; Coe 1990) represented the next major advance within the Peten in gathering data about the Preclassic. In particular the excavations in the North Acropolis at Tikal exposed a long and continuous sequence of temples and tombs that in some cases preceded the accepted date for the start of monumental architecture and tomb construction in the Classic period. These excavations also pointed to the Late Preclassic period as the phase of most rapid development of the institutions and artistic manifestations of Classic Maya civilization. This work was complemented by other large-scale excavations at Altar de Sacrificios (Willey 1973) and Seibal (Willey *et al.* 1982), and large-scale surveys in the Belize River Valley (Willey *et al.* 1965), which not only provided further indications of the antiquity of Maya occupation in the Lowlands (as we saw earlier) but added new fuel to diffusionist theories concerning the origins of Maya civilization.

The defining characteristics of the Classic Maya were polychrome ceramics, masonry architecture and hieroglyphic writing. Vaulted masonry buildings had now been found with increased frequency in Preclassic contexts. This was especially clear in the building sequence of the North Acropolis at Tikal, where several temple structures dated to the mid-Late Preclassic period (circa AD 100). These were lavishly decorated with mural paintings and stucco masks depicting supernatural beings apparently related to Classic Maya deities, along with ancestral figures related to rulers' iconography. In addition, richly furnished tombs were found inside the foundations of these early temples, suggesting the association of early architecture and ancestral rulers' veneration, a few centuries prior to the first-known dynastic rulers.

It was increasingly obvious to many that the institutions of Classic Maya civilization and their material manifestations had made their first appearance at places like Tikal in the Late Preclassic. The period of 300 BC onward was believed to be one of rapid growth until the "crystallization" of the institution of divine kingship and state organization near the 1st century AD (Adams and Culbert 1977; Willey 1977). As a corollary of this assumption, many saw the passage from village farming communities to Classic Maya city-states as a sudden phenomenon. Once again, there were indications that the sources of this rapid change could be found outside of the Lowlands.

Polychrome ceramics were a stylistic choice and technological innovation that appeared more or less suddenly at the end of the Late Preclassic period and were believed to be an important indicator of, if not a factor in, significant changes in the structure of Lowland Maya society. The earliest set of Lowland polychrome ceramics was first identified at Holmul during the 1911 Harvard excavations (Merwin and Vaillant 1932). The polychrome decoration consisted of abstract symbols and stylized supernatural forms in red, black and yellow, on an orange slip background. The new painted decoration appeared on new forms such as bowls, dishes and vases having mammiform supports, as well as on Z-angle profile vessels. Both painted styles and vessel forms appeared unrelated to previous types of Preclassic decoration, which favored red monochrome slips and simpler vessel forms. Prior to the Holmul excavations, no Preclassic ceramics were known. The early polychromes were found in two sealed tombs in a temple building (Rooms 8 and 9, Building B in Group II) and were identified as the starting point of the Maya cultural sequence—the Holmul I phase. Later, the Holmul combination of forms and polychrome paint began to be called the Q complex (Merwin and Vaillant 1932). As became clear later, these tombs also contained red monochrome vessels of common Late Preclassic types next to the polychromes. The subsequent Uaxactun excavation encountered ceramics of much earlier date. The Mamom and Chicanel Preclassic phases demonstrated a long, albeit slow, sequence of local development prior to the appearance of polychrome painted ceramics. The Holmul I types, however, were curiously absent from the Uaxactun corresponding early Classic phase, the Tzakol phase, or even the previous Chicanel phase. The Uaxactun polychromes instead included vessel forms such as basal flange bowls and painted decorations similar to the Holmul II ceramic period at Holmul. The first systematic regional survey in the Maya Lowlands, the Belize River Valley survey directed by Gordon R. Willey in 1954, recovered a much larger sample of Holmul I polychrome vessels amid abundant Late Preclassic complexes (Willey et al. 1965). This was denominated the Floral Park complex.

The naming of Holmul I ceramics as a ceramic complex had important implications. A ceramic complex is a complete set of vessels used at any one time in a site or region, and the introduction of a complex implies a major change in vessel manufacture and style. This led Gifford to hypothesize that a

Figure 2.3 Ixcanrio polychrome tetrapod (Terminal Preclassic), Holmul, Building B,
Burial 10, excavated in 2003 from the earliest dated context with such
vases at Holmul (AD 150)

Source: © Holmul Archaeological Project

new group had arrived in the Belize River Valley, bringing their new Floral
Park (Holmul I) ceramic style with them (Willey and Gifford 1961).

Increasingly, as research on this issue progressed, the Holmul I ceramic style
appeared to be irregularly distributed in the Lowlands and to cluster mostly
in eastern Peten and Belize (Pring 1977, 2000). To the south, mammiform
vessels and polychrome decorations found at Altar de Sacrificios and Seibal
marked a separate cluster or the limit of distribution of this style (Shook and
Smith 1950). Related tetrapod-form vessels with orange slip decoration,
however, were known to predate the Lowland Holmul I style in the Maya
Highlands. Based on specific stylistic ties and the precedence of the vessel
forms and orange slip technique in the Highlands, Sharer and Gifford (1970)
suggested that the Holmul I style had been brought into the Lowlands by
groups of Highland migrants from the centers of Kaminaljuyú in central
Guatemala and Chalchuapa in western El Salvador. The migrations were
said to have followed the same routes as the much earlier ones, which had
brought Xe ceramics and agriculture to the Lowlands, and were believed to
be responses to increased competition for resources among an overgrown
Highland population, a supposition attested to by the sizes of Kaminaljuyú
and Chalchuapa. The discovery of a Holmul I-related style of ceramics in the

intermediate northern Highland region of Salama, Alta Verapaz (in connection with early inscriptions and sculpture), suggested that they may have moved north with a wave of migrants with hieroglyphic writing and complex political institutions via the shortest route (Adams 1971; Sharer and Gifford 1970; Sharer and Sedat 1973).

Another possible motive for this migration could have been the eruption of the Ilopango volcano in El Salvador, which perhaps sent waves of refugees north and west (Sharer and Gifford 1970; Sheets 1971). This eruption was also correlated with the termination of temple construction and stela carving at Kaminaljuyú and Chalchuapa. Elites from these centers would have fled into the Lowland centers with which long-standing relations already existed. The new influx of foreigners would have overlaid a new high-status class of individuals upon a society with less developed ranking. This process was evident in the appearance of "rich" polychrome vessel types—in addition to the existing "poor" Preclassic forms—concurrent with other elite features, such as the stela cult, Long Count calendar systems, and more elaborate tombs at some Lowland centers. Study of the Ilopango eruption and the ensuing widespread destruction of settlement in western El Salvador added weight to this theory (Sheets and Grayson 1979). It was widely adopted when the Ilopango eruption was dated to AD 260. The eruption was later re-dated to AD 400–550 (Dull et al. 2001). However, in either case, the Ilopango catastrophe was a couple of centuries too late to have caused the influx of Holmul I ceramic style in the Maya Lowlands, which was believed to have occurred in the first century AD (Pring 1977, 2000). Nevertheless, most scholars continued to accept the migration theory as fact.

The period from AD 50 to 250 was believed to represent a major transition from the Preclassic to the Classic period and the "crystallization" of Classic Maya civilization. It was termed the "Protoclassic" (Gifford 1965; Willey and Gifford 1961). Exactly what significant cultural and social changes this transition entailed was to be a matter of discussion for some time.

Even in the face of widespread ceramic influences from the Highlands, some doubted that such similarities should be attributed to significant population movements into the Lowlands. In an overview of this issue Gordon Willey (1977) pointed out that the Late Preclassic period was a time of growth in population as well as in cultural complexity in the Lowlands. The Holmul I-style ceramics appeared at the end of this period but no corresponding population increase was discernible in the archaeological record. However, Willey also noted that some areas, such as the northern plains (Dzibilchaltun), experienced a decline, while other areas continued their progress towards the early Classic with a total lack of Holmul I-style ceramics (Willey 1977; see also Ball 1977).

Protoclassic or Holmul I-style ceramics were clearly present at Tikal (Culbert 1977). The Highland-inspired polychrome techniques and the Usulutan-like (Highland-inspired) negative/resist or double-slip painting technique at Tikal marked a gradual increase in sophistication and overall status differentiation locally extending back to the Late Preclassic period. Willey (1977) believed, as Morley (1946) did before him, that the existence of early carved dates (Baktun 8: i.e. pre- 9.0.0.0.0/AD 435) primarily in the Tikal zone was of paramount importance for understanding the development process of Classic Maya civilization. While the "ideas" of the stela cult and polychrome decoration may have been introduced through contact with the Highlands, Morley (1946) believed these were innovations of a local emerging elite centered at Tikal. Once formed, the Tikal kingdom assumed an expansive mode, attempting to build an "empire" in the Peten. This would have explained the introduction of elite innovations at Tikal first, such as the carving of Long Count inscriptions on stela monuments there, and the radiating distribution of early-dated monuments at sites in the central Tikal region, as well as in surrounding areas to the east (Holmul and Belize), west (Usumacinta region) and south (Pasion region). This zone also largely overlapped with the spotty distribution of Holmul I ceramic styles, and, as Hammond (1977) noted, included northern Belize, probably because of its strategic resources and river routes to the sea. Long-distance trade connections were also believed to be radiating from Tikal during the Protoclassic and Early Classic period, due to the increased complexity of the local system.

Willey (1977) noted that it was probably not coincidental that the earliest signs of Teotihuacan interest in the Maya Lowlands were found at places along the Lowland routes, such as Altun Ha on the Belizean coast (see also Pendergast 1971). The distant center of Teotihuacan might have had an influential role in the formation of the Classic Maya state. Sanders and Price (1968) proposed that Classic Maya society was the product of a process of secondary state formation emanating from the area of primary state formation, the central Highlands of Mexico. This process was viewed from an evolutionary perspective, envisioning Late Preclassic Highland centers such as Kaminaljuyú being transformed into state-organized societies after the arrival of elite emissaries from Teotihuacan. Subsequent penetration of Teotihuacan traders and accompanying military groups, similar to the Aztec *pochteca*, into the Peten region would also have transformed the Preclassic Tikal chiefdom into an Early Classic Maya state. Evidence of Teotihuacan-style temple architecture and richly furnished tombs in Early Classic Kaminaljuyú (Kidder *et al.* 1946) was interpreted as a sign of a foreign enclave of elite merchants at that site. Similarly, the mounting evidence of Teotihuacan-style architecture and ceramics at Tikal brought to light by the Pennsylvania excavations inspired many scholars to envision a strong Teotihuacan influence on the locals at the opening of the Classic period (Coe 1965; Coggins 1975; Proskouriakoff 1993).

The Preclassic Maya behemoth

The discovery of the Preclassic Maya center of El Mirador and a score of other large Preclassic centers in northern Guatemala in the last 20 years of the 20th century turned many theories of foreign influence about the origins of the Maya Lowlands on their heads.

The site of El Mirador was known to airplane pilots in the 1930s as a clear peak emerging from the rather flat forested landscape of northern Peten. The fact that this was a man-made feature—massive pyramids later called the Danta complex—was subsequently established by oil prospectors, chicle gum collectors, and finally by solitary Maya explorer Ian Graham in 1962. Graham first mapped the site and reported that El Mirador was a predominantly Late Preclassic construction, and the largest Maya site thus far known. In fact, the Danta complex is the largest Mesoamerican pyramid. The idea that a site of these proportions dated to before the Classic period was largely dismissed by the academic community but later confirmed by excavations. The first archaeological explorations were conducted in the 1980s by Brigham Young University (Matheny *et al.* 1980) and briefly by Harvard University (Demarest 1984). Research at El Mirador and nearby sites continues with an inter-disciplinary project led by Idaho State University's Richard Hansen (Hansen 1990, 1998, 2005).

The site's map shows a vast ceremonial core stretching along an upland area for over 2 kilometers from east to west and more than 1 kilometer from north to south. This area was likely completely paved with plaster flooring and punctuated by massive temple complexes. The largest of these was the Danta complex at the east end of the site. It featured a Triadic Group of temples, a common feature at El Mirador, whose eastern temple rose 73 meters above the group. The group rested on a gigantic platform over 600 meters wide, rising in three broad terraces. The lowest terrace is occupied by a large pyramid on the west and an elongated platform on the east. This type of arrangement was first identified at Preclassic Uaxactun Group E, and is known at other Maya sites as the E-Group plaza type (see Chapter 3). The Danta complex stands in relative isolation with respect to the central and western parts of the site, which constitute a more compact area of connected plazas, platforms and temples. A large moat and embankment encircling the central and western part of the site gives the impression that the Danta complex was thought by the Maya themselves to be separate from the rest of the site. Within this main area are a number of very impressive temple complexes, such as El Tigre, the second-largest Triadic complex (53 meters maximum height), located at the western extreme of the ideal axial line bisecting the site from east to west and passing through the Danta pyramid. Of the major Triadic Groups, the Monos Group, located at the south end of the core, is the third largest in volume and height. Following these are a number of smaller complexes, including the Tres Micos. As many as 15 complexes at El Mirador repeat the Triadic arrangement,

Figure 2.4 Artist's reconstruction of the central area of El Mirador, as it may have appeared circa AD 100

Source: Courtesy of the National Geographic Society

with east–west (as Danta and Tigre) or north–south axes (as Monos and Tres Micos). An elevated complex mixing Triadic temples and probably some non-temple groups dominates the central area of the site and is known as the Central Acropolis. To the north of this is the main E-Group plaza at El Mirador, the Leon Group—one of the largest in the Maya Lowlands.

El Mirador was not only a ceremonial center on a previously unseen scale, both in area and number of buildings, but the focus of a network of large centers connected by a system of paved causeways within a large area now known as the Mirador Basin. This is a region of upland karst, the highest elevated plateau of the Yucatan karst, covering over 2200 square kilometers. Two major rugged hill ridges provide geographical barriers along the east and west, enclosing a roughly triangular area between. To the north, the upland gently dissolves into a region of lower karst. The basin is largely occupied by wetlands punctuated by islands of upland soil containing the tallest forest vegetation. Such upland locations are occupied by El Mirador and all the major Preclassic sites in the region. One major causeway connects El Mirador with the second-largest center in the region—Tintal—18 kilometers to the south across vast wetland *bajo* areas. Other major causeways radiating out of El Mirador connect to Nakbe, 12 kilometers to the southeast, and unknown centers to the west and northwest. One causeway possibly connects El Mirador with Calakmul, 40 kilometers to the north. This causeway system testifies to the massive scale

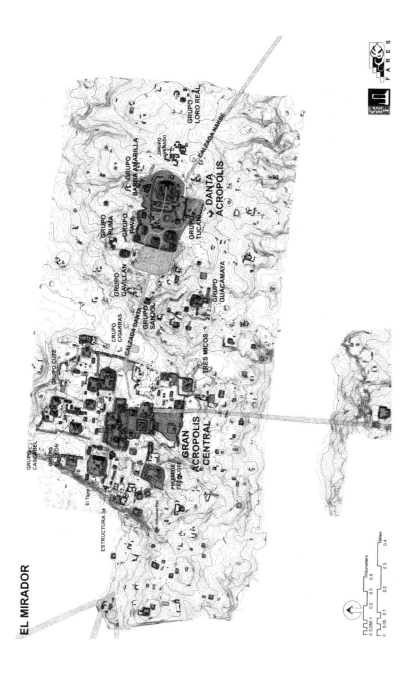

Figure 2.5 Map of El Mirador

Source: After Hansen *et al.* 2008b; © FARES; courtesy of Richard D. Hansen

of ceremonial works in the region and the central role played by El Mirador in integrating centers in other parts of the basin into a single ritual and perhaps political system (Hansen 2005).

Hansen's reconnaissance in the Mirador Basin has produced a large inventory of Preclassic centers, work that has been matched by Ivan Spajc on the Campeche side of the border (Hansen *et al.* 2008b; Sprajc 2002). Most reached their building apex during the Late Preclassic, before being subsequently abandoned, as at El Mirador. Each of these is impressive on its own terms for scale and complexity of architecture. Carved monuments in Lowland Preclassic style have been found at El Mirador, Nakbe and Tintal. The latter site is known for its massive Triadic Group of temples, the second largest outside of El Mirador, and the huge watered ditch encircling its main plaza groups. The site of Wakna, with a 200-meter-long eastern platform and tall western pyramid, lies southeast of El Mirador and boasts major architecture as well as the largest E-Group complex. Its Triadic Groups also house mural paintings yet to be completely uncovered. Other major sites are El Porvenir, La Florida, La Muralla and Zacatal, all yet to be fully explored (Hansen 2005).

Perhaps the most striking new fact added to our presently limited knowledge of the Preclassic Lowland Maya is that the monumental architecture at the site of Nakbe largely—as it has been mostly attributed to the late Middle Preclassic Ox (late Mamom) phase (600–350 BC; Hansen 1992, 1998)—predated that of many other basin sites, including El Mirador. The earliest Nakbe architecture includes a ball-court and an E-Group.

In Richard Hansen's (2005) opinion, several centers emerged simultaneously and then competed with one another in the Middle Preclassic period, with Nakbe perhaps being the largest. The relatively homogeneous ceramics of this epoch, the Mamom pottery, would reflect the increased interaction and political integration of the Maya Lowlands at this time around selected centers, such as Nakbe in the Mirador Basin. The process of centralization and integration was accentuated during the Late Preclassic period, when El Mirador overshadowed all other centers and extended its trade connections far across the Yucatan Peninsula. Other large centers with mainly Late Preclassic architecture became known outside of the Mirador Basin. These were Seibal, in the Pasion region of Peten (Willey 1970), Nohmul (Hammond 1985), Cerros (Freidel 1982) and Lamanai in northern Belize (Pendergast 1981), Becan in southern Quintana Roo (Webster 1976), San Bartolo (Saturno *et al.* 2005b) and Cival in northeastern Peten (Estrada-Belli *et al.* 2003a, 2003b). All these sites display a primary Late Preclassic occupation followed by permanent or temporary abandonment. Some of them—Cerros, Becan and Cival—boasted large-scale defensive moats or stone walls. At other sites an important Late Preclassic building component was recognized by excavations such as those at Seibal, Altar de Sacrificios and Tikal, and more recently at Calakmul, Rio Azul, Yaxha and Naranjo, Caracol and Cahal Pech. Among these, Tikal's sprawling periphery was enclosed within vast earthworks (moat and embankment) in the Late Classic period (Webster 2004). Curiously, the moat was apparently missing in large sections and the circle around the city may never have been finished.

The new political geography of the Late Preclassic Maya Lowlands and the great similarity in architecture and art were doubtless the result of intensive interaction. The possible prominence of El Mirador amid less organized Lowland polities, combined with the similarities in art and architecture and the great homogeneity of the Chicanel phase ceramics across Lowland regions, led Hansen (Hansen and Guenter 2005) to speak of El Mirador as the first Maya state. As El Mirador's massive temples, carved monuments and hieroglyphs clearly demonstrated, a Preclassic Maya state was no longer a fantasy. To state the matter more broadly, many lines of evidence now indicated that "Preclassic Maya civilization is no longer a contradiction in terms" (Hammond 1980: 189).

3

MAYA STATES BEFORE
THE CLASSIC PERIOD

The rise of the first Lowland states

For Mayanists, as for experts in other ancient cultures, the scientific definition of "civilization" is normally tied to several material traits. Among the most commonly mentioned are social hierarchy, craft specialization or forms of interdependence among population segments, monumental architecture, complex ideology and public rituals, and writing systems. Maya archaeologists long believed the first appearance of these traits coincided with the onset of the Classic period (AD 300–900). For the Lowland Maya, the Classic period's defining criteria were held to be the first appearance of writing in the form of carved stelae, craft specialization in the form of polychrome painted ceramics, and masonry architecture in the form of corbeled-vault roofed buildings. These categories were admittedly arbitrary and broad. They were largely based on the findings of these traits in the excavations of Uaxactun in the 1930s, and the AD 292 date of Tikal Stela 29, which is the earliest monument bearing a calendar date in the Lowlands. For decades, these markers served to guide archaeologists who attempted to make sense of disparate findings from 3000 years of development throughout the Yucatan Peninsula.

As often happens, once fixed classifications are created, exceptions begin to emerge. Even as early as the Carnegie excavations at Uaxactun during the 1930s, exceptions emerged that suggested that monumental architecture and painted ceramics predated the AD 300 cut-off date. Even though the earliest writing in the Lowlands dated to AD 292 (Tikal Stela 29), it appeared with such sophistication and complexity that many postulated that it must have evolved long before Stela 29's date. On the other hand, many scholars in the first half of the 20th century firmly believed in the greater antiquity of writing systems in the southern Highlands and the Pacific Coast of Guatemala. They were not surprised by the mature style of the early Lowland stelae and explained it by proposing that the Lowland Maya had simply adopted the writing system developed by their southern neighbors (an opinion still held by some scholars even today, in spite of linguistic data to the contrary). The adoption of writing necessarily had to coincide with the time in which the

Lowland Maya had reached a sufficient level of complexity for them to make use of such an advanced tool. As we will see in the following section, this expectation was recently put to rest by the discovery of Preclassic texts in stone and other media. But even prior to these discoveries, many scholars challenged this position by pointing out that many "higher civilizations" of the ancient world had little or no use for a writing system. One often-invoked example was the great Mesoamerican civilization of Teotihuacan, where most researchers find no signs of a fully functioning writing system, despite the glyph-like signs used in iconography. Many have pointed out that the content of Mesoamerican writing systems was related to dynastic histories and propaganda. The absence of writing at Teotihuacan and the absence of any images of rulers were found to fit with the prevailing model of Teotihuacan being ruled by a corporate system (Pazstory 1997). Other ready examples of great civilizations lacking writing were the Inca and the Andean civilizations that preceded them. (The Inca did, however, have a complex recording system, the *quipu*, which combined the recording of tribute and economic transactions with oral communications in encoded messages that only the elite could decipher.)

Until recently, many scholars agreed that the Lowland Maya lacked several important characteristics of "civilization" prior to AD 300. The most important was the non-existence of kings or other individualized and centralized institutions. Many adduced the Classic period's custom of burying rulers in underground chambers with rich furnishings and human sacrificial victims as terms of reference. When such elaborate tombs failed to appear at Preclassic sites, despite intensive excavation, many felt forced to conclude that the Preclassic Maya must have had forms of rulership that did not include individual kings until the end of the Preclassic period. It was thought that these people were probably ruled by a class of religious leaders (theocracy) such as the one postulated to have ruled over Teotihuacan (Thompson 1970), or by a system similar to the *multepal*, an assembly of lineage leaders who ruled the statelets of northern Yucatan just prior to the arrival of the Spanish conquerors (Roys 1957: 6; Marcus 1993: 118–120). Replacing a corporate system with an individualized system of governance would represent a significant cultural change—a "conjuncture," a term used by Annalist historians for a moment of social change with widespread ramifications for the organization of economic, ritual and power relations (Knapp 1992b).

In the line of the founder: Preclassic royal burials

The excavations at Tikal by the University of Pennsylvania began to turn up evidence that challenged earlier assumptions about the lack of kings in Maya society prior to the Classic period. Beneath the massive Late Classic temples of the North Acropolis, archaeologists documented a sequence of rich burials (tombs) dating to the Late Preclassic period (Coe 1990). These were often placed in axial position under the basal platform of temples, as if they served to venerate the interred individual. It was thought that most of the first 22 rulers of Tikal were interred in this location. The earliest burials in this complex date to the Middle Preclassic, and more elaborate tombs began to appear in the Late Preclassic period. Among them, Burial 85 was outstanding for its rich furnishings, including a repertoire of decorated vessels. Many scholars believe this to be the tomb of the ruler identified by Simon Martin (2003) as *Yax Ehb Xook*, named in later Classic period inscriptions as the founder of the Tikal dynasty (Coe 1990; Jones 1991). A revision of archaeological and epigraphic evidence has now placed his death near AD 100, identifying the remains in Burial 85 as likely to be his (Martin and Grube 2000; Martin 2003).

The tomb was at the bottom of a deep, 2.5-meter shaft reaching into the bedrock layer. A chamber built with roughly shaped blocks and beveled stones formed a corbeled vault. It accommodated an adult male with a rich funerary cache of vessels. The body was found headless and in a seated position. Several missing bones indicated that it had been deposited as a defleshed bundle. A jadeite mask had been placed on top of the bundle in lieu of the head. This represented an individual wearing the trilobed *hun* royal crown. Shell and coral inlays were used for his eyes and teeth. Twenty-six vessels of various forms and decoration accompanied the body. Many of these were adorned with red or brown painted wavy lines on an orange background, reminiscent of the Usulutan resist technique more common in the southern Highlands in the Late Preclassic. Among the most extraordinary vessels was a tall spouted effigy jar, also decorated with wavy lines. Aside from the elaborate decorations that recalled foreign influences, three brown-black incised bowls found in the tomb were imports from the Highland center of Kaminaljuyú. Also, in the interred cache were shell and jade ornaments, stingray spines for bloodletting, and paper-thin painted gesso fragments that may have been the remains of a codex. The latter is a rare item associated with royal burials in the Classic period. Once the tomb had been deposited and the shaft filled, a small platform was built over it, Structure 5D-Sub 2. This was a small pole-and-thatch structure that may have served as a commemorative shrine for the interred. It is one of several such shrines built over burials that preceded and followed Burial 85.

If this individual was in fact the person later Tikal kings recognized as the founder of their dynasty, and if Tikal had indeed some prominence in formalizing the institution of kingship among Lowland Maya, then the beginning of Lowland Maya "civilization" must indeed have coincided with this ruler's accession to new levels of power. Many agreed that this burial and the concomitant appearance of badges of royalty such as the *hun* crown in the iconography marked the beginning of kinship, and by extension of Maya civilization, to about AD 100.

However, what is lacking from Burial 85 is as interesting as what it contains. We would expect the burial of the founder of a new regime, one that

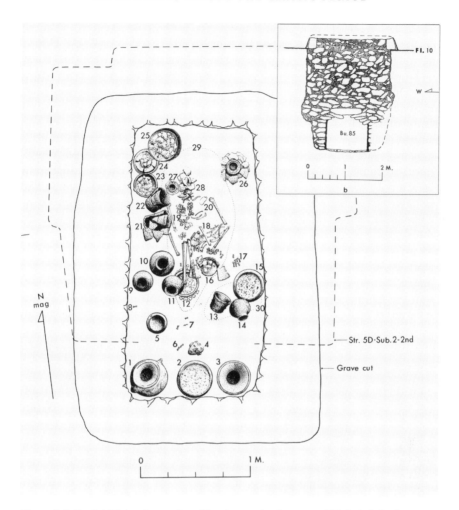

Figure 3.1 Burial 85 in plan and profile view under Structure 5D-Sub 2-2nd

Source: After Coe 1990, Tikal Report 14; courtesy of the University of Pennsylvania Museum of Archaeology and Anthropology

involves the concentration of the polity's political power (and, at least for the later Maya, of the public ritual ceremonies) upon the person of the ruler, to correspond with major changes in the way such rituals and politics are performed at the site. This in turn should require a change in the arrangement of the building in and around which the rituals and state offices are performed. There is no such change in the layout of the Northern Acropolis that immediately precedes or follows the Burial 85 interment. Instead, we discover a marked continuity and incremental improvement in a long-established pattern of ritual buildings.

Other rich burials were placed in the North Acropolis even before Burial 85, during the general 1st century AD of the Late Preclassic period. One of these is Burial 166, a tomb containing the body of a middle-aged woman and the bundled remains of a young woman accompanied by 21 vessels. Several of these closely match vessels in Burial 85, such as the tall Altamira fluted jars and one spouted tall-necked chocolate jar, and there is frequent use of Usulutan wavy line decoration, although there is less variety of decoration and imports. The tomb was placed on the open western side of the acropolis plaza and a low platform was built above it (5D-Sub 11). In terms of its position in time, this tomb was separated from Burial 85 by two re-paving episodes on the acropolis plaza, so it is likely that this important lady and her bundled younger relative were ancestors of that male individual rather than his contemporaries.

Another predecessor of Burial 85 was interred on the eastern side of the acropolis plaza at roughly the same time, or shortly prior to AD 100. This tomb (Burial 167) was cut through the plaza floor immediately in front of the eastern temple (Structure 5D-9). In the same fashion as Burial 85, it stood in front of the acropolis's main (northern) temple (Structure 5D-1). A deep (2.4-meter) vertical shaft through the floor of the plaza terminated into an

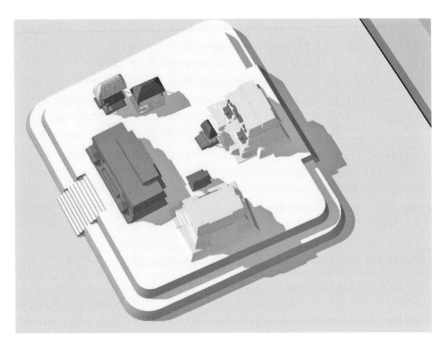

Figure 3.2 Tikal North Acropolis circa AD 70 with shrines facing temple buildings

Source: From Loten 2007; courtesy of the University of Pennsylvania Museum of Archaeology and Anthropology

east–west-oriented chamber. The walls and the vault were built with roughly squared and beveled stones and covered with a coat of dark mud. In it were three individuals: a principal adult male, in extended position; a bundled female arranged in a pot on the chest and right arm of the male; and an infant laid in a vessel at the male's side. The 17 accompanying vessels resembled the Burial 85 assemblage in variety of form and decoration. In addition to the wavy line Usulutan decorated tall-necked bowls and jars, there was an example of two imported black-brown incised bowls identical to the three in Burial 85.

These correspondences in the artifacts contained in Burials 166 and 167 are undoubtedly due to the close spacing in time of these interments, as well as their close familiarity during their lifetimes. According to the plaza's stratigraphy, Burial 167 was an important male, possibly a ruler, whose date fell in the years between the women in Burial 166 and the male (founder) in Burial 85. His body was not adorned with jade ornaments, as in the others' interments, but with shell necklaces and pendants. However, his tomb was marked by a more substantial platform shrine than the others. Above the burial shaft was a small vaulted building (Structure 5D-Sub 10-1st). The preserved rear wall of this two-room building was decorated with a beautifully colored mural depicting two figures standing amid red cloud-like scrolls below a sky-band motif. The iconography seems to be evoking the celestial deities whom the interred was to join in the afterlife. As in the other two examples described above, this shrine stood in front of a major temple, effectively occupying a prominent position within the plaza.

These tombs of the end of the Late Preclassic period were but a sample of several earlier interments in this location within the main acropolis plaza. Indeed, the individual in Burial 167 could be the ruler immediately preceding Burial 85, the Tikal dynasty's founder. Because of similarities in the furnishings and honorific placements of these tombs, we must assume that no significant breaks in the genealogy of Tikal's rulers occurred when the "founder" took the throne. Instead, these elites buried in the North Acropolis were the inheritors of high status from a long line of rulers, reaching back into the beginning of the Late Preclassic. This leads to several questions. Why was Burial 85, or *Yax Ehb Xook*, or another ruler from the period around AD 100, proclaimed the "founder" of the dynasty by later kings? What was his relation to the several earlier rulers buried in the North Acropolis and elsewhere at Tikal? And why did his reign not result in any extensive renovation of the North Acropolis, but rather a continuation of the *status quo?*

Approximately 100 years passed after the deposition of the "founder" in Burial 85 before significant renovations occurred on the acropolis, in what Tikal archaeologists' refer to as Time Span 10 (Coe 1990). The next construction episode in the acropolis involves the massive burial of all existing temples up to their roofs, with over 5 meters of vertical infilling, and the expansion of the platform area. New temples were built on this higher and wider space above the older ones, denoting great continuity in ritual behavior. This episode

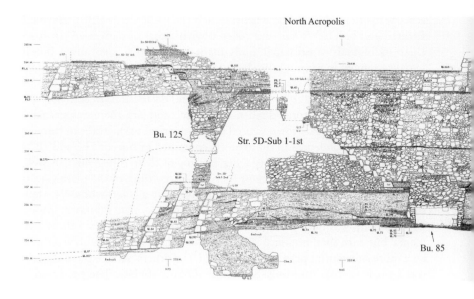

of major renovation certainly reflects a period of prosperity and political integration at Tikal, if not consolidation of power in the hands of the rulers. More than one ruler must have been responsible for this renovation, but only one was found buried in the central axial location that earlier rulers had chosen, Burial 125. This burial was placed in front of the new northern temple of the North Acropolis, in the most prominent location, as was his Burial 85 predecessor. The tomb was cut deeply into the acropolis and the shaft sealed by a low, south-facing platform (5D-Sub 7), in all ways similar to the one above Burial 85 (5D-Sub 2). According to William Coe (1990), who directed the Tikal excavations, this individual may have been one of the successors of the founder who commissioned the final stages of the renovation; although, given the lengthy period evident from the various additions, other rulers before him must have contributed to it. There was also a stark absence of any offerings in Burial 125. This led Coe (1990) to propose that it could represent a non-royal individual or a sacrificial victim interred as a dedicatory offering to the new building. In either case, this deposition would represent the final outcome of an extended period of prosperity rather than being the result of a single watershed project. The other most important ritual area of Tikal—the Mundo Perdido astronomical complex—experienced significant renovation and increase in the size of its buildings and in the elaboration of the art that decorated them. High-status burials were deposited there after AD 200 (Laporte and Fialko 1990).

The significance of later kings at Tikal naming a founder around AD 100 is still not clear. The date of his death is indeed independently corroborated by several king lists and the best candidate for Burial 85 remains *Yax Ehb Xook*.

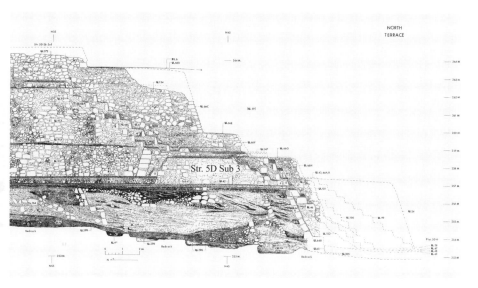

Figure 3.3 Profile of the University of Pennsylvania Museum trench across the North
Acropolis showing major infilling that buried the pyramids associated with
Burial 85 (at center)

Source: From Coe 1990, Tikal Report 14; courtesy of the University of Pennsylvania Museum
of Archaeology and Anthropology

It is clear, however, that some of his successors witnessed far greater changes
in the city, or at least more tangible ones, and had more resources at their
disposal. The continuity in the temples and royal interments in the North
Acropolis of the Late Preclassic, which were effectively emblematic of the ideology of the living rulers and their forebears, is also clear. It is possible that
the period following AD 100 represents the beginning of a period of unprecedented prosperity at Tikal rather than a "conjuncture" in which major changes
were made to the ancient Maya system of governance.

Preclassic kingdoms and the AD 100 "conjuncture" across the Lowlands

We must then look outside of Tikal for any evidence of major changes that
may coincide with the installation of new rulers or new forms of rulership.
Elaborate burials have been found at many Preclassic sites across the Maya
Lowlands. There is, however, a general lack of well-furnished burials such as
Tikal Burial 85, in spite of an abundance of other impressive traits of complexity, such as monumental architecture and iconography of rulership. Most
glaring is the absence of burials from some of the greatest sites of this period,
such as El Mirador. The majority of relatively richly furnished Preclassic

burials come from some of the smaller sites of the period, and the richness of their funerary offerings is often commensurate with the size and relative importance of the site in which they are found. The smaller Lowland sites have historically received far more research than the larger ones of the central Lowlands (i.e. in northern Peten, and adjoining remote areas of Campeche and Quintana Roo, Mexico). This is due to the difficulties of accessing architecture and interments deeply buried underneath massive construction at large sites.

One must consider the possibility that different burial practices that did not require the disposal of personal wealth with the ruler's body and the placement in public buildings may have been in operation prior to the end of the Preclassic period. Generations of archaeologists have been accustomed to the richness of Classic Maya royal burials but one must question whether those levels of personal display of wealth represent an absolute standard or a characteristic typical of the Classic period (i.e. tombs are equally rare in the Postclassic period). Nevertheless, there are several indications that relatively elaborate burials were not as uncommon in most Late Preclassic sites as is generally believed. While most Preclassic burials do not include the spectacular array of artifacts found in Tikal's tombs, this lack may also be due to the nature of the excavated sample, biased as it is towards main temple groups and plazas. In addition to being located at the base of temples, there is a good possibility that earlier generations of rulers were buried in residential contexts and that these remain covered under less obvious constructions, as is the case in smaller sites.

The best examples of burials of Preclassic high-ranking individuals have been found in residential contexts at smaller sites, such as Cuello, an unassuming Preclassic community in northern Belize. Here, thanks to more than 20 years of excavations, indicators of social status have been found in burials dating to the earliest phases of the Middle Preclassic (1000–800 BC) including jade and shell ornaments associated with both children and adults. Several high-status burials appear in a sequence in specific residential loci over periods of time. Among them, one stands out, Burial 160, which dates to 500–400 BC. The individual was buried in a simple cist and was accompanied by two ceramic vessels and ornaments. Of particular note were tubes made of deer bone decorated with the mat design later associated with royal power, and a plaque carved into a face from the top part of a human skull. Thus, the excavators concluded that this individual, like others buried with such symbols of power, was among the Middle Preclassic rulers of the small Cuello community. That the locus of these burials had special significance for this community was demonstrated by the later conversion of the residential patio into a raised ceremonial platform supporting a small pyramid temple (Hammond *et al.* 1992).

The discovery of a rich burial at San Bartolo offers another significant example of Preclassic elite mortuary practices. San Bartolo Tomb 1 was found in a residential group (Grupo Jabali), located to the northwest of the main public site core (Pellecer 2006). The tomb was placed in front of the western structure of the group, an elite residential platform, in a chamber sealed by horizontal slabs. In the funerary cache were six vessels, including an unusual orange effigy censer, effigy bowls decorated with Usulutan style wavy lines and other Late Preclassic vessels of the finest quality among Lowland burials of the period (e.g. see Tikal Burial 85). Also with the body was a small greenstone figure similar to several examples of "royal" diadem jewels from Cerros and Nohmul, Belize (cf. "bib-heads", Freidel *et al.* 2002; Justeson *et al.* 1988). Judging from these funerary offerings, this person may have been one of the Late Preclassic rulers of San Bartolo. Another high-status burial was recently found in the residential area of K'o—a site with significant ceremonial architecture on the outskirts of Holmul. The funerary offerings included eight fine vessels and a small effigy bowl depicting the maize god head wearing the royal *hun* jewel (Estrada-Belli 2009). These sporadic finds of high-status burials in unassuming residential locations indicate that rulers and elites were not buried in temple-pyramids prior to AD 100.

We might then expect that discoveries of ruler burials from the Late Preclassic period may be forthcoming, as research progresses at the greater centers of the Mirador Basin and central Peten, on both residential and ceremonial platforms. Many of the high-ranking burials may have been lost to looting and erosion but some may lay undetected. Good examples of the sorts of tomb that may have remained undetected at large centers until now are Tombs 1, 2 and 3 at Wakna, reported by Richard Hansen (1998) and dated to the Terminal Preclassic period (AD 150–300). Unfortunately, these interments had already been looted at the time of discovery. The three tombs were placed at the base of each of the temples atop a Triadic complex. The now half-emptied tombs were built with finely cut blocks to form an unusual pentagonal cross-section vault and their interiors were lined with stucco. The most elaborate of the three, located under the northern temple, was built within a series of recessed walls at the entrance, adding to the effect of monumentality. The contents included Late Preclassic vessels of the Sierra, Flor and Polvero groups. Hansen noted that this type of vault matched a Terminal Preclassic tomb in the Mundo Perdido at Tikal (PNT-021 in Structure 5D-86; Laporte and Fialko 1990). This suggests an estimated Late Preclassic–Terminal Preclassic date for the Wakna tombs as well. Hansen also noted that the looters had excavated many additional trenches in other Triadic Groups across the Mirador Basin in the hope of locating similar tombs, but to no avail. Given that monumental construction was fairly common throughout the Preclassic period at these sites, and the earlier patterns of residential interments noted above, the overall absence of tombs in monumental settings could indicate that the pattern of burying important individuals under major temples was a late development.

Elaborate Preclassic burials have been encountered at several other sites. Some of these have unfortunately been looted and emptied of their contents, so their classification as "tomb" relies on the presence of a vaulted chamber. In

Figure 3.4 Late Preclassic tomb in Building B's Room 8 at Holmul, photographed by
Raymond Merwin in 1911

Source: Merwin and Vaillant 1932; courtesy of Peabody Museum, Harvard University

other cases the context is well documented by the richness of the furnishings.
But in general the classification of the interred as a ruler or member of a
high-ranking elite is dubious. Among the sites with vaulted chambers,
those at Cival, Seibal, Rio Azul, Holmul and Altun Ha are among the best
known (Krejci and Culbert 1999; Estrada-Belli 2004). We must await further
research at the largest sites in the Lowlands before ruling out the presence of
royal burials in the earlier Preclassic periods.

The dawning of a new era: Tikal

There are other important changes to consider in the period following AD 100
that might shed some light on the events leading to the formal founding of a
dynasty at Tikal. Around AD 100 most of the greatest and longest-lived centers of the Mirador Basin, including El Mirador, Tintal and many other centers
across the Maya Lowlands, entered a period of decisive decline. Shortly after
the burial in Wakna Tomb 1, and those in similar high-ranking tombs at
other sites, many areas of the central Lowlands appear to have experienced

devastating population losses. The large Triadic Groups and plazas at El Mirador, Tintal, Wakna, Uaxactun, Cival, Cerros and Becan, to name a few, received their last renovation around this time and then were left to decay. In the course of the following 100 years, many of these sites would be completely abandoned. In some cases, small populations continued to occupy a selected portion of the once-public plazas, but with a much reduced profile. Some of these groups appear to have maintained their privileged standard of living, but the vast majority of the population seems to have migrated to better pastures (Hansen *et al.* 2008a). Recent studies have correlated the clear and widespread decline between AD 100 and 200 with environmental stresses, such as deforestation, soil erosion and water shortages induced by overuse of the landscape (Hansen *et al.* 2002, 2008a; Wahl *et al.* 2006b).

It is not clear, however, why certain sites and not others were affected by this phenomenon. Defensive works of various kinds were built at many Preclassic sites, suggesting civil unrest and endemic warfare as possible causes of their demise (see Chapter 6). While the debate continues, it is fairly clear that Tikal made the transition through the second and third centuries AD unscathed. Quite remarkably, this period corresponds with increased prosperity and some of the most ambitious construction projects of all Maya times in the North Acropolis at Tikal, as was noted above. New polychrome ceramics begin to appear at this time (after AD 150), and their distribution is highly skewed to the east of the Tikal area. Many have concluded from this correlation that Tikal may have contributed, at least in part, to the failures of other Late Preclassic centers in northern and eastern Peten by controlling important trade routes and therefore restricting competing sites' access to trade (Hansen *et al.* 2008b; Reese-Taylor and Walker 2002; also see Chapter 6). This would certainly have resulted in greater prosperity and a population increase at Tikal. After AD 100, the Tikal rulers claimed greater status than their predecessors, and required larger ritual spaces while keeping with the old tradition. The new layout of the acropolis certainly reflected the rulers' heightened success and ambition, but also continuity in the location and orientation of the main temples. The successes of Tikal's rulers in the century that followed the "founding" of the dynasty enabled them to stand as equals among the rulers of the greatest centers in the Maya Lowlands for the first time.

Perhaps the more elaborate treatment of rulers' interments with rich offerings and location under temples is a symptom of stresses on the system of governance at the end of the Late Preclassic. The founding of new dynasties represented more idealized renewals of power than mere shifts in power relations. But we must await more adequate evidence with respect to power relations during and after the Preclassic period. Possibly, once extensive trenching and tunneling has been done at the largest Preclassic sites, as has been done at Tikal, we may better understand the treatment reserved for deceased rulers and high-ranking individuals, and how these features of Maya society may or may not be correlates of political institutions.

In sum, there are good indications that Tikal's new dynasty emerged as a fresh player among long-established and more powerful states in the 2nd century AD. These same indicators demonstrate that civilization in the Maya Lowlands began much earlier than the widely accepted date for the "founding" of Tikal's dynasty—AD 100. As noted earlier, these indicators include craft specialization, monumental architecture, complex ideology, writing, site planning and ritual performance—all of which correlate not only with complexity but with the known symbols and ritual ceremonies of the Classic period. These features of civilizations are known to be present at large and small Preclassic sites prior to AD 100 and to be preceded by an earlier and equally complex tradition dating back several centuries.

4

PLANTING THE SEED
OF CIVILIZATION
The making of sacred ground

Preclassic Maya site planning

In general, the layouts of Preclassic sites appear to follow a more regular pattern than those of the Classic period. This is immediately noticeable when observing a site map, especially when the Preclassic architecture is not concealed by later substantial constructions. During the Classic period, centuries of incremental accretion and the addition of new temples and platforms may have distorted or completely transformed the original plaza arrangements of Preclassic times. One obvious commonality in the layout of Lowland sites with largely undisturbed Late Preclassic architecture, such as El Mirador, Tintal, Nakbe, Wakna, Cival, San Bartolo and Cerros, among many others, is the general arrangement along an east–west axis. Despite centuries of accretions of buildings, this pattern is generally maintained and elaborated. A primary east–west pattern has also been noted at early sites in neighboring regions of Highland Chiapas, and has led to some discussion of migrations to, or Highland influences on the early developments of, Lowland Maya civilization (Lowe 1989; Clark *et al.* 2000; Clark and Hansen 2001).

Another commonality of Preclassic sites, especially in the central Lowland region (Peten, southern Campeche, Quintana Roo and Belize), is the presence of two distinct types of building arrangement. These are known as E-Groups and Triadic Groups and are known to have served ritual functions. Both have widespread distribution at large and small sites. E-Groups are generally formed by a western pyramid with radial stairways to the west and an elongated platform with one or three small substructures on the east side of the plaza. Their name is derived from Group E of Uaxactun, which was the first of this type to be recognized (Morley 1946; Ricketson and Ricketson 1937; Smith 1950a). Triadic Groups are normally situated on an elevated platform and are formed by a main pyramidal temple flanked by two smaller ones facing each other. The most common orientation of Triadic Groups is west-facing, although other cardinal orientations are not uncommon, especially at sites where several Triadic Groups are present (such as El Mirador, Nakbe, Lamanai, Cerros and Cival).

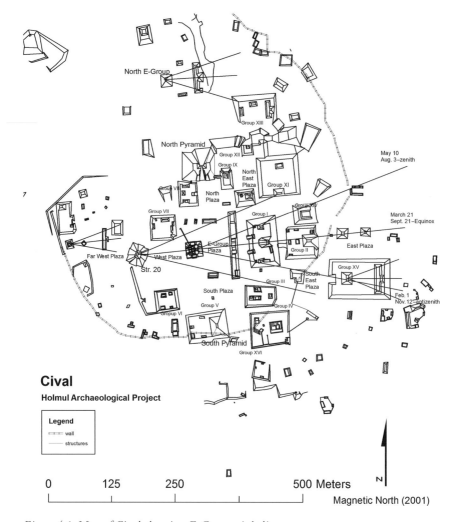

Figure 4.1 Map of Cival showing E-Group sightlines

Source: © F. Estrada-Belli and Holmul Archaeological Project

E-Group architectural arrangements appear to have greater antiquity than the Triadic Group, at least in its monumental form, and it seems that both types continued to be built upon during the Late Preclassic and Early Classic periods. While the first to be recognized, Uaxactun's Group E, dates to the Late Preclassic and Early Classic, this type of complex has great antiquity and is demonstrably the earliest form of space for public rituals in the Lowlands. The earliest examples of E-Groups have been dated to the Middle Preclassic period (800–600 BC) at several sites, including Nakbe, Tikal

(Mundo Perdido), Cival and Cenote (Hansen 1998; Chase and Chase 1999). Triadic Group architecture, when secure dating is available, dates to the Late Preclassic period (El Mirador, Nakbe, Tintal, Wakna, Tikal, Uaxactun, Calakmul, Caracol, Lamanai, Cerros, Cival and many others) and is also known in the northern Yucatan region (Hansen 1998; Andrews 1965). At several sites, such as Nakbe, Tikal, Uaxactun, Lamanai and Cival, extensive trenching has shown that Triadic Groups can be augmented by several (three to six) subsequent construction episodes, ultimately resulting in considerably larger height and mass than the original. El Mirador has the largest number of Triadic Groups, as many as 15, and also the groups of greatest size. The largest is the Danta Group, with a total height of 73 meters, several platform levels, and a maximum length of 600 meters at the base (see Figures 2.4 and 2.5, above). The second largest at El Mirador and in the Lowlands as a whole is the El Tigre complex, with its main temple reaching 53 meters above the plaza. Structure 2 at Calakmul was almost as large a Triadic Group in the Late Preclassic. After some remodeling in the Late Classic it stood at 55 meters. Smaller examples range from 20 to 50 meters in maximum height. Surprisingly, some of the larger El Mirador Triadic Groups, such as El Tigre, have been found to be the result of a single construction effort during the late phase of the Late Preclassic period.

At El Mirador, as at other Preclassic sites, the Triadic Groups appear to be positioned at the ends of the ritual centers and are often connected with other groups and plazas through broad ceremonial causeways. E-Groups tend to be located most commonly near the center of the site's ceremonial area (e.g. at El Mirador, Tikal and Cival) as well as at the axial extremes (e.g. at Nakbe). Often, early examples of E-Groups are also found to occupy the most prominent and broad hilltop or knoll, which, if topography allows, remains the central focus of later site planning.

In several cases it is possible to demonstrate that the orientation of the E-Group also corresponds to the main east–west axis of the sites, which is maintained in later expansions of ceremonial core. This is noticeable at El Mirador and Nakbe, where the site's main axis is parallel to, albeit not exactly centered upon, the east–west orientation of the E-Group's main structures (El Mirador's Leon Group as well as Danta lower platform's E-Group; see Figure 2.5, above).

A good example of coherent site orientation and planning being followed throughout the Middle and Late Preclassic times can be found at the recently mapped center of Cival, Peten. Cival's ceremonial core occupies an artificially leveled 500-meter wide, two-hilltop area near an aguada which gives the site its name. The site core is dominated by four major temple buildings, each located at the end of the site's cardinal axes, plus one near the center. The tallest buildings are the Triadic Group (Group 1) to the east (33 meters high), then the North Pyramid (21 meters high), followed by the Western Pyramid (Structure 20, 19 meters high), and the South Pyramid (12 meters high).

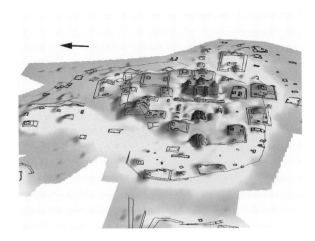

Figure 4.2 Virtual view of Cival's central area from the west based on GIS data

Source: © F. Estrada-Belli and Holmul Archaeological Project

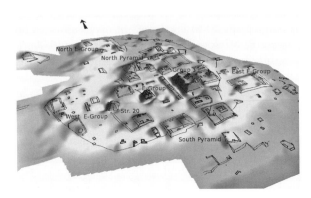

Figure 4.3 Virtual view of Cival's ceremonial complex from the southwest based on GIS map data

Source: © F. Estrada-Belli and Holmul Archaeological Project

At the very center of the four-pyramid orthogonal axes is an E-Group plaza. Its western radial pyramid rises 18 meters above the plaza and faces a 130-meter-long eastern platform supporting an outset central building. Two smaller (4-meter-high) rectangular buildings close the north and south ends of the plaza.

Just to the north of the plaza is a ball-court which was first built in the Late Preclassic and follows the general north–south axis orthogonal to the E-Group's main east–west axis. To the east of the ball-court is a 3-meter-high platform (Group VII, 38 × 45 meters) supporting five small mounds. Excavations at the base of the Western, North and South pyramids, as well as in the E-Group, have documented the first leveling of the entire area enclosed by these buildings in the early Middle Preclassic (circa 900 BC), with a series of subsequent floors laid out in the Late Preclassic period.

To the north, the natural descending ground is modified by a series of platforms and ramps to facilitate a more formal access to the ceremonial area from

70

that direction. On the north side of this depressed area the ground rises again to a knoll occupied by a small plaza with a distinctive E-Group-type arrangement of buildings. The 8-meter-high Western Pyramid faces a 48-meter-long platform with a central outset building at the opposite end of the plaza. Two smaller structures close the north and south sides.

Cival's east–west axis was maintained for the duration of the Late Preclassic by subsequent residential and ritual platforms. Immediately to the east of the Triadic Group is a large platform (Group II, 52 × 52 meters) supporting an 8-meter-high temple on its far eastern end and a number of low platforms for masonry buildings. The main site axis passes through the center of this temple, as well as the Triadic Group's main pyramids, Structure 7 and the Western Pyramid (see Figure 4.1, above). Behind Group II, the ground drops sharply. At the base of the slope one finds a plaza area (the Far East Plaza) with two small temple buildings (8 meters and 5 meters high) also aligned with the main east–west axis.

The orientation and distance between major buildings along the site's axes denote deliberate planning.

Structure 20 and the Triadic Group form the east–west end points of a cross-shaped pattern with the North and South pyramids. The distance between these two pyramids is 308 meters, while the distance between the western Structure 20 and the Triadic Group's eastern structure is 259 meters (from top to top). The orthogonal axes of these temples effectively form a kan-cross pattern. The center of this idealized kan cross falls in the center of the E-Group plaza, as defined by the intersection of the axes of its north and south buildings and the Western Pyramid with the eastern platform. The arms of the idealized kan cross formed by the four outer pyramids are unequal. On the other hand, their distances bear direct relationship to the distances between opposing buildings of the E-Group and appear to be an expansion upon that original (earlier) pattern. In the E-Group, the distance from Structure 9 to the eastern platform is 86 meters and the distance between the north and the south end structures is 103 meters. The nourt–south (308 meters) and east–west (259 meters) arms of the cross formed by the outer pyramids are therefore exactly three times the corresponding axial distances of the E-Group structures. Because the stratigraphy at the four extremes of the site cores shows that these areas were leveled at one time in the Middle Preclassic—that is, at roughly the same time as the first version of the E-Group was laid out—it is possible to surmise that the axial relationship was the result of the site's initial planning. This would have involved the laying out of additional plazas outside of the E-Group, whose cardinal extremes perpetuated not only the axial orientation established by the E-Group but the harmonious relationships among the four parts of the E-Group extrapolated onto the entire ceremonial area.

These sorts of canonical proportions are also found at other Late Preclassic sites in the Cival region (also known as the Holmul region), such as T'ot, Hahakab and Holmul (Estrada-Belli 2003a).

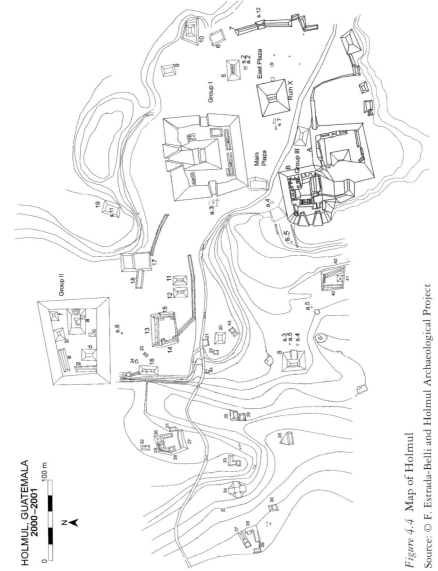

Figure 4.4 Map of Holmul

Source: © F. Estrada-Belli and Holmul Archaeological Project

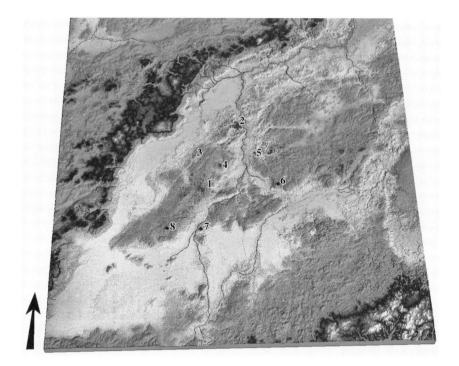

Figure 4.5 View of sites with E-Group complexes in the Holmul region

Source: Topography based on AIRSAR data courtesy of NASA; © F. Estrada-Belli and Holmul Archaeological Project

Note: 1 = Holmul; 2 = Cival; 3 = Hahakab; 4 = Sisia'; 5 = Hamontun; 6 = T5; 7 = Riverona, 8 = T'ot.

At Holmul, the layout of the East Plaza in its current form dates to the Late Classic. Test excavations showed, however, that at its base are earlier Late Preclassic buildings and plaza floors. The orientation and distance between the western pyramid (Ruin X) and eastern platform (Structure 7), as well as the north and south end structures in this plaza, replicate the axial distances (102 meters north–south and 86 meters east–west) of Cival's main plaza E-Group. The only exception in this case is that the south end structure is not present, due perhaps to its removal at a later time to expand the plaza area in that direction. However, the 51-meter distance between the north structure and the plaza's midpoint (Stela 1) possibly indicates that the original north–south length of the plaza was 102 meters, as at Cival.

Other smaller versions of E-Groups exist at the minor centers in the same region, denoting a consistently shared pattern of site planning among neighboring centers during the Late Preclassic, as mentioned above.

The orientation and general size of E-Groups are highly variable across the Maya Lowlands, and such patterns of standardized planning as observed in the

Cival surrounding area probably reflect political integration or interaction as well as religious conformity. We might expect a similar regional recurrence of site planning patterns across the Lowlands, when adequate data are available. In a recent study of E-Groups, Aveni *et al.* (2003) note that the general astronomical alignments of E-Groups are highly variable across the Lowlands and were likely subject to change over time as well as space. In this sense, many of the modifications variously made to E-Groups across the Lowlands during the Early and Late Classic periods would effectively obscure any regional regularities in their proportions.

In its basic forms, the E-Group's western-pyramid-facing-the-eastern-platform layout is also known outside of the Lowlands, even at earlier times. Similarly arranged early Middle Preclassic examples occur in Highland Chiapas (e.g. Chiapa de Corzo, Finca Arizona, San Isidro; Lowe 1977, 1981, 1989) and can even be detected in the layout of sites in Pacific Coastal and Highland Guatemala (Takalik Abaj; Popenoe de Hatch 2002).

The earliest monumental works and the making of a civilization

As noted above, E-Groups first appear in the Lowlands in the Middle Preclassic period and are demonstrably the earliest forms of large plazas where public rituals were likely performed. Archaeological evidence connects E-Group ritual complexes with the later emergence of monumentality and several other elements of what we recognize as hallmarks of Maya civilization.

Cival's earliest E-Group plaza floors document one of the largest and oldest such complexes in the Lowlands (Estrada-Belli 2002a; Estrada-Belli *et al.* 2003b). A looters' trench in Structure 7 demonstrates that the first version of this E-Group's eastern platform was actually a modified bedrock knoll, an early feature also noted at Tikal and other sites (Coe 1990; Laporte and Fialko 1990). Altogether, the Cival eastern platform and its central outset structure (Structure 12) were remodeled six times, the last two dating to the Terminal Preclassic period—AD 150–250. The first construction, however, was much earlier and may take us back to a very early period of Maya sedentary life—the 9th century BC.

Archaeological excavations have shown that the construction of the Cival E-Group and of other E-Groups across the Lowlands in the Middle Preclassic period (Tikal, Nakbe and elsewhere) are intimately related to the actual founding of centers of ceremonialism. The birth of Cival as a ceremonial center was the result of the laborious leveling and infilling of a broad (500-square-meter) hill. At times, this involved raising the surface by as much as seven meters in the south, and by about 4 meters in the north and west. At the same time, in the middle of this vast hilltop plaza, a modest-sized E-Group architectural complex was built (Estrada-Belli 2006). In it, a small (1–2-meter-high) radial platform faced a low platform on the east. The latter was not built of masonry but carved out of a natural rise in the soft limestone bedrock, and was itself no more than 1–2 meters in height.

The stratigraphy of various parts of the hill reveals that the leveling of the hill and the construction of the low-profile E-Group complex to its present height did result from a gradual process of accretion through Preclassic eras, as might be expected. Instead, it seems that there was a single episode of construction over a very short period of time—probably as little as 50 years. The date of this construction episode probably centers on the year 800 BC, but it could be as early as 900 BC. It is bracketed by two anchoring dates. The first of these is an 840–800 BC AMS radiocarbon date derived from a well-preserved human skeleton (Burial 33,[1] buried unceremoniously in a storage chamber beneath the first paving of the plaza under the North Pyramid). The second comes from a piece of charcoal from the plaster capping of the jade offering (Cache 4; see below) for the inauguration of the E-Group complex. Its most probable date range is 790–760 BC.[2]

The amount of material brought in to fill the sides of the hill and thus create a wide, flat, open space was estimated by comparing the shape of the underlying bedrock surface and observed strata of fill and floors in plaza excavations.[3] The calculated volume of the single Middle Preclassic plaza leveling project observed in the excavation profiles, including the material used in the E-Group eastern platform (carved in bedrock) and the small (2-meter-tall) western radial pyramid, is 1,304,026 cubic meters. The areas of the hill where greater amounts of fill were deposited are along the hillsides. The maximum depth of the fill was about 7 meters in the south and 4.5 meters in the north. Unlike later construction projects composed mostly of oversized limestone boulders, the type of material used consisted of rocks too large for one person to lift and haul. Little marl was added to the rocks. The first floor of the plaza was 5–10 centimeters thick and of great quality and hardness, compared to later examples. It was laid out throughout the hilltop, forming a 500-meter wide plaza, including the E-Group platforms in its center. Our limited soundings of the lowest levels of the plaza do not permit us to determine whether other structures existed on the hilltop outside the E-Group. So, at the moment, we can also surmise that this modest, astronomically oriented complex lay in the middle of an immense white plaza.

The Middle Preclassic construction of the E-Group and associated plaza leveling project were greater than all subsequent construction projects combined. In the Late Preclassic period, beginning at roughly 350 BC, several pyramid complexes were built on each side of the plaza: Triadic Group I at the east; the North Pyramid; the South Pyramid; and Structure 20 (the Western Pyramid) at the western end. Each pyramid lay axially with another pyramid at the opposing end of the plaza at the exact distance of 305 meters (see Figure 4.3, above). Once again, the pyramids were laid out in a cross pattern. Each of their present-day volumes is the result of multiple incremental construction episodes occurring throughout the Late Preclassic period—from 300 BC to

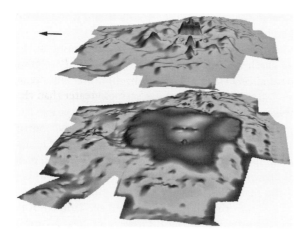

Figure 4.6 Three-dimensional views of Cival's volumetric input during the Middle
Preclassic (below) and Late Preclassic (above) periods

Source: © F. Estrada-Belli and Holmul Archaeological Project

Note: Shading indicates the relative amounts and where material was brought in

AD 100. So far, our excavations have been able to document five construction
episodes for Triadic Group I and three each for the North Pyramid and
Structure 20.

The first version of Triadic Group I dates to circa 350 BC and rose to no
more than 3 meters from plaza level. Its width is unknown but the group
likely included all the architectural components of the latest version: a
broad platform supporting three pyramidal platforms on the east, north
and south, with the eastern one being slightly taller than the other two. In
addition, there were two small stepped platforms on the west end of the complex, flanking the group's large inset stairway (see Figures 4.1, 4.2 and 4.3,
above). This architectural pattern, which includes five main structures, is
perhaps unfairly named "Triadic" and is one of the earliest forms of pyramidal
building at Lowland sites such as Nakbe, Wakna, El Mirador (Danta Pyramid)
and Uaxactun (Group H), among others (Hansen 1998; Laporte and Valdés
1993).

The North Pyramid, rising to 23 meters in its last version, was a large, two-
stage pyramidal platform, with the upper section set back from the lower one,
forming an intermediate terrace. At the top stood a third, smaller pyramidal
platform. A broad inset stairway led to the top through the various terraces.
The volume of the first of its five construction episodes is not known but was
likely much smaller and shorter than the latter two. Because our excavations
did not penetrate to the center of this structure, it can only be supposed that
the North Pyramid, like Triadic Group I and many other large platforms at
Cival, was remodeled at least five times.

In sum, the currently visible mass of Late Preclassic architecture is the cumulative result of several construction episodes between 350 BC and AD 100. The calculated combined volume of all Late Preclassic buildings and platforms on the Cival main hill, not including the first Middle Preclassic version of the E-Group, is 555,721.3 cubic meters. Therefore, the volume of the single Middle Preclassic construction phase is 2.45 times greater than the combined volume of all subsequent architectural projects.

In terms of construction volume per labor investment, the frequent remodeling of pyramids and platforms during the Late Preclassic period meant that the investments in each episode were much more modest. The volume of construction per 50-year period was 61,726 cubic meters or a mere 1234 cubic meters per year. The population of Cival responsible for the public works of the Middle and Late Preclassic periods can be estimated from the available maps of over 200 residential groups (patio hilltop groups) located in the surrounding area. A preliminary population estimate for the Late Preclassic ranges between 2000 and 5000 people. A maximum figure of 10,000 people is not out of the question for the greater supporting area of Cival in a 3-kilometer radius. In our mapping and excavation sample about one-fifth of all residential groups revealed Middle Preclassic occupation. These simple figures emphasize even further the extraordinary investment in material and labor of the initial, smaller Cival community when they established a ceremonial center.

The longevity of the first plaza layout and E-Group is also remarkable. An estimated 400-year period saw only one remodeling of the E-Group platforms and plaza floor. Thus, all the above elements may reflect fundamental differences in kind and scale between the first and all subsequent construction projects at Cival. The difference in scale is obvious. The difference in kind has to do with the fact that the foundation of the hilltop complex represented something new and grandiose, certainly oversized for the modest Cival community. We must surmise that it served as a gathering place during religious functions for a much greater community of residents from beyond the 2-kilometer radius of the Cival settlement we have mapped. The nearest large Middle Preclassic center, Yaxha, lay 30 kilometers to the south; Tikal is 35 kilometers to the west. Emerging centers such as Cival, Yaxha and Tikal lay at the center of communities of widely dispersed hamlets and villages within a half-day walk. The first construction project marked a threshold moment in the creation of these broad communities: the foundation of regional polities within bounded landscapes which, once established, were constantly recreated through ritual practices.

In sum, perhaps the most important juncture in the long-term history of the Lowland Maya occurred when several villages convened to modify the Cival hilltop and created a large plaza for ritual performances. I see this type of major construction project, with associated architecture and offerings, as laying the foundations for a new form of community with local ties and identity. At the same time, the earliest monumental architecture, with astro-nomical orientation and cosmological symbolism evoking cosmic forces, appeared in similar forms across the Maya Lowlands. These similarities in form and ritual (and in an increased similarity in ceramics across the Lowlands) sug-gest a new narrative—perhaps introduced by emerging elites—and a stronger interconnectedness across regional boundaries.

The earliest plaza rituals: activating the Maya cosmos

The position of the rising sun behind buildings on E-Group plazas had long been noted and was often cited to describe E-Groups as astronomical obser-vatories (Blom 1924; Ruppert 1940). Several scholars have been skeptical of their functionality as time-reckoning devices, due to the fact that too much variability exists around the "canonical" equinoctial alignment.

As noted earlier, E-Group types of building arrangement have great antiquity in the Lowlands and were used and expanded upon for more than a millennium. A great deal of variation in basic features is therefore not sur-prising. The size and axial alignments of E-Groups can be highly variable from site to site as well as over time. A survey of the alignments of a large sample of E-Groups from the southern Lowlands by Aveni *et al.* (2003) has shown that in the majority of cases the sightlines through buildings do not target the equinoctial or solstitial sunrise but other, intermediate points on the horizon. This study showed that in spite of the variability of orientations, E-Groups as a class were used to target points on the horizon separated by regular day intervals. The intervals between sightline targets were shown to correspond with specific day intervals in multiples of 20 preceding and following the passage of the sun through the zenith. Also, at Uaxactun, devices were incised on the floors of the Early Classic A-V elite group. These are known as "pecked crosses" and mark the divisions of the year based on the passage of the sun through the zenith in relation to the equinox (inner circle) and the four intervals between the equinoxes and the solstices (outer circles). While in the sample of Lowland E-Groups analyzed in this study the equinoctial and solstitial target points were generally found not to be the norm, the targeted positions did mark specific 20-day intervals (or multiples of) in relation to the sun's passage to the zenith, thus underscoring the paramount importance of this solar phenomenon in providing meaningful time-markers in the calendar (as expressed in pecked crosses) and public rituals (as indicated by E-Group plaza offerings).

The first passage of the sun at its zenith in the southern Lowlands roughly corresponds with the advent of the rainy season, near May 10. The second passage of the sun at its zenith occurs near August 2, corresponding to the arrival of the second wave of monsoons in the Maya Lowlands. A short (10-day) period of diminished rain precedes the second part of the rainy season, known today in Guatemala as "canicula" (after the constellation Canis), which tends to occur in late July/early August. In ancient times, as in the present, Maya farmers plant their first maize plot in April in preparation for the arrival of the rains in May, and plant the second crop in July taking advantage of the canicula.

Both the pecked crosses and the E-Group plaza layout underscore the importance of tracking the sun's movement in relation to its zenith for the Lowland Maya, with the aim of correctly scheduling the rituals associated with the agricultural and solar cycles. Through the use of these devices, the Lowland Maya were able to maintain the congruence of the ritual *tzolkin* calendar and *haab* solar calendars with the pace of the seasonal and agricultural cycles (Girard 1966). Thus E-Group plazas with their buildings aligned to the cardinal position and also their mainly east–west alignments underscored the quadripartite construct of the calendar and served as the environment for rituals related to it. Unsurprisingly, once the alignment of an E-Group was established at a site, this positioning was carefully followed by most subsequent site planning episodes, reinforcing the E-Group's importance in reflecting the Maya's most fundamental cosmological vision.

Evidence of public rituals of great antiquity is often found in E-Groups. The earliest evidence occurs in the form of caches or ritual deposits placed in cists, stone boxes or lip-to-lip vessel pairs, dating to the Middle Preclassic. The offerings are often placed along the major east–west axis in connection with the stairway of the eastern platform. In the later phases of the Late Preclassic and Early Classic periods, burials are placed along this axis or at the summit of the eastern platforms, in the place usually occupied by offertory deposits. Such burials can be interpreted as dedicatory in themselves (Chase and Chase 1999). Good examples of this practice are child burials and mass graves. Stelae were dedicated in the plaza area in front of the eastern platform in the Late Preclassic and Early Classic periods at Uaxactun, Tikal, Nakbe Wakna and Cival, for example. In many cases the stelae found in E-Groups are among the earliest to be found in all of the Lowlands. Stela 1 at Nakbe and Stela 2 at Cival, for example, date to the Late Preclassic period. Although these were not found *in situ*, they were likely erected on the E-Group main axis. The pattern of stela dedication in E-Groups continued through the early part of the Early Classic period. At Tikal, Stela 29, carved in AD 292, is believed to have been placed originally in the Mundo Perdido E-Group complex in front of the eastern platform and later thrown into a nearby ravine (Laporte and Fialko 1990); Stela 39 (AD 376) was found broken and buried in the upper room of the eastern temple of the Mundo Perdido complex (5D-86-5th). At Uaxactun, Stela 9, the site's earliest, is believed to have been originally erected in Group E before being moved later (Valdés *et al.* 1999). The earliest ritual offerings that so consistently occur in the E-Groups' axial location, beginning in the Middle Preclassic, were perhaps dedicated to building renovations and in many cases were specifically connected with calendar event rituals (e.g. Cival Cache 4; see below). This pattern continued in the Early Classic period, as this location was the primary ritual space for calendar rituals such as the commemoration of *katun* cycle completions (*katuns* 8.14 through 8.17) marked by monuments and Long Count inscriptions dedicated by royal individuals (Coggins 1980).

In sum, there was a progression of ritual behavior in E-Group plazas from cache offerings to carved monuments through the Preclassic and Early Classic phases.

This phenomenon is perhaps best illustrated by recent finds at Cival. Several major features deposited in the plaza floors in front of the E-Group's eastern structure (Structure 7) mark major stages in the history of this sacred space. The first evidence of ritual activity dates to the Middle Preclassic, between 700 and 600 BC[4] and comes in the form of five water jars, five upright celts, and 114 jade pebbles placed in a three-level cruciform cut in the soft limestone bedrock. The second event, also in the Middle Preclassic, was the burial of a large, defaced stela across the center line of the eastern platform. Subsequently, at the beginning of the Late Preclassic period, a low rectangular platform was built on this axial space in front of the eastern platform's stairway. This platform was used to elevate Stela 2. Later, in connection with an enlargement,

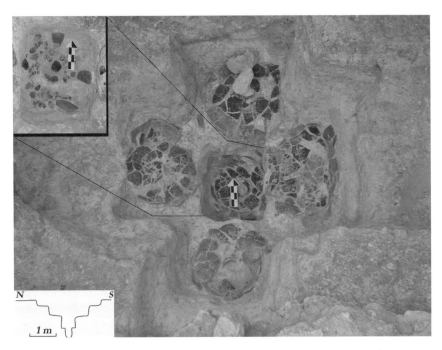

Figure 4.7 View of Cache 4 at Cival with jars deposited in *k'an*-cross-shaped pit on the east–west axis of the E-Group

Source: © F. Estrada-Belli

Note: Inserts show the pit's peculiar profile and arrangement of jades in the lowest cavity

Figure 4.8 Rendering of Cache 4 at Cival (circa 800 BC)

Source: © F. Estrada-Belli

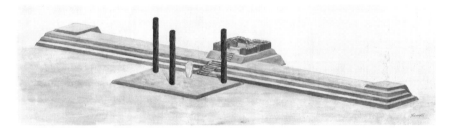

Figure 4.9 Rendering of Cival's E-Group Plaza, Structure 7, Stela 2 and wooden posts
(300–200 BC)

Source: Drawing by Joel Zovar; © Holmul Archaeological Project

four large timber posts were placed in cardinal arrangement around Stela 2. In the final stage, the monuments were toppled and some were smashed, with the fragments buried in this platform. Low platforms in front of E-Group plazas' eastern structures have been documented at Tikal and Uaxactun. The platform in the Mundo Perdido at Tikal was also associated with a mass burial (Laporte and Fialko 1990). These and other signs of violent events and drastic changes across the Lowlands are perhaps symptomatic of the tumult at the end of the Preclassic period.

81

The symbolism of the offerings in the Cival E-Group plaza is fascinating testimony to the development of the Preclassic Maya's complex ideology. Cache 1 was placed in a cruciform pit. The space inside the pit was further subdivided in three levels. The first level was a shelf on the outer arms of the cross dropping 40 centimeters from the original bedrock surface. Three black jars and a red one (in the south) were laid on these shelves. The second level was a squared pit in the center of the cross-shaped opening in which a fifth (black) jar was placed. Next to this central jar four 25-centimeter-long celts were placed upright in correspondence with each of the cross's arms. Underneath the jar were an additional 30 green-blue jade pebbles and 84 green jade pebbles. Finally, a round hole in the center of the squared pit formed the third level of the cruciform pit. Here was a magnificent green-blue jade celt, the finest of the assemblage. After these objects were deposited, the jars were smashed and the pit filled with gray marl up to the level of the original bedrock surface. Finally, a round post was erected in the center of the filled pit.

The carefully oriented pit and its contents of various materials and shapes present an intriguing cosmological message and are clearly the result of a sumptuous ritual which involved the arranging and burying of these objects in the earth. The jars most likely contained water but other fluids—such as *balche* (mead) and *chicha* (a maize-based brew)—were sometimes used in Maya rituals. According to Taube (2000), Olmec jade celts represent sprouting corn plants. Celts or axes are also related to the rain god. The Maya lightning god *K'awiil* is represented as a personified axe, or with an axe sprouting from his forehead. Aztec codices depict rituals dedicated to the birth of maize in which five Tlaloc rain gods holding axes pour water on axe-like maize sprouts. The position of axes in a quincunx represents the cosmological order and the *axis mundi* often personified by Mesoamerican rulers (Reilly 1991). Therefore, the vessels and the jade celts placed in a symbolic primordial sea suggest a ritual dedicated to cosmological order, water as a life-giving substance for maize, the essence of human sustenance and the *axis mundi*.

This Maya construct has close parallels in Olmec rituals. According to Coggins' (in press) interpretation of the Olmec statuette from Las Limas, the four celtiform heads incised on its shoulders and knees possibly represent celts and as such have calendrical significance by framing the central newborn baby-jaguar/maize god in a quincunx. As the centerpiece of this symbolic construct, the newborn represents the embodiment of the maize life cycle. Again, the maize cycle and the Mesoamerican calendar are closely related in religious symbolism. In the Postclassic period, the Yucatec Maya celebrated the new year as the birth of the *winal*, the basic 20-day unit of the Mesoamerican calendar. In Classic times the seating of a new Maya ruler was celebrated as the birth of the new *winal*-based year and the rebirth of the maize god, all in one (Coggins in press).

In sum, Cival's cruciform cache and the quadripartite sun-oriented space of the E-Group in which it is located relate not only to the quadripartite division of the Maya universe but to the fundamental construct of the Mesoamerican calendar and the agricultural cycle of maize.

The final act of the Cival Cache 4 ritual was to place a wooden post above the jade cache. Wooden posts, world trees and maize plants are often equated in Olmec and Maya iconography (Taube 2003). Classic Maya rulers and their Olmec precursors often portrayed themselves as world trees, as in the famous statuette from Rio Pesquero and Pacal's sarcophagous lid (Reilly 1991), or as a centerpiece of a quincunx in ritual landscapes, such as the La Milpa cosmogram, of which the ceremonial core and the royal throne are the center (Tourtellot *et al.* 2003; Estrada-Belli 2003a).

The time–space cosmological vision of the Preclassic Maya was rooted in agrarian ways of life that their earliest rulers appropriated to form an ideology of central authority based on the primacy of the maize god as the *axis mundi* and the giver of sustenance to the people. Early in this process, Preclassic Maya rulers began to portray themselves as the *axis mundi* of the Maya cosmos.

5

EARTH–MOUNTAIN–CAVES
AND SKY–SERPENT–BIRDS

Meta-narratives of Preclassic Maya art

Cival's Preclassic Stela 2 was found a few centimeters away from the Middle Preclassic Cache 4 jade offering along the east–west axis of the plaza. In style, it predates the earliest monuments from Nakbe and El Mirador (Estrada-Belli 2003a). Although found on the surface, its oval-shaped setting pit was identified during excavation. It originally stood on a small rectangular platform in front of the stairway of Structure 7, the E-Group's eastern platform (see Figure 4.9, above; Estrada-Belli *et al.* 2003a; Bauer 2005). A vessel found in an offertory cache placed under the oval-shaped pit suggests a probable date for it of 300–200 BC. It is carved in simple low-relief outlines. The figure wears a jade bird-head pectoral with three plaques. This avian motif is often worn by rulers as a pectoral or a headdress on Preclassic/Protoclassic monuments at Kaminaljuyú, Abaj Takalik, in the Maya Highlands, on the Pacific Coast, and on the Gulf Coast of Mexico (e.g. La Mojarra, Stela 1; Parsons 1986; Winfield Capitaine 1992). This image has many parallels with scenes of the maize god wearing the feather costume of the Principal Bird Deity (PBD; Bardawil 1976) and performing a dance described by Taube (2009). These images are common, for example, on Holmul dancer-style vessels produced in this same area during the Late Classic. In them, a maize god impersonator wears a feather backrack. In a famous Early Classic vessel from Kaminaljuyú an individual wears a full avian costume and is captured in a spinning motion. The meaning of this dance may have to do with the superior importance of the PBD among all Maya supernaturals (see below) and the taking of his headdress and other accouterments by the maize god in Classic and Postclassic Maya mythology. The Late Preclassic mural of the West Wall of the Pinturas Sub1A structure at San Bartolo may depict an early version of this myth that culminates with the crowning of the maize god with the foliated headdress of the PBD. This scene in turn serves as mythological precedent for the accession ceremony of a mortal ruler vested with the avian crown by the maize god himself wearing an avian cape and headdress as well (Taube 2009). Traditionally, scenes in which the maize god faces the PBD are most readily compared to the mythological episode of the triumph of the maize god over the avian impostor *Vukub Qakix*

"Seven Macaw" of the Popol Vuh creation story (Tedlock 1996). However, the actions and identities of the characters in Classic and especially Preclassic art may refer to mythologies not preserved or only partially preserved in the Popol Vuh and thus unknown to us (see, for example, interpretations of the PBD alternative to *Vukub Qakix* in Bassie-Sweet 2008). Regardless of the exact mythological reference, the Cival stela could be the oldest representation of the ritual dance performance that was so important to Maya royal ceremony. Finally, it is also worth noting that this stela's tapered shape recalls upturned jade celts such as those in the cruciform cache, a feature noted in early stela monuments in the Gulf Coast as well, suggesting once again a ruler/maize god/world tree identification in the person of the ruler (Taube 2000). In sum, at the time of the Cival Stela 2 dedication, circa 300–200 BC, the ideological charter of Maya kings was fully in place.

The first monumental sculpture and the first portraits of rulers appear at the onset of the Late Preclassic period in the Maya Lowlands. At Cival the dedication of Stela 2 in the 3rd century BC coincides with the construction of the site's Triadic Group (Group 1) platform.

Large platforms supporting Triadic Group temples were built across the Lowlands at this time and throughout the Late Preclassic period. These three-pyramid complexes often stood to the east of E-Groups and followed the same

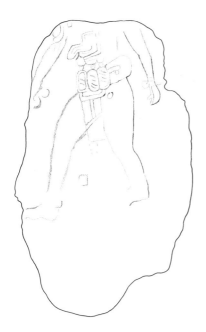

Figure 5.1 Cival Stela 2

Source: Drawing by N. Grube; courtesy of Nikolai Grube

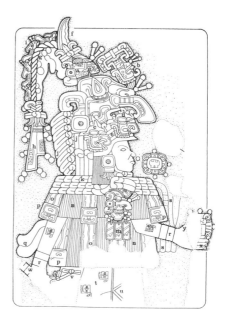

Figure 5.2 La Mojarra Stela 1

Source: Drawing by G. Stuart; courtesy of George Stuart

Figure 5.3 Avian dance on Kaminaljuyú vessel

Source: After Kidder, Jennings and Shook 1946; courtesy of the Pennsylvania State University Press

east–west alignment. The main structure typically faces west. Examples of this distinctive arrangement of pyramids on a site's east side are found at Nakbe (Eastern Group), El Mirador (Danta Group) and Yaxha (Northeast Acropolis). At many sites, however, Triadic Groups also exist independently of E-Group complexes and can face in any direction. Few of these complexes have been excavated, so there is a limited amount of evidence to give clues to their function. It appears that the three upper buildings, often supported by steep pyramidal platforms, served a ritual rather than an elite residential function. All three temples, or sometimes just the major (eastern) one, were decorated with monumental sculpture. The decoration typically includes a low-relief frieze on the upper half of the temple building, painted designs on the outer walls, and large deity masks adorning the platform's terraces alongside the central stairway. These monumental sculptures are rarely completely preserved, and even in those fortunate cases where they are, their complexity renders their interpretation difficult without the aid of direct written sources (but see below for a discussion of their iconography).

In the southern Lowlands, some of the best-known examples of Preclassic monumental sculpture are found at El Mirador, Nakbe, Calakmul, Tikal, Uaxactun, San Bartolo, Cerros and Cival. Several studies have attempted interpretations of the rich imagery of masks and friezes, proposing that these are the personified or zoomorphic versions of places of creation, such as the sacred mountain, or celestial bodies and deities identified with them, such as the sun or Venus and the hero twin sons of the maize god. But the stories of Maya creation that have come down to us are of much later date and any interpretation is bound to be revised when more adequate data become available. The so-called masks are usually large-scale, often gigantic representations of anthropomorphic or zoomorphic beings. The best-known examples feature the Principal Bird Deity (Nakbe Structure 1; Bardawil 1976; Hansen 1992), an avian/reptilian creature characterized by a long snout or down-curving beak, and various versions of a personified mountain (*witz*, "flower mountain" or "cleft mountain"; e.g. at Uaxactun and Tikal; see Taube 2004). Both types of being represent important places and actors of the first creation. Also represented are other deities that are more difficult to identify, usually described as sun gods or the sun god of the underworld. These masks often have some feline traits. Some long-nosed masks combine avian and feline traits and have been variously attributed to Venus or other celestial bodies (e.g. the Cerros masks; Schele 1998). Some more anthropomorphic masks may be identifiable with the maize god because of their more human appearance (Calakmul Structure 2; Carrasco and Colon 2005). In summary the themes expressed by these monumental sculptures seem to recall the places and actors of creation and the birth of the maize god, as told in the Classic period inscriptions and in the Colonial period Popol Vuh book of the Maya-Kiche' (Freidel *et al*. 2002). In specific cases, the meaning of the masks has been related to rituals performed in the temple with which they are associated (Reese-Taylor 2002). These interpretations stimulate more in-depth analysis of the function of Preclassic temples as foci of rituals related to the ideology of kingship, and therefore serving political as well as religious purposes.

The Nakbe Structure 1 masks of a long-nosed creature identified as the Principal Bird Deity by Richard Hansen (1992) are the largest stone-and-stucco examples of Preclassic monumental art, measuring 11 meters in width and 5 meters in height. Here, the PBD combines avian and serpent traits.[1] It is sometimes identified as a scarlet macaw, and thus equated with the "false" sun god of the Popol Vuh creation story, *Vukub Qakix* (Tedlock 1996). In Late Preclassic Lowland Maya art, it has a massive beak, squarish or L-shaped eyes,

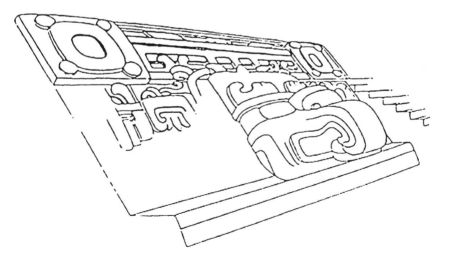

Figure 5.4 PBD mask on Nakbe Structure 1

Source: Drawing by T. Routledge; courtesy of Richard Hansen

flamed eyebrows, J-shaped fangs, and large ear flares decorated with circles in each corner. Its full-bodied forms can include widely spread wings that terminate in serpent heads, as in Nakbe Structure 1 bird masks, for example (Hansen 1992). The wings are sometimes subsumed into a rectilinear set of symbols known as the "skyband." The band stretches on either side of the PBD's head and terminates in serpents' heads at its ends. The wings may carry cartouches containing the *k'in* glyph (for sun) on one side and the *akbal* sign (for darkness) on the other. These signs may convey the dual essence of this entity as the daytime and nighttime sky. The *akbal* sign—often worn by this deity (as God D, see below) as a flowery jewel—may be associated with divination (Taube 1992a) or "dark waters" of creation (Bassie-Sweet 2008). Such traits strongly suggest that this creature is a celestial deity or the personification of the various aspects of the creator god of the sky, and a cognate to a number of separate Mesoamerican deities, such as the feathered serpent deity and the wind god. Among other attributes often associated with its full-figured form are a jade necklace and a *yax* shell jewel. Twisted ropes are often held in the mouth. In some cases, these twisted ropes are represented as two intertwined serpents, a motif which is believed to be related to rain-making rituals (Guernsey Kappelman and Reilly 2001); and in the context of the PBD, twisted ropes may relate to the source of rain.

On Altar 10 at Kaminaljuyú, the Late Preclassic Highland Maya carved a cartouche containing a sign that some refer to as God C on the belly of the PBD. As a glyph, this sign is read as *ku*, the generic word for "god." It is also found in a quatrefoil-shaped cartouche on world trees, and is clearly shown on the bodies of rulers impersonating world trees and wearing the PBD headdress, as on Kaminaljuyú Stela 11 (where a tree sprouts from a shell on the headdress). In Preclassic and Classic Maya art the PBD is often perched atop world trees, suggesting that these may be different aspects of the same entity. In Pacific Coast Maya art, the PBD is represented either in full figure at the top of the composition to represent the sky or in zoomorphic form as a head with a skyband in lieu of wings terminating in serpents' heads (Takalik Abaj Altar 12; Hansen 1992). In Late Preclassic Izapan art, the PBD is stylized and replaced by its basic identifying attributes—the outflaring J-fangs, U eyelid and flamed eyebrow—and is known as the Izapan skyband (e.g. Izapa Stela 12). In the Classic period the PBD is also associated with the old god (God N), God D (Taube 1992a; Guernsey 2006) and Itzamnaaj, who, among the Colonial period Yucatec Maya, was the high god. In Classic period art he is sometimes depicted on a throne as an aged king. He wears an oversize necklace and the *yax* diadem (Taube 1992a; Martin 2006; Thompson 1970). In other instances, the aged god wears a net headdress and an *akbal* flower and is associated with scribes, the art of divination and pool water (dew). Based on the overlapping associations between God D, God N and the PBD and the Maya bird–serpent, Karen Bassie-Sweet (2008) has argued that these may actually be different manifestations of the same deity. This would be equivalent to the creator god identified as "First Father" in the Popol Vuh, and to the present-day Tzutuhil Maya god Mam, the old god of the mountains, rain and childbirth (see also Thompson 1950, 1970; Carlsen and Prechtel 1991).[2] In addition to the qualities listed above, this creator deity is associated with mountains and rain, the essence of divinity. As such, in its primordial form, it possibly also corresponds with the first among the Maya creators Kukumatz and Tepeu (Quetzal Serpent and Sovereign; Tedlock 1996) to appear at the moment of creation in the first pages of the Popol Vuh myth, as well as with the personification of kingship. The various associations of the old god and the PBD underscore the multi-faceted nature of Maya deities that have often been misinterpreted as separate gods by western scholars.

The Nakbe Structure 1 avian mask closely follows the pattern of Late Preclassic PBD imagery. Above its main avian head component is a massive frieze consisting of J-fangs, straight teeth and diagonal brackets representing the skyband, as noted earlier. In addition, at each end of this frieze are two massive ear flares. Below them are the eroded profile heads of two serpents emerging from the skyband. In essence, the Nakbe mask repeats the motif of avian–serpent creature in flight posture with fully spread wings arching above the bird's head and forming the arch of the sky, and represented by a double-headed serpent in a fashion that is similar to Late Preclassic Takalik Abaj Altar 12 (Graham *et al.* 1978) and Classic period building façades such as Palenque's House E (Maudslay 1889–1902: Plate 43).

Figure 5.5 Kaminaljuyú Altars 9 (above) and 10

Source: After Parsons 1986; courtesy of the Dumbarton Oaks Research Library and Collections, Washington, D.C.

Figure 5.6 Kaminaljuyú Stela 11

Source: After Parsons 1986;
courtesy of Dumbarton Oaks
Research Library and Collections

Figure 5.7 Izapa Stela 12

Source: After Norman 1973; courtesy of the New
World Archaeological Foundation

The avian–serpent attributes of the PBD are the badge of royal power in Classic period iconography. In Late Preclassic monumental art, they are combined with the maize god as the personification of kingship. This is seen in Preclassic headdresses and costumes combining avian features with maize god attributes, such as in a Kaminaljuyú stucco vessel (Kidder *et al.* 1946; see Figure 5.3, above) and in the costume of the Holmul dancer as painted on Late Classic polychrome vases (Merwin and Vaillant 1932). On Cival Stela 2, the ruler, now unfortunately headless, wears a long-nosed avian pectoral. At Cerros, four masks adorned the terraces alongside the stairway of south-facing Structure 5C-2nd. Schele and Freidel (1990) have interpreted the lower masks as the jaguarian sun god Yax Balam while the upper long-nosed avian masks are believed to be two aspects of the PBD, as the celestial bird Itzamnaaj and as the water fowl of the underworld (see Freidel *et al.* 2002 for alternative interpretations of the Cerros masks).

Figure 5.8 Eastern masks on the terraces of Structure 5C-2nd at Cerros (circa 50 BC)

Source: Courtesy of David Freidel

At Uaxactun, masks adorned every building on the Late Preclassic Triadic Group H. Many of these masks are difficult to identify, but they fall in the broad categories of deities and places of creation outlined above. One set of these masks on Structure H Sub-3 is especially well preserved. At Uaxactun, as at Cerros, two masks are stacked on terraces alongside the frontal stairway leading to a temple. The lower mask appears to be an anthropomorphic creature with reptilian flamed eyebrows. Flower sprouts emerge from the sides of its head. Wavy scrolls emerge from the sides of its open maw while either fish or turtle heads[3] float within them. A third fish or turtle head is inside the creature's open mouth. The flower sprouts and the fish motifs identify this mask as "flower mountain"—the place of creation emerging from the primordial sea (Taube 2004). The turtle heads are references to both the old god as *witz* ("mountain") and the earth, which is often represented as a turtle's carapace.[4] On the upper terrace and also conceptually at a higher level is another

91

mask with its mouth open. A serpent emerges from each side of the mask. Inside the mouth is a small deity's head with L-shaped eyes and a mirror over the mouth.[5] The mask in which it is contained could be the celestial version of the flower mountain or another cosmic entity associated with the sky, such as the PBD. These masks adorned the easternmost and dominant temple in the triadic Group H at Uaxactun. The meaning expressed by this art is strongly related to the creation story and creator deities as both zoomorphs and mountain locations.

One example of monumental sculpture from Holmul is among the earliest and more striking variants of the pyramid-as-sacred-mountain theme in Preclassic Maya iconography.

Two large *witz* masks decorate the earliest version of one of the longest occupied buildings at Holmul, Building B, dating to 400 BC, and remodeled five subsequent times in the following 800 years. Building B's first phase was a beautiful six-room temple edifice standing atop a 6-meter-tall, three-terrace pyramid. Its front measured 13 meters at the summit and stood one step lower than the rear half of the building. This rising of rear rooms one step above the

Figure 5.9 Masks on the terraces of Structure Sub 3 in Group H at Uaxactun (Late Preclassic)

Source: Drawing by Linda Schele; courtesy of David Schele

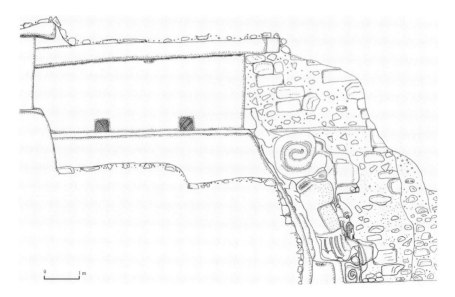

Figure 5.10 Profile elevation of Building B-1st, Holmul (circa 400 BC)

Source: Drawing by N. Neivens Estrada; © Holmul Archaeological Project

front rooms, known as T-shape layout, gives the appearance of two buildings stacked against one another. This is a common feature in early Maya public architecture and is mirrored by Cival's Triadic Group Structure 1. In this case, the temple was fortunately preserved almost in its entirety up to the cornice of the roof, and was not looted in modern times.

The temple's walls and façade were coated with a thick layer of cream-white plaster. Red hematite paint bands ran horizontally along the outer cornice of the building. Vertical red bands also framed the two windows that opened on to the front of the building. Next to the west window were traces of black-line paint. An upward-looking human face appears to have been part of this incomplete, graffiti-like figure. Also in this area of the wall two handprints were made with red paint. These were apparently unrelated graffiti.

This south-facing pyramid was decorated with large mask sculptures on either side of a narrow central stairway, which was inset into the body of the structure. The mask sculptures represented three different beings in a complex composition. The upper half of the composition is occupied by a large zoomorphic being with an open maw. This head is surmounted by a stepped protrusion and flanked by two bracket-like reliefs. In lieu of ears or ear flares, there are two high-relief crossed bands over a human skull on the sloping panels on either side of the main mask. The eyes of this being are oval and deeply recessed. The eyebrows are composed of a stepped motif ending in large clockwise scrolls while parallel streaks appear to descend from the corner of the eye. The teeth are regularly shaped and human-like. The top protuberance

Figure 5.11 Façade of Holmul Building B-1st

Source: Drawing by N. Neivens Estrada; © Holmul Archaeological Project

Figure 5.12 Masks and temple room, Building B-1st, Holmul (circa 350 BC)

Source: © F. Estrada-Belli

and the side bracket motifs help identify this carved head as a *witz* (mountain), in many ways similar to those from Uaxactun H Sub-3, described earlier.

From the open mouth of the *witz* monster emerges a human head, also with his mouth wide open. Deep lines are incised on either side of the mouth as if to represent age lines. Inside this man's mouth is a low-relief symbol made of a down-turned "Y" sign and two diagonally placed dots. This sign appears to be unique to this composition and remains undeciphered, although it may represent a mirror, as the Uaxactun Sub-3 upper mask does. His hands grasp the edge of the orifice as if he were literally pulling himself out of an opening on the head of the third entity in this composition. This is a pointy-nosed zoomorph with almond-shaped eyes and no lower jaw. Contrary to the *witz* monster, deeply carved scrolls are below the corners of the eyes while straight carved lines stretch upward from them, resembling the familiar flamed-eyebrow motif. No teeth are visible in the upper part of its mouth, nor is the lower part of the mouth represented.

Like the Uaxactun H Sub-3 masks, the Holmul sculpture appears to represent a sacred mountain. This, however, does not appear to be the flower mountain of creation, but a mountain associated with the dead (as symbolized by skulls), from which an old man emerges. The crossed-bands motif is often

Figure 5.13 View of zoomorphic head in profile (from west) and human skull (lower left), Building B-1st, Holmul (circa 400 BC)

Source: © F. Estrada-Belli

intended to mark portals in Preclassic Mesoamerica (see Grove 2000; Joyce 1980) and conveys the idea of the cave in this mountain as an entrance to the world of the dead. As he rises from the cave, the old man appears to be carried on the back of a large serpent-like monster. The latter image suggests the frequent representations of ancestors, rulers and gods emerging from the mouth of serpents in Maya art of all periods.

In Mesoamerica, serpents and caves are thought of as conduits to the underworld. Preclassic and Classic Maya sculptures often depict serpents within the mouths of *witz* monsters, identifying these as portals associated with gods and ancestors. Many Mesoamerican myths relating to man's journey from birth (emergence) to death feature passage through these caves. Tikal's Early Classic Temple 5D-33-2nd was decorated by two sets of *witz* monsters. The upper one was decorated with the bracketed-cleft motifs, the added beads resembling corn-kernels to reinforce the idea of the maize god's place of emergence, the flower mountain (Taube 2004). In this case, however, the mouth is closed. Curiously, a serpent emerges from its teeth and passes through a four-bossed ear flare. In Classic Maya inscriptions this sign is a phonetic compound that can be read as a two-syllable word, *och* (Yucatec for rattlesnake; or "to enter") and *bih* ("road") or *ochbih* ("to die") (Stuart 1998). In Maya thought ear spools are symbolic portals—like caves and other liminal spaces, like pools—and are related to breath and wind (and rain). Serpents emanating from jade ear spools represent the breath of life in Classic and Preclassic Maya art. Rather then representing final breath and therefore death, when gods appear in the mouths of serpents rising from ear spools, they are being conjured up, according to Karl Taube (2005). In Taube's analysis of Preclassic and Classic iconography *och b'ih* (literally "enter the road") also concerns rebirth and resurrection of fire, flowers and the celestial path of the sun.[6] Symbols of gods such as *k'in* for sun god or actual images of gods are often carried on the bodies of serpents, therefore being conjured. According to Karl Taube, one prominent example of this Maya and Mesoamerican iconographic convention is the Pyramid of the Feathered Serpent at Teotihuacan. On each terrace, the headdresses of the War Serpent are carried by serpents undulating amid water symbols and emerging from flower-centered rings (Taube 2005). Sugiyama (2005) and Taube (1992b) suggest the iconography of the headdress and feathered serpents symbolizes rulership and the office of war as well as the metaphor of warriors being transported into the sky on the celestial path of the sun. In light of the many similar images of gods being carried by serpents, I believe the Pyramid of the Feathered Serpent sculpture may also be simply a metaphor for the close relation between the flower mountain, the place of creation, and the storm god who presided over it, represented by the headdress. Not surprisingly, there is some evidence that the temple that once stood on the summit of the pyramid was dedicated to Tlaloc (Sugiyama 2005: 76–86), the most important deity at Teotihuacan and indeed a god of war and rulership there as elsewhere in Classic and Postclassic Mesoamerica. Attributes of Tlaloc and feathered

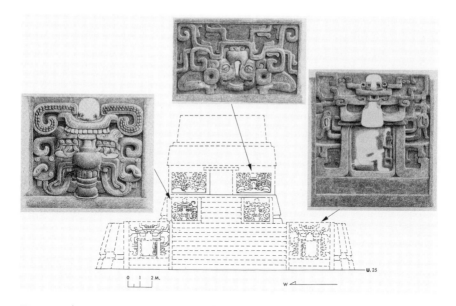

Figure 5.14 Structure 5D-33-2nd, profile with masks, Tikal

Source: After Coe 1990, Tikal Report 14; courtesy of the University of Pennsylvania Museum of Archaeology and Anthropology

serpents are often depicted in association in Teotihuacan art, especially on headdresses.

The lower mask of Temple 5D-33-2nd displays the motif of a cleft mountain. A small god's head in the cleft appears to be that of an aged man, repeating that this pyramid is the image of the old mountain/god. The *witz* is a place of emergence (birth or rebirth) but this time a seated ancestor or god is within the monster's open mouth. This is probably a depiction of an ancestor in the underworld. One of the most important rulers in the history of Tikal, *Sihyaj Chan K'awiil*, was buried below this temple. He greatly expanded the hegemony of his kingdom in the Early Classic, an achievement that was honored by later kings through the burial of his stela (Stela 31) in this temple prior to its rebuilding on a more monumental scale in the Late Classic.

The concept of emergence from mountains/caves in the Preclassic is clearly depicted on the North Wall of the San Bartolo Structure 1A Mural, dating to 100–50 BC. Here a large feathered serpent, the earliest clear representation of it found thus far in Mesoamerica, emerges from a cave opening into a mountain zoomorph surmounted by lush vegetation and wild animals. Thus the serpent is emerging from the flower mountain/cave, the place of creation. As it exits the cave the serpent carries on its back eight human figures, including the maize god and his female attendants, recalling the myth of emergence of the maize god retold in the Popol Vuh and in Late Classic Maya art. The flower

97

mountain is the place of birth and the origin of all things (Taube *et al.* 2004). In Classic and Postclassic Mesoamerica the feathered serpent is often depicted as transporting figures of warriors and merchants (see the Cacaxtla Portico A and Red Temple murals, for example; Uriarte 1999). Through the breath emanating from its mouth, the feathered serpent conveys the idea of steam and rain-clouds emerging from mountains/caves.[7] Streams meandering out of mountains also mimic snakes and pathways into the underworld. The latter metaphor has an epigraphic correspondence. Taube *et al.* (2004) equate the (smaller) serpent emerging from the San Bartolo Mural's cave with the Classic Maya inscriptions' *lok-yi* glyph for "to emerge." In Classic Maya texts, this word is expressed by a serpent rising from a cleft sign (Houston 1993: Figure 4-11). In the Madrid Codex the skeletal death god emerges from a serpent accompanied by a textual caption that includes the *lok-yi* sign "to emerge" (Taube *et al.* 2004).

The old man emerging from the mountain on the Holmul masks could represent the old god, God N, who differs from God D in having almond-shaped (as opposed to L-shaped) eyes. As was noted above, in Classic period imagery the aged god is often associated with the sky and Itzamnaaj and the Principal Bird Deity (known to us as God D). Here, instead, is an aged god associated with mountains and the earth and thus the world of the dead (known to us as God N; Taube 1992a). When he appears with *kawak* ("stone" or "earth") signs on his body, the aged god is identified with the four directional *pawatuns* (or mountains that support the sky).[8] The Classic Maya represented this old god supporting the sky as emerging from a mountain, or a monster with *kawak* (earth) symbols. One such representation is on the corners of the entrance of Copan's Temple 22. Similarly, in the Sepolturas Group at Copan, he is carved on the supports of a bench holding it as if it were the sky. Here this deity literally holds up the skyband. As was mentioned earlier, this old god was referred to as Mam by several Colonial period and modern Maya peoples. Among them, as well as among the Classic Maya, he

Figure 5.15 San Bartolo North Wall mural: mountain/cave scene

Source: Courtesy of William Saturno

was associated with lightning and thunder and was often a malevolent god (Bassie-Sweet 2008; Taube 1992a). The word *mam* is also found in Classic Maya inscriptions and it is read as "grandfather," "ancestor," or "honorable" (Stuart 2000b). As a hieroglyphic sign, it is the profile head of an aged, toothless man with age lines around his mouth and hair falling forward from his forehead. The old god (God N) is also often associated with turtle carapaces, which is a symbol for the surface of the earth (Bassie 2002).[9] In Classic inscriptions, there are instances of "God N Yellow Turtle"; and in the Postclassic Dresden Codex (p. 37) God N wears a turtle carapace on his back with the kan sign for "yellow/precious" (read *Itzamkanahk*; Stuart 2007a) but which also represents the cleft in the earth/mountain associated with the emergence of the maize god and the world tree (Taube 1992a).[10]

Figure 5.16
Sepolturas sky bench, *pawatun* support, Copan (Late Classic)

Source: ©
F. Estrada-Belli

Karen Bassie (2002; Bassie-Sweet 2008) and Allen Christenson (2000) have also argued that God N is associated with the god of lightning, *K'awiil*, and the "First Father" god, *Xpyacoc*. The association with lightning stems from God N emerging from the leg/serpent of *K'awiil*. In this aspect he appears to be evoked during births and healings in Classic Maya art and among the modern Maya as well (Stuart 2000b; Foster and Wren 1996). In Classic Maya texts the glyph for Mam is sometimes substituted by a bird. As an old man, he appears in scenes depicting women giving birth emerging from the serpent/leg of *K'awiil* (Stuart 2000b). In addition, in some contexts, elements of God N appear as a mix of the Principal Bird Deity, feathered serpent with water-lily flowers, and the God N net headdress. In Classic inscriptions the elements of the water-lily feathered serpent are combined to spell phonetically the name *Yax Chit* or "First Father" (who is the same creator/grandfather as the Popol Vuh's *Xpyacoc*): Water Bird Serpent. Thus the feathered serpent and the creator grandfather god were aspects of the same deity to the Classic Maya and most probably to the Preclassic Maya as well. In other words, what western scholars may have perceived as a collection of separate deities associated with different parts of the Maya cosmos may have been understood by the Maya as a multifaceted supernatural entity that had manifestations in the three cosmic domains of earth, sky and underworld.

Because of the various related aspects of the Maya old god, Holmul's Building B imagery, displayed as a badge on the front of the structure, seems to identify this pyramid with the old god/mountain of creation and the world of the dead. It was also possibly a place in which to evoke ancestors. Enabling communication between the world of the living and the world of ancestors and supernaturals was one of the prerogatives of the Maya ruler, as *axis mundi*, and it is possible that this temple materialized the link between dead rulers, the supernatural world and living rulers who identified with them in the present world. When rulers wore the iconographic elements of the old god— the PBD headdress, the large yax diadem, the water lily, the hair net and so on—they claimed his overarching powers as creator. We can imagine a ruler standing at the entrance of this temple wearing the insignia of the Principal Bird Deity (as the old god and creator) as the embodiment of the supreme deity of sky and earth.

The fact that other Mesoamerican cultures of the Middle Preclassic left images of their rulers in just this type of iconographic composition supports our hypothetical reconstruction of Building B's function associated with royal power. The large Olmec stone monuments that are believed to be massive thrones—such as Altar 4 at La Venta, for example—may have been stood or sat upon by Middle Preclassic Olmec rulers. Altar 4's iconography identifies it as a mountain saurian monster with flowers emerging on the sides of its mouth/cave. From it emerges a human being, possibly a dead ruler or a god, wearing a bird headdress. Any individual standing or seated atop this throne would have formed an axis between the living and the ancestor/god appearing

in the cave. Monument 22 at Chalcatzingo, Mexico, is an oversized architectural version of the La Venta altar. In this case a large patio in front of it
substituted for the cave entrance to the earth, as a gigantic open maw. Finally,
a Middle Preclassic mural from Oxtotitlan, in the Highland state of Guerrero,
Mexico, shows a ruler wearing a full-body bird costume in a dance pose, seated
on an earth monster. In this case the mouth of the cave is not depicted, because
the mural itself was painted above the entrance of a cave (Grove 2000). Thus,
for the Maya of Holmul at circa 400 BC, as for the rulers of Middle Preclassic
La Venta and Highland Mexico, temples such as this were places in which they
positioned themselves axially with gods and mountains/caves and presented
themselves as embodiments of those supernatural forces.

In summary, the image of the old man in the maw of the mountain monster
(*witz*) from Holmul evokes a number of religious concepts (or, following the
previous discussion of western interpretations, deities) that are related to the
Maya creation story as well as to the ideology of the earliest Mesoamerican
rulers. One important component of this relation is the concept of the sacred
mountain as the earth and its association with the world of the dead and
ancestral spirits. Two related notions are the mountain/old god as the sky
bearer and the mountain/old god as the sky, associated with the Principal Bird

Figure 5.17 La Venta Altar 4
Source: © F. Estrada-Belli

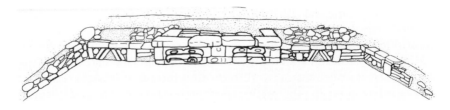

Figure 5.18 Chalcatzingo Monument 22
Source: After Grove 2000; courtesy of David Grove

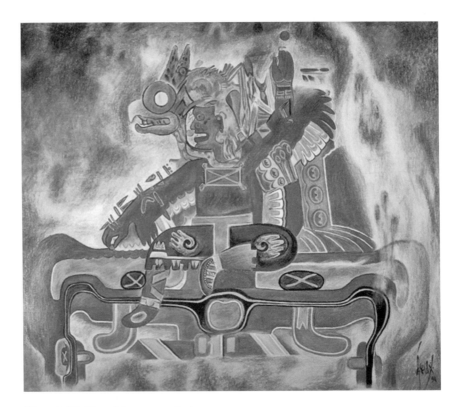

Figure 5.19 Oxtotitlan cave painting
Source: Drawing by A. Moreno; courtesy of the New World Archaeological Foundation

Deity, the iconic symbol of kingship among the Preclassic and Classic Maya. Thus the pyramid as the image of the mountain/old god straddles the three cosmic dimensions of the Maya worldview—sky, earth and underworld. As was noted earlier, among the present-day Maya the old god is a god of healing and birth as well as of malevolent magic. These aspects relate to his powers as creator of life, reinforced by the specific association with the omnipresent water-lily feathered serpent and "First Father," the supreme creator of the universe depicted in Classic and Postclassic Maya iconography.

The above examples show several common traits that help in the identification of the main ideological program behind the construction of Preclassic Lowland Maya monumental art. It is apparent that most traits are related to the story of creation, at least as much of it as we can see reflected in the Popol Vuh account of the Colonial period and in Classic period inscriptions and painted ceramics. It is rare to find a series of archaeological features, such as caches or burials associated with monumental art, that can provide a more coherent view of the development through time of such buildings and of the ritual activity that took place among them than those at Cival, north of Holmul.

The discovery of stucco sculptures at Cival decorating one of the Triadic temples facing the E-Group plaza, where many caches were deposited, offers more details to illustrate the ideological program of Preclassic monumental art from the time of its earliest manifestations. The Triadic Group 1 of Cival is a steep-sided platform rising 20 meters from the plaza. It measures 70 meters on the front and 39 meters on the sides. It supports three temple pyramids forming a Triadic Group (see Figures 4.1, 4.2 and 4.3, above). The main temple on the eastern side is 13 meters high. Two stepped temples flanking it on the north and south sides of the platform are 5 meters high. Attached to the eastern and southern temples are two low rises which could be the remains of low rectangular building platforms. In addition to these three main temples, on the west there are two 4-meter-high pyramidal structures flanking an inset stairway on the front of the platform. Finally, on the northwest and southeastern corners are two small rises, which could be the remains of small single-room buildings (5 × 3 meters wide). Because of its imposing volume and location blocking the eastern horizon on the site's east–west center line, this new Triadic Group was probably the most important focus of ritual performance at Cival during the reminder of the Late Preclassic period. Over at least 400 years it underwent five major remodeling episodes, the last one around AD 100. The construction of this group represented a major change in the scale and nature of ritual architecture at Cival, from horizontal to vertical. It may have made some rituals secluded, but nevertheless a large audience standing in the plaza would have had an impressive view of the ceremonies carried out on this elevated space framed by towering temples.

The second-to-last stage of the eastern temple of the Triad consisted of a temple pyramid fully enclosed within the latest stage of construction. Its upper temple would have risen 6 meters from the platform's top and 26 meters from the plaza below it. Its pyramidal platform consisted of three terraces decorated with sloping apron-moldings and a 2-meter-wide inset central stairway, all of which were coated with a 5-centimeter thick stucco lining. This pyramid is decorated with two large and identical stucco masks, each of which measures 5 meters in width and 3 meters in height. They are placed on the

Figure 5.20 Northern mask on Cival Structure 1–4th
Source: © F. Estrada-Belli

sloping face of the upper (third) terrace of the stepped pyramid. It is interesting to note that while the upper sloping terrace measures 3 meters in height, the first two are only about 1.3 meters high. The first terrace (1.1 meters wide) was much narrower than the second. The terrace above it (4.15 meters wide) clearly created a broader space in front of the mask to accentuate it.

The giant masks are anthropomorphic. Their identifying characteristics are down-turned, L-shaped slit eyes, a single tooth (central incisor) with bifurcated ends, cross-band signs on the cheeks, flamed-eyebrow and curled motifs on the cheeks, and ear-flare assemblage. The L-shaped slit eye is often related to solar and sky deities.[11] This mask closely resembles Cerros's lower masks from Structure 5C-2nd, in spite of being separated by at least two centuries (Cerros's masks date to about 50 BC; Freidel 1986). However, there are also apparent differences, especially in the cross-band motif on the face, instead of a *k'in* sign, but these are often interchangeable in early Maya art. Moreover, the slit-eye and flaming-eye compound of the Cival masks is similar to that of an unidentified bundled figure appearing in the San Bartolo Mural and several examples of Olmec sky dragons/serpents (Taube *et al.* 2004: Figure 2; see Figure 5.15, above). On a carved vase from Tlapacoya, the cross-band motif is inside the mouth, identifying this being as the sky or the center of the sky, the

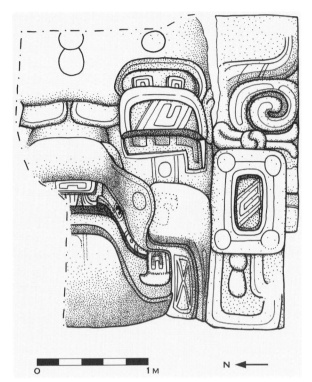

Figure 5.21 Southern mask on Cival Structure 1–4th

Source: Drawing by H. Hurst; © H. Hurst and Holmul Archaeological Project

interception between the Milky Way and the elliptic, according to Joralemon (1971), or as a portal to the world of supernaturals, according to Grove (2000: 289). This concept is similar to that of the "Heart of Sky" of the Quiche Maya, an epithet often used in the Popol Vuh for the hurricane god. The Heart of Sky was the being that initiated the moment of creation and it has many equivalents among creator deities of the Mesoamerican pantheon (Tedlock 1996: 341). The compound formed by the flaming eyebrow, expressed by the double-merlon motifs, and the diagonally bracketed U sign often appears together on carved Olmec heads and on Izapan stelae as a skyband, as a *pars-pro-toto* of the sky dragon or Taube's (1995) avian serpent. This composite motif for the Preclassic Maya became a glyphic compound for *ahaw*. As such, according to Freidel *et al.* (2002), it probably refers to the heavenly or holy nature of *k'uhl ahawob*. It is interesting to note that the San Bartolo bundled beings, which are probably ancestral bundles, are enveloped by scrolls, possibly representing clouds. Another important detail of the Cival mask is the curled motif on the cheek. This motif is similar to that in the corner of the eyes. According to Taube (1995), it represents a stylized version of the Olmec paw–wing motif of the sky dragon. A similar mask/figure is repeated multiple times on Izapa Stela 1 (Norman 1973). This being has the curl on the cheek and flamed eyebrow

(Taube 1995). Diagonal brackets are upturned on the forehead rather than on the eyelid, perhaps due to the profile view, and it has a scrolled ear-flare compound. It has a decidedly anthropomorphic appearance, with its puffy cheeks and furrowed forehead, like the Cival masks. It has been interpreted by Taube (1995) initially as an early form of rain god (*chaak*). However, the bracketed U signs on eyelids and ear spools may be related to the idea of shining brilliance (Taube personal communication 2010), which would be consistent with other solar attributes on this mask, such as the *k'in*-cross bands and L-shaped eyes, although not sufficient to identify it with the Preclassic sun god. Finally, it should be noted that two dots and an exclamation-point water sign are incised on the Cival mask forehead and two bracketed dots are incised below the mask's eye. In Olmec iconography this motif is interpreted as representing teardrops from the rain gods (Reilly 1991).

The Cival masks were placed atop the highest temple on the plaza's east horizon, the direction of the rain-laden storm winds. As such, they could represent the earliest surviving Maya representations of the rain/lightning sky gods of creation (Tedlock and Tedlock 1985).

In addition, two blocks found in the rubble covering the masks show remains of black-painted signs. These appear to be representations of the Lamat or Venus star sign, common in Preclassic Isthmian and Maya scripts. Finally, in two separate locations, painted on the temple terrace aprons and on a block in the rubble above the masks, were two profile almond-eyed faces with squared mouths similar to the masks and wearing elaborate headdresses.

Above these masks was a temple room painted in red on the outside and with polychrome figures and black star signs in the interior walls. The painted blocks found in the rubble covering the masks may be remains of doorjambs tossed down at the moment of the termination and rebuilding of the temple.

Although much of this temple was destroyed by looters, parts of the walls are sufficiently preserved for us to determine that this structure was a two-room vaulted building. The front room was accessed by three wide doorways. The rear room was accessed through a central doorway and was raised 30 centimeters above the front room. The front walls were painted red, while the doorjambs, now largely lost, were painted with polychrome murals. Inside, the lateral walls were painted white, while the frontal wall(s) were painted in a tan color. On the inner (east) side of the wall separating the front (west) from the rear (east) room of the temple, several small figures were painted in black. Fifteen of these have survived on a section of this wall. Four are situated about 50 centimeters from the floor and three more are aligned at about a meter above it. Figure 1 is the best preserved. It is a human figure in striding position facing left. He has almond-shaped eyes with dark facial paint in the upper nose and eye areas. His mouth consists of a straight upper lip and fangs; he has curls on either cheek and wears nose beads and a large four-dotted ear flare. Below the chin is a trilobed ornament (or bib) that may be a form of shell or *yax* (first/green) sign. These facial traits are consistent with those of the maize god.

Figure 5.22 Figure 1 of Mural 1 on Cival Structure 1–4th (circa 200 BC)

Source: Drawing by H. Hurst; © H. Hurst and Holmul Archaeological Project

He wears a foliage-shaped cap and a large headdress consisting of a long-beaked avian head, with L-shaped eye and flamed eyebrow, bifid tongue, and an *ahaw* sign as ear ornament. He has a long hair braid emerging from the top of his head. The only ornaments on his body are a large-bead belt and bracelets on the upper arms. Overall, this figure is consistent with other images of the maize god in Late Preclassic Maya art. In this case, he wears the PBD/Itzamnaaj headdress, indicating his identification with the concept of the old god reviewed above, the world tree, the *axis mundi*, and the supreme power of the creator. This image directly recalls the portrait of the ruler on Cival Stela 2 wearing the PBD royal pectoral, which was erected in the plaza below this temple. According to available evidence, Stela 2 may be 100 years earlier than Figure 1 (300–200 BC), but in the absence of more precise dating, they should be considered contemporary.

Figure 13 is a full-figure portrait of the maize god in a striding posture, wearing a feathered cape (see Figure 5.27, below, for a similar costume). The style of Figures 1 and 13 is particularly similar to the roughly coeval painted images of the maize god in the North and West Wall murals of San Bartolo Structure 1. In the West Mural, the saga of the maize god culminates in his wearing the avian headdress and ascending to absolute power as a result of his defeat of the PBD. In Figure 2 from Cival Mural 1 we have a similar facial portrait. This time a simple headband is worn by the maize god with a central

Figure 5.23 Figure 13 of Mural 1 on Cival Structure 1–4th (circa 200 BC)

Source: Drawing by H. Hurst; © H. Hurst and Holmul Archaeological Project

Figure 5.24 Figure 2 of Mural 1 on Cival Structure 1–4th (circa 200 BC)

Source: Drawing by H. Hurst; © H. Hurst and Holmul Archaeological Project

trilobed diadem, the *hunal*, which is the royal symbol *par excellence* in Maya iconography. Figure 3 of Cival Mural 1 is a portrait of the maize god wearing the simple foliage-shaped cap. In Figure 4 only the facial traits are preserved, and in Figure 5 only the upper part of the head is preserved, revealing a cross-band sign on the foliage-shaped headdress.

These figures reveal a certain variance in particular traits when representing the common theme of the maize god as the *axis mundi* and the image of divine kingship itself. Judging from the slight variations in line styles, different artists participated in painting these images, or they were painted at different times by several artists. Given the highly restricted location of the painting, it was conceivably visible only to a small, elite group involved in performing rituals at this location. Given their extemporaneous arrangement, it is likely that the paintings resulted from repeated rituals evoking the maize god, rather than a single planned mural composition.

Altogether, the masks and the mural fragments are evidence of the cosmological theme of this Cival temple: rain-bearing sky gods supporting a temple decorated with images and symbols associated with the sky, making this pyramid the image of the center of the world of creation and birthplace of the maize god. In a review of the iconography of the Cerros masks, Freidel *et al.* (2002) propose that the masks may represent constellations of the night sky during the birth of the maize god prior to the day of creation, August 14, 3114 BC, and leading to the birth of the maize god. At Cival, celestial beings represented on the masks and the star symbols decorating the upper temple do appear to relate to various elements of the Itzamnaaj/PBD/old god, the sky-and-earth creator deity. According to Kathryn Reese-Taylor (2002), Late Preclassic Triadic pyramid complexes, such as Uaxactun Group H and Cerros Group 6, mirror a place described in the Palenque texts as the Raised-up-Sky/Eight House Partitions, where the three realms of the universe were separated as the sky was being raised. The Cival example appears to support this interpretation in the sense that its focal pyramid represents the main deity of the first creation who elevated and supports the sky (see also Freidel *et al*. 1993).

To summarize, in light of the above-discussed offertory caches and monumental sculptures, it is apparent that, across the Maya Lowlands and as early as the Middle Preclassic (circa by 900–800 BC), the E-Group plazas are the earliest monumental settings for rituals related to the Maya worldview, the agricultural cycle, the maize god as *axis mundi*, the creator deity (the PDB) and their centrality in Maya ideology as the prototype and patron of kingship. While monumentality by itself does not equate with civilization, the appearance of a programmatic new narrative that coopted creation stories and symbolism in the 9th century BC reflects a new sense of community throughout the Maya Lowlands at that time. What used to be a patchwork of regional ceramic styles, in the Pre-Mamom phase, was replaced by a more widespread phenomenon, place-making at ritual centers and setting a new communal identity across regions accompanied by more widely shared ceramic styles (i.e. broad regional variants of the Mamom ceramic style). The presence of monumentality, elite rituality and a novel narrative does not necessarily correspond with the existence of a fully articulated hierarchical (stratified) society of the sort we typically associate with the term "civilization." Rather, from the reconstruction of the timing of adoption of ceramics, the formation of villages and the creation of ritual space at Cival, I see the appearance of these elements as signaling the accelerated development of Maya civilization around 900 BC. The monumentality and associated narrative provide the catalyst for this process. But the rise of hierarchical structures in their society likely was a drawn-out process for the duration of the Middle Preclassic period. Subsequently, during the early part of the Late Preclassic period (circa 300 BC), as the resources available to Maya communities increased, large temple complexes were erected and the themes of creation focused more on the maize god as the source of worldly power. These themes were expressed more evidently in the context of royal ideology. The greatest monumental complexes of this time were erected in the Mirador Basin, at such sites as Nakbe, El Mirador, Tintal, Xulnal and Wakna.

In the region surrounding the Mirador Basin, Cival was but one among many ceremonial centers in which monumental construction took place. The progression seen in the Cival record, from E-Group rituals to the monumental art of Triadic temples, provides a particularly compelling case for the continuity of ideological programs associated with the elite narrative from which royal ideology emerged. In spite of apparent idiosyncratic variation in the monumental art of this period (Late Preclassic) across the Lowlands, the theme of cosmic creation, the creator gods and the saga of the maize god appear to be most consistent themes.

The role of hieroglyphic writing in Maya (royal) narratives

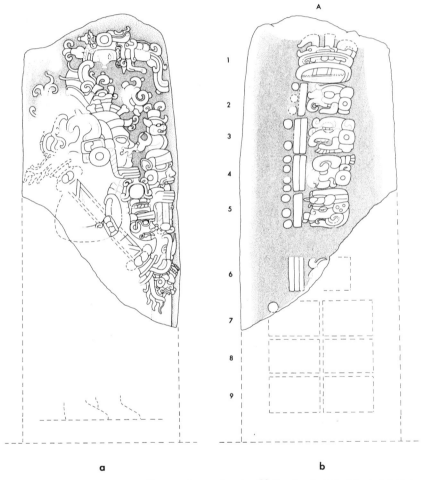

a   b

Figure 5.25 The earliest carved Long Count date in the Lowlands, Tikal Stela 29 (July 8, AD 292)

Source: After Jones and Satterthwaite 1982; courtesy of the University of Pennsylvania Museum of Archaeology and Anthropology

Note: a=front; b=back

110

The earliest-known dated inscription[12] in the Maya Lowlands remains that of Stela 29 at Tikal, having a Long Count date of July 8, AD 292 (8.12.14. 8.15 13 Men 3 Zip). On it is a portrait of the Tikal king Foliated Jaguar (Proskouriakoff 1993; Martin 2003). While this is the earliest Long Count date to be found, hieroglyphic writing predates it in the Maya Lowlands by centuries. There are unreadable hieroglyphs on El Mirador Stela 2. Its date is difficult to establish without knowing its original placement, but stylistically it appears to date to the Late Preclassic period and certainly prior to AD 150: that is, before El Mirador was finally abandoned. On El Mirador Stela 2's surviving fragment is a large head figure of the PBD floating amid scrolls. To the right is a vertical panel with two columns of small, incised hieroglyphs (Hansen 1991). What remains of the inscription suggests a historical text (Hansen 2001).

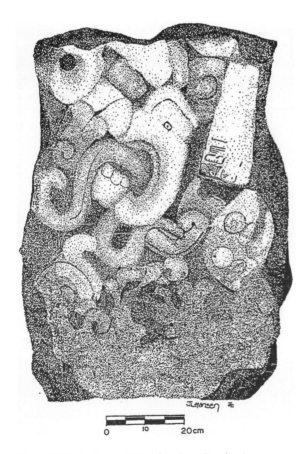

Figure 5.26 Stela 2, El Mirador (Late Preclassic)

Source: Drawing by J. Hansen; courtesy of Richard Hansen

111

Until recently, early inscriptions were known only from the Guatemalan Highlands. Monument 1 from El Porton, in Baja Verapaz, is possibly the earliest known, with an associated radiocarbon date of circa 400 BC (Sharer and Sedat 1973). On the left side of the monument is a single column of glyphs, preserved but not legible. Next to the text is a large eroded area that was likely occupied by one or more standing figures. It therefore likely represents a caption or other type of historical inscription describing the ritual or action depicted in the main scene. Other texts from the Highlands share similarities with the El Porton monument. Stela 10 from Kaminaljuyú, for example, has one of the longest surviving inscriptions and it includes cartouched day names, which we unfortunately cannot translate in our calendar. Stylistically, it can be placed with a certain confidence in the Late Preclassic period. However, it was moved after being carved, and like many other Highland monuments it was not found associated with Late Preclassic material. Despite its length, this inscription is also largely undeciphered. Some of the signs, however, resemble examples from the Classic period, which has led some to suggest that Highland Maya writing of the Late Preclassic period is closely related to the C'holan language of the Lowland Maya (Schele and Freidel 1990; Fahsen 2001; Mora-Marín 2005). The same type of script is also found at Late Preclassic sites on the Pacific Coast of Guatemala. Ceramic and architectural styles there are similar to those of Kaminaljuyú and therefore suggest that there were at

Figure 5.27
Kaminaljuyú Stela 10
(Late Preclassic)

Source: After Parsons 1986; courtesy of the Dumbarton Oaks Research Library and Collections, Washington, D.C.

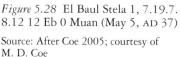

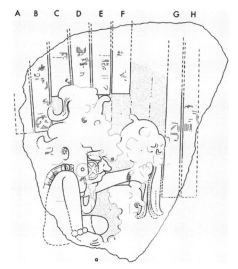

Figure 5.28 El Baul Stela 1, 7.19.7.
8.12 12 Eb 0 Muan (May 5, AD 37)

Source: After Coe 2005; courtesy of
M. D. Coe

Figure 5.29 Chalchuapa Monument 1

Source: After Sharer and Sedat 1973; courtesy of
R. Sharer

least enclaves of Maya speakers on the coast at these sites. The distribution of early texts on the coast is quite spotty and may also denote the presence of Maya enclaves amid non-Maya speakers. The earliest carved dates are from Chiapa de Corzo, El Baul (AD 37; Parsons 1986) and Takalik Abaj (AD 126). Interestingly, to the west and south of these sites are many centers that boast sculptural art but no inscriptions (e.g. Izapa, Ujuxte and Monte Alto), as if the use of writing were tied to ethnic affiliation and/or elite connections with Highland centers. These few dated monuments are complemented by many undated ones that may be stylistically earlier. At Chalchuapa, El Salvador, for example, is an undated but stylistically Preclassic inscribed monument (Monument 1; Sharer and Sedat 1973). This suggests that there was an extensive tradition of hieroglyphic writing in the Highlands and Pacific Coast by the 1st century AD. This likely developed primarily at sites occupied by Maya speakers since the Middle Preclassic Period. The El Porton text seems to date to the period in which Maya writing was first developed.

It is reasonable to conclude from the above that the art of hieroglyphic writing was known to Maya-speaking people just to the south of the Maya Lowlands for quite a long time. Until recently, it was believed that before the beginning of the Christian era the Lowland Maya did not have the sufficient socio-political complexity to require the use of a writing system. However, the recent discovery of several texts at the site of San Bartolo has confirmed the existence of a Lowland writing tradition coeval with the earliest Highland texts discussed above. At San Bartolo, several columns of hieroglyphic texts accompany the figures in the North and West Wall murals, as captions or descriptors of the figures. These texts have been dated by radiocarbon samples associated with the murals to the 1st century BC (Saturno *et al.* 2006). Another inscription was found on a painted block that was associated with an earlier construction stage of the same temple where the well-known murals are located (the Pinturas structure). Charcoal samples found in the rubble that contained the painted block date to between 400 and 100 BC (Saturno *et al.* 2006). While it is difficult to ascertain the exact date of the inscription even in this well-documented case, it is clear that there was writing prior to the 2nd century BC in the Maya Lowlands. This writing system appears to be coeval with the great architecture of the Triadic Groups of El Mirador, Nakbe and many of the other major sites, and with the monumental sculptures that adorned them.

Given that the currently known earliest texts, those from San Bartolo, are conservatively estimated to date from 300–200 BC and represent a well-developed usage of signs, it is likely that future research will uncover even earlier Maya texts attesting to the earliest stages of development of the writing systems. Elsewhere in Mesoamerica, in Oaxaca and on the Gulf Coast, the

Figure 5.30 Hieroglyphs from a painted stone block found in the rubble of the Pinturas structure at San Bartolo

Source: After Saturno *et al.* 2006; courtesy of William Saturno

114

earliest writing appears to have developed out of simple calendrical and icono-graphic signs around 500–400 BC (Marcus 1992; Pohl *et al.* 2002). This was a time when monumental buildings adorned with complex iconography were erected at Nakbe in the Maya Lowlands. It is possible that the earliest forms of writing in the Lowlands also developed in the 5th century BC. Because we know that complex forms of glyph-like iconographic motifs were already being used on a monumental scale at the Highland Maya site of El Porton by 400 BC, it is possible that future research will uncover earlier Lowland inscrip-tions.

The relationship between the Preclassic Maya writing system and the Classic period hieroglyphic script is not clear. Some epigraphers have noted that the Preclassic Lowland and Highland scripts are closely related (possibly two stages of development in the same writing tradition), and that they may have been used by speakers of the same C'holan–Maya language family (Fahsen 2001). Others have pointed out that the Lowland texts have greater similarities with the epic-Olmec script used to the west, along the Gulf Coast (Saturno *et al.* 2006). This similarity may simply be due to the early date of the San Bartolo text. Although many of the Preclassic signs are unintelligible to us, others are easily recognizable as precursors of Classic types. The *ahaw* sign, for example, is repeated several times in the San Bartolo texts and is clearly recognizable as an archetype of the Classic period sign (Saturno *et al.* 2006). Other examples of Preclassic signs with a Classic equivalent are those for accession to the throne, or "be seated" (*chum-laj*), expressed by a sim-ple seated figure in profile, and the signs for month or twenty (*winal*) and mountain (*witz*; Fahsen 2001). Verbs are also expressed in similar ways by hand-signs in the Preclassic and Classic scripts.

There is very strong evidence, therefore, that the Preclassic and Classic Maya scripts represent stages of development in a single Maya writing system. The Maya script underwent major changes from the Classic period to the Postclassic. The same might be expected from the Preclassic period to the Classic. One problem is that our Preclassic sample is too small and there is a two-century gap between the Preclassic and Classic scripts, so we appear to be missing a transitional phase. As new texts are uncovered, it is likely that additional equivalent signs will be found. These in turn will facilitate the decipherment of even more signs. But only when a sizable corpus of text is available will we be able to begin deciphering them in earnest.

While the Preclassic and Classic scripts may have been read in the same language, and while one appears to be ancestral to the other, the small samples we have of Preclassic writing remain largely unreadable. The Preclassic script appears to have been in use until approximately AD 150, after which a large number of Preclassic centers were abandoned and the Maya Lowlands were affected by a general reorganization of the centers of power. There was then a period of between 100 and 150 years for which we do not have texts, between the last securely dated Preclassic inscriptions and the earliest Classic Maya text on Tikal Stela 29 (AD 292), although a number of unprovenienced texts on portable objects may date to this period. At the end of the Preclassic period, Maya hieroglyph writing was in widespread use from the northern Lowlands (e.g. the Loltun Cave; see Andrews 1981a) to the southern Lowlands, and the southern Highlands.

In the Preclassic period, the knowledge associated with writing was certainly restricted to a small group of high-ranking specialists within Maya society, perhaps more so than in the Classic period. Early scribes probably preferred paper books or other perishable media to stone, which might explain the paucity of surviving inscriptions from this period. Its highly restricted use and the fragile media in which it was transmitted may also explain the rapid changes in many of its notational signs before the Classic period. Based on available evidence, it is possible to surmise that knowledge of writing quickly evolved during the 150-year span of the Terminal Preclassic. During this period, the carving and painting of inscriptions may have been interrupted by widespread warfare and a generalized crisis in Maya society, which uprooted elites from their palaces. Whatever the causes, this short but intense period of turmoil would effectively have resulted in the loss of many inscriptions, especially those written on perishable material, in a way similar to the deliberate destruction of Maya books by Spanish missionaries. As the literate elites were evicted from power in favor of non-literate or semi-literate military factions, books and any knowledge relating to them may have quickly been lost.

After this brief dark age around AD 250, order and elite tradition were restored within the Lowlands when new dynasties consolidated their power at sites outside of the Mirador Basin, such as Tikal. The new elites simply adopted what knowledge had survived of the ancient writing system and then continued in a new tradition.

6

THE PRECLASSIC–CLASSIC MAYA TRANSITION

A new beginning?

A "Protoclassic" or "Terminal Preclassic" to Classic transition

The Preclassic and Classic periods are arbitrary temporal divisions set by archaeologists half a century ago, at a time when we knew little about the antiquity of Maya civilization (Willey and Sabloff 1974). These divisions were based on the occurrence of certain traits in Maya culture around the year AD 300. The perception was that, with the appearance of these traits, the Maya had reached full-blown civilization. Tikal Stela 29 carried the earliest Long Count date (AD 292) and provided a convenient fixed, if completely artificial, boundary between the two periods. In addition, it was recognized that at roughly the same time, polychrome-painted ceramics and corbel-vault buildings also made their appearance.

Archaeologists have since recognized that a temporal division at AD 300 does not accurately reflect the actual first appearance of those traits in the Maya Lowlands. For example, it has been known for some time that polychrome ceramics and vaulted architecture existed in the Preclassic period, at least a couple of centuries before the first inscriptions (Hammond 1992). Moreover, Long Count date inscriptions that pre-existed Stela 29 by at least a couple of centuries had been known from the southern Maya Highlands and Pacific Piedmont (Sharer and Sedat 1973; Hammond 1977), and some early but unprovenienced examples can be attributed with some level of confidence to the Maya Lowlands (e.g. the Hauberg stela; Hammond 1977). Nevertheless, archaeologists chose to ignore these problematic indications in favor of the well-established chronological divisions. However, it is now widely accepted that the appearance of those cultural traits (and others) in the centuries preceding the Classic period indicate that the beginnings of Classic Maya civilization occurred considerably earlier, in the Preclassic period.

The decipherment of hieroglyphs during the 1980s steered the debate towards the iconographic symbols and hieroglyphic systems used by Classic Maya kings, and to the question of origin: that is, where and when they were developed. In a series of influential articles published at the end of that decade, archaeologists and epigraphers pronounced that the institution of divine kingship so closely associated with Classic Maya civilization was a likely product of the intense population growth at many Lowland centers during the Late Preclassic period and of the attendant "crystallization" of social norms that occurred in the last century prior to the Christian era (Freidel and Schele 1988; Stuart 1988; Fields 1986).

At the same time, as research at El Mirador (Matheny *et al.* 1980), Becan (Ball 1977), Cerros (Freidel 1986) and other Preclassic sites began to produce results in the late 1970s and early 1980s, new issues regarding the timing of specific site histories emerged but were largely overlooked. For example, neither Cerros nor El Mirador showed signs of Classic period occupation, Preclassic Becan was encircled by a moat, and polychrome ceramics appeared at some very specific locations in the two centuries from AD 100 to 300. A new debate ensued on the nature of this transitional period. Was it a dark age or a period of innovations spurred by migrants, who, along with ceramics, brought a new political system—Maya kingship? In the same influential article in which David Freidel and Linda Schele (1988) suggested that the "crystallization" of Maya kingship, the institution of the *ahaw*, occurred in the 1st century BC, they also echoed the widely shared perception that the subsequent transition of the Preclassic into the Classic period fundamentally altered that institution. But how this alteration should be manifested in the archaeological record was not clear. An important ingredient of this transformation was the stela cult and the associated Long Count calendrical system, which were said to have travelled from the Maya Highlands to the Lowlands. In Freidel and Schele's view, the mixing of the esoteric knowledge of Lowland village-level shamans with the writing and calendrical system of Highland elites gave rise to the Classic form of Maya kingship. As noted earlier, though, the recent discovery of a parallel Lowland writing tradition in the Late Preclassic period put this idea to rest (Saturno *et al.* 2006).

The idea of migrations from the Highland regions of Guatemala and El Salvador, where polychrome and modeled ceramics (as well as Long Count dates) prevailed prior to the Lowland Classic tradition, was another point of great contention. The debate was stimulated by an ever-improving data set of ceramics from good, datable contexts (architecture and ritual cave deposits) and continued through the 1990s, when finally an agreement (of sorts) was reached. Brady *et al.* (1998) proposed that polychrome bowls and vases with distinctive supports (mammiform modeled) and orange glossy background paint were products of a local development (see Figure 2.3, above). The proposition that the so-called "Protoclassic" orange polychrome ceramics comprised a full ceramic complex (i.e. a full set of storing, cooking and serving wares) rather than a ritual/burial sub-complex was viewed with great suspicion. Indeed, numerous documented site contexts showed this proposition to be untenable. The new polychromes served a minority of ritual and burial functions, at least initially. Eventually, over the course of the two-century transition from the Preclassic to the Classic (approximately AD 75 to 250), the style became more sophisticated as well as accessible to non-elite ritual contexts. But perhaps the single most significant fact about these ceramics was that in both style and technology they had developed out of a pre-existing tradition of monochrome red Late Preclassic ceramics (Brady *et al.* 1998; Pring 1977) and initially coexisted with it. A recent study by Callaghan (2008) has highlighted this, showing that in the Holmul region the same variety of clay recipes was used for Preclassic red and Early Classic polychrome orange vessels. Because of these new developments, the term "Protoclassic" was retired.

The period between AD 75 and 250 was renamed "Terminal Preclassic." But since not all sites exhibit early polychrome vessels, it was to be used as a marker of localized ceramic development rather than a pan-Maya cultural period. In fact, certain locations outside of the central area of Peten lacked polychrome technology for some time and Preclassic monochromes were said to have persisted well into the 4th century AD (Kosakowsky 1987; Kosakowsky and Pring 1991, 1998). However, sites like Cuello and Nohmul, quite close to one another, differed in the presence or absence of early polychromes. The meaning of these discrepancies is not clear. It is possible that they may be attributed to the abandonment of certain sites during the transitional period while others near by may have prospered through connections to the most active trade networks (but not migrations, as was once proposed; Willey *et al.*, 1965). And so the temporal lag of certain sites that lacked early polychromes may be apparent rather than real.

In any case, this temporal lag rendered any broad generalizations about the correlation of ceramic and socio-political innovations problematic, so the transition between the Preclassic and Classic periods remained obscure.

The eclipse of El Mirador and the rise of Classic kingdoms

So what do we really know today about what happened in the two centuries prior to AD 300? Admittedly, not much. But one thing is clear: new kings and dynasties appeared in new places, as the major sites of the earlier era, first and foremost El Mirador, were abandoned. With new kings and dynasties in "unusual" places, a novel, more individualistic form of iconography appeared in art and architecture. Because of this, the period in question became the focus of study by epigraphers. Once the whole corpus of inscriptions for a given site could be examined, it was possible to reconstruct its dynastic history. We now have king lists for most major kingdoms in the southern Lowlands—Tikal, Calakmul, Palenque, Yaxchilan, Piedras Negras, Naranjo, Caracol, Dos Pilas and Copan—and Quirigua in the southern Highlands. It also became apparent that while several Preclassic sites were abandoned, new dynasties were being founded in nearby locations.

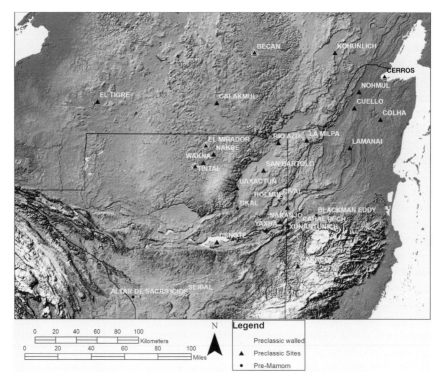

Figure 6.1 Preclassic sites, including those walled and abandoned at the onset of the Classic period

Source: © F. Estrada-Belli, Topographic data courtesy of NASA SRTM mission

There were exceptions to this rule. The Mirador Basin, a large sector of the Maya Lowlands, is largely devoid of Early Classic occupation. Given that the last 20 years of continued research in this region have not uncovered any Early Classic inscriptions, it is doubtful that this is an accident of discovery. To the east and to the north, there were inscriptions dating to the 4th and 5th centuries AD, at Naachtun and Uxul, for example. As a result, new research was initiated there to establish the link between these sites and the abandonment of El Mirador (Grube and Paap 2008; Reese-Taylor and Walker 2002). But, the fact remains that most of the Mirador Basin was largely abandoned at the onset of the Early Classic period. Remarkably, Uxul and Naachtun lie just outside its geographic margins and it is not yet clear whether their environment was different than the Mirador Basin's and whether that played a role in these sites' survival.

Tikal was another exception that might require explaining. It thrived during this transition and most importantly, at the end of it, boasted the earliest dated inscriptions among all Maya centers. As we saw earlier, Tikal's

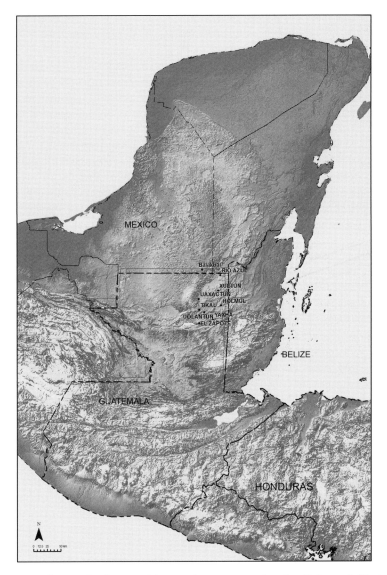

Figure 6.2 Lowland sites with carved monuments bearing Baktun 8 (Cycle 8) Long
Count dates (i.e. earlier than AD 435)

Source: © F. Estrada-Belli, Topographic data courtesy of NASA SRTM mission

Classic period scribes' retrospective texts referred to a ruler named *Yax Eb*
Xook as the first in the line and therefore founder of the same dynasty
that controlled the kingdom during the Classic period (Jones 1991; Martin
2003). Unfortunately, we do not have inscriptions from his reign, estimated
at circa AD 100, and his identification as first in line occurs centuries later, and

121

therefore remains tenuous, at best. Whether *Yax Ehb Xook* was revered as the first "real" king of Tikal by his own contemporaries, as he was much later by his successors, remains to be determined.

Tikal's is perhaps the most ancient Classic period dynasty in the Lowlands. Few other sites appear to have had rulers who carved inscriptions prior to AD 435 (the Long Count Date 9.0.0.0.0), including those kingdoms (such as Naranjo) with dynastic founding dates set far back in mythological time (Grube 2004). All of the Lowlands' early inscriptions and kingdoms are located within a short distance—a day's march—from Tikal. It is possible that Tikal's ruling lineage may have been the first to adopt a new royal ideology after the fall of the great El Mirador kingdom. Indeed, because of their distribution and chronological sequence, subsequent early inscriptions of the central Peten appear to be spin-offs from this innovating center. The process may have been one of political expansionism by the Tikal elites. We know from later inscriptions that such a process was an ongoing feature of the Tikal kingdom throughout the Classic period. The Terminal Preclassic and Early Classic elites of Tikal were also the possessors of some of the finest new polychrome ceramics of this era, the orange gloss wares (Culbert 1993). This innovative style was a departure (albeit not a technological one) from the waxy red monochromes of the previous era. We now know, after several stylistic and provenience studies, that in the Late Classic period, polychrome ceramics were exchanged by elites across kingdoms, to solidify friendly relations and to build reciprocity during ritualized visits. As an innovation, orange polychrome ceramics were the result of a similar motivation—the desire of emerging elites to solidify a new network of political alliances and friendly relationships by exchanging and imitating a new style of ceramics. Tikal may have been one such center of innovation, and the ceramics either distributed or imitated within developing trade and alliance networks (see Reese-Taylor and Walker 2002 for a discussion of this scenario in greater detail).

The rise of new Maya kings and the Teotihuacan "entrada"

Tikal, then, is the rising star of the turbulent post-Mirador interlude years from AD 100 to 376. During this period, the kings of Tikal, after a reorganization of their own kingdom around new elite lineages (possibly unrelated to the El Mirador alliance networks of the previous era), established a hegemonic network of friendly smaller kingdoms around themselves. These were the kingdoms with Cycle (*baktun*) 8 inscriptions and/or places in which the early orange polychrome ceramics were traded and imitated. Intensity of commitment varied with distance and level of shared economic and political interests, but the network may have included a great number of large and small places in the northeastern Peten and southeastern regions. These were located along the main trade routes to and from the Caribbean. The development of this

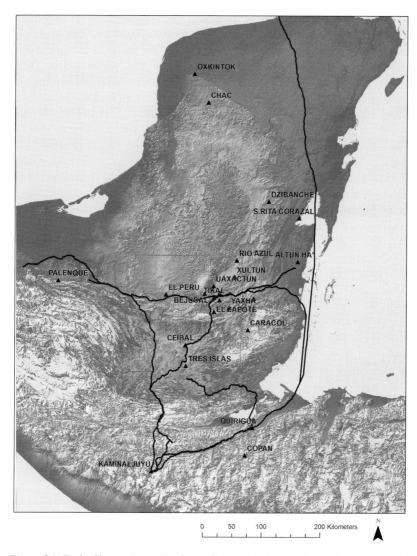

Figure 6.3 Early Classic sites related to Tikal or Teotihuacan "entrada" and least-effort routes computed by GIS algorithm

Source: © F. Estrada-Belli and Holmul Archaeological Project, Topographic data courtesy of NASA SRTM mission

hegemony was not an entirely peaceful process, as is indicated by captive imagery on the early Tikal monuments (Stela 39, for example). Tikal's expansionism came to a culminating moment with the appearance in the Lowlands of Teotihuacan warrior imagery and textual references to a legendary man from "the west" named *Siyaj K'ahk'* (Proskouriakoff 1993; Stuart 2000a). After the so-called Teotihuacan "entrada" in the Lowlands, Tikal appears to enjoy much greater direct and indirect control over much of the southern Lowlands and its trade routes. Tikal-style architecture and/or Teotihuacan imagery often accompany textual references involving 4th-century Tikal kings outside Tikal. *Siyaj K'ahk'* himself is mentioned at a number of sites strategically located to control the main routes (see Figure 6.3). El Peru/Waka', Bejucal, El Encanto, Uaxactun, Holmul and Rio Azul are among the places where he is named (Stuart 2000a; Estrada-Belli *et al.* 2009). Other sites simply display Teotihuacan-style imagery in stone or ceramics. Among these are Tres Islas (Tomasic and Fahsen 2004), Yaxha, in Peten, and Santa Rita Corozal (Chase and Chase 1981), Altun Ha (Pendergast 1971) and Baking Pot (Colas *et al.* 2002) along the Rio Hondo and Belize River routes.

First identified as a possible Teotihuacan conqueror by pioneering epigrapher Tatiana Proskouriakoff in the 1960s (Proskouriakoff 1993), the figure of *Siyaj K'ahk'* has remained elusive and the nature of the Teotihuacan-style

Figure 6.4 Tikal Stela 39 showing ruler *Chak Tok Ichaak* standing above a captive (Early Classic period)

Source: Courtesy of Simon Martin

imagery controversial for a long time. Thanks to a great deal of new information gained from excavations at Tikal and other sites, as well as the reading of
Maya hieroglyphs, we can now safely rule out speculations that *Siyaj K'ahk'*
was a mythological figure or a title of the ruling Tikal king *Yax Nuun Ayiin*.
Both the archaeology and epigraphy agree on certain aspects of this issue.
According to several Early Classic monuments, *Siyaj K'ahk'* arrived at Tikal
(from the west), bringing with him several insignia of power (such as the
eighteen-snake-headed "manikin sceptre" headdress of the god *K'awiil*[1]). The
day of his arrival is expressed by the shortened date 11 Eb 15 Mak, and is
recalled by many Maya kings (not only at Tikal) as a milestone in Maya history.
On this day, the ruling king of Tikal *Chaak Tok Ichaak* died. One year later, a
boy named *Yax Nuun Ayiin* would take the throne, having traveled to an
unknown location in which he was ritually invested with the symbols of royal
power (possibly Teotihuacan). It is during his one-*katun* reign that Teotihuacan
imagery and his likeness are found outside of Tikal. About this point, the texts
do not tell us all that was going on, of course. In fact, excavations in various
elite residential compounds at Tikal (Groups 6C-16, 6C-5 and others) show
that there was a substantial, if small, resident population that built its homes
and made use of material culture carrying Teotihuacan symbolism at least from
AD 250 (Laporte and Fialko 1990; Laporte *et al.* 1992). So the arrival may

Figure 6.5 Uaxactun Stela 5—a
possible portrait of *Siyaj K'ahk'*

Source: Drawing by Ian Graham, Corpus
of Maya Hieroglyphic Inscriptions,
Volume 5, Part 3, Uaxactun; courtesy
of the President and Fellows of Harvard
College.

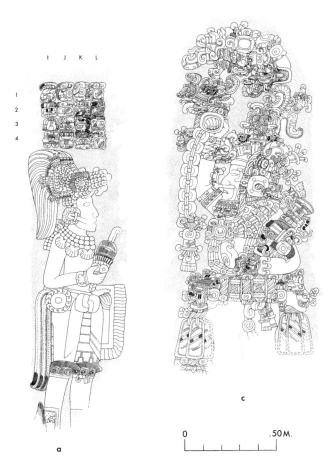

Figure 6.6 Tikal Stela 31 depicting *Siyaj Chan K'awiil* and his father (left) *Yax Nuun Ayiin* (dedicated in AD 445, or 9.0.10.0.0)

Source: After Jones and Satterthwaite 1982; courtesy of the University of Pennsylvania Museum of Archaeology and Anthropology

not have been literal but figurative, meaning the accession to power of a new faction, perhaps with the foreigners' support. Some have suggested a Tikal takeover by a foreign army. Although that is possible, and there are indications of raids at Early Classic Tikal (e.g. early monuments are missing), based on the available data and known practices of later Mesoamerican states (and empires), it is perhaps more likely that foreign help was sought by a local faction aspiring to dethrone an existing ruler. And thus a long-distance alliance with Teotihuacan was probably more a by-product of a local struggle than a motivation for or cause of it. In the end, though, these various details do not change the substance of what happened next.

During approximately the next 100 years, Tikal, with the support of its Teotihuacan allies, successfully consolidated its hegemonic control over much of the Lowlands by securing key places. Aside from obvious episodes of conquest, part of this process may have involved inserting new dynastic centers (with one of their own as founder) in areas void of occupation or between unfriendly neighbors. The most notable case is that of Copan, Honduras, whose founder, the Teotihuacan-affiliated *Yax K'uk' Mo'*, in the year AD 426 made an arrival similar to that of *Siyaj K'ahk'* at Tikal, displaced the existing ruler, and founded a new royal center a short distance from the earlier cere-monial plaza (Figure 1.15, above). He thus secured a distant province near an important Lowland–Highland trade route. Along it traveled such vital resources as obsidian and jade. The nearby kingdom of Quirigua was founded by a vassal of the Copan king shortly thereafter to secure this same route. Following the Motagua River, it was now possible to travel the route from the Highlands to the Caribbean Sea and coastal Yucatan, encountering various Tikal–Teotihuacan-friendly kingdoms along the way.

Both inscriptions and archaeology seem in agreement on the central Peten origin of these kingdom founders (Sharer 2003; Looper 2003; Martin and Grube 2008). A surprising new discovery came when an obscure early text from Caracol, one of the most fearsome enemies of Tikal in the Late Classic, indicated that it was first established through the influence of Tikal. This information, and the occurrence of the Witz'/Caracol place name near that of Yax K'uk Mo', led David Stuart to hypothesize that the Copan founder may have originated there, rather than at Tikal itself, as might be expected[2] (Martin and Grube 2008; Stuart 2007b; Buikstra *et al.* 2004; Sharer 2003). This new discovery, while reinforcing the notion of early Tikal aggressiveness in estab-lishing outposts and a new hegemonic order in the Lowlands, also underscores the short-lived nature of political allegiances in the Maya Lowlands.

But did the rapid ascent of Tikal bring down the colossal kingdom of El Mirador? Even with the help of the greatest foreign power, this would perhaps have been an impossible feat for an upstart kingdom such as Tikal in the 2nd century AD. There is some evidence that El Mirador may have come under attack, and that the attacker left many green obsidian points and blades from central Mexico on the ground. The evidence is currently confined to the Tigre and Danta pyramid complexes, but absent from much of the rest of the site (Hansen 1990; Hansen *et al.* 2008b). This evidence could have been created by a massive attack or a skirmish on the slopes of two of the greatest complexes fairly late in the history of El Mirador, possibly around AD 300. At that time the great kingdom was already on its knees for undetermined reasons and its population was likely confined to the high-rise areas of the site. Why the attack? It may have been an attempt by the rising power (Tikal) to squash the last elites of this great and previously all-powerful kingdom. Their mere existence and influence could have represented a formidable obstacle for Tikal kings as they were establishing their kingdom as the new powerhouse in the

Maya Lowlands, with the help of Teotihuacan, the greatest powerhouse in the whole of Mesoamerica.

The puzzling end of El Mirador

This plausible political scenario does not provide all the answers, by any means. The other side to this story concerns the causes for the decline of El Mirador, independent of the ascent of Tikal. These causes may be found in changes in the Mirador Basin climate and environment. These alone, as current consensus suggests, could have caused the collapse of the Preclassic colossus and initiated a chain reaction of failing centers of power throughout its alliance networks. Environmental science has found evidence for certain changes at this juncture, but neither their causes nor their effects on the local population are easily inferred. More data are needed. From what we know, at El Mirador, as at Cival, large and small water sources contracted towards the end of the Preclassic period (Wahl et al. 2006a, 2006b; Estrada-Belli et al. 2007; Wahl and Estrada-Belli 2009). The changes in water level and concomitant droughts may have affected the hydrological regime of the swamps, causing major problems in agriculture. Some scholars argue that increased sedimentation of swamps and lakes, providing the sustenance for most sites in the Mirador Basin and elsewhere at this time, may also have reduced their productivity (Jacob 1995; Beach et al. 2006; Kunen et al. 2000; Hansen et al. 2002). Simultaneously, the population may have reached critical levels at least in the more populated areas (El Mirador). The environmental crisis, when it manifested itself, may have been too great and too rapid for the ruling class to handle effectively. This scenario is controversial, even though the available evidence points to environmental changes at this time. The complete and utter abandonment of not only the Mirador Basin centers but much of that water-rich environment (in spite of relative reductions in water level) in which they were located is certainly dramatic, as well as puzzling.

Whatever the exact causes, a much-weakened power structure seems to have persisted at El Mirador through the 4th century, before eventually coming under fatal attack. The archaeology of El Mirador is clearer about this. The final abandonment of the site happened rapidly—domestic utensils were even left inside buildings (e.g. Structure 34; Hansen et al. 2008a), a pattern typically associated with Maya sieges (see the Aguateca rapidly abandoned structures; Inomata et al. 2002). Its diminished hegemonic reach beyond the Mirador Basin may have left some of its allies and trade partners to fend for themselves, thus causing a more widespread decline of centers across the Lowlands. The diminished influence of El Mirador on its allies may also have enabled Tikal's Teotihuacan-supported local faction to gain power.

Warfare was probably a frequent affair in Maya politics, even in the Preclassic period. It is possible that El Mirador may have enforced a relative peace within its hegemonic sphere of influence. Although that may have been accomplished through military action (just as the *Pax Romana* was in the 1st-century Mediterranean). But conflict appears to have spiraled upward during the final centuries of the Preclassic period. With the failure of the great hegemony and the rise of new centers, new technological and ritual innovations led to new material culture and new iconography in the Maya Lowlands.

It is fair to conclude that these scenarios are not mutually exclusive, as decades of debate in the field of Maya studies have implied. Taken together, they may provide a more informed explanation than the outright rejection of one or the other.

Environment, politics and friends in high places

In the Holmul region, we have found concrete evidence of the interplay of environmental and political changes at the end of the Preclassic era. Even though we do not have all the answers, some preliminary inferences can be drawn. The environment of Cival is similar in all respects to that of El Mirador, and their occupation ended at the same time. Some parallels should be drawn from these two, among many sites that fared similarly. Cival, like many other Preclassic centers, is located on a broad hill, overlooking a vast seasonal swamp

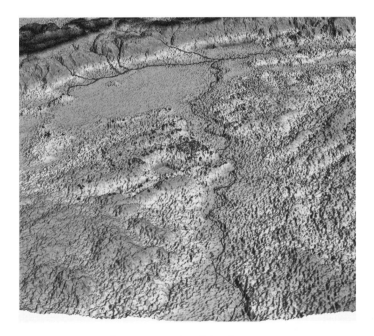

Figure 6.7 View of the topography of Cival

Source: © F. Estrada-Belli and Holmul Archaeological Project

Note: Dark spots identify built areas. Terrain data courtesy of NASA

(to the north and west). Unlike El Mirador, it also overlooks a river, the Rio Holmul, to the east. Today, as in ancient times, this river does not flow for much of the year, its course being dotted by frequent water holes, spots in which the water table is at the surface. These small ponds, known locally as *aguadas*, are the sources of water for anyone traversing or camping in the forest today. In ancient times, they were equally important as sources of drinking water, perhaps the most important sources for much of the population. This likelihood is implied by the location of important sites along the river course and in connection with *aguadas*—Holmul, Cival and Nakum, for example. The absence of other major sources of water, such as lakes and man-made reservoirs, suggests that the population that was dispersed around the ritual center got their drinking water from *aguadas*. Cival did have one other major source of water, an oval-shaped sink-hole, a cenote of gigantic size, 400 meters across, with steep ridges ringing it on three sides and connected by an outlet to the Holmul River to the east. In ancient times, when the forest had been removed, the whole place would have looked like a meteor crater, with some of the elite residential groups settled on its edges, enjoying a view of its interior water. Testing the sediment of a nearby lake (Yaloch) revealed that it received large amounts of siltation during the Preclassic and Classic periods (Maya clay). After these periods, the sediment input declined sharply. Additional testing showed that the water level of the lakes declined significantly around 1700 years ago. This pattern was also observed in other Peten lakes (Beach *et al.* 2008). We do not know what caused this phenomenon, but both climate change and sediment input during the Preclassic period might have played a role. The effect of this reduction in lake water level on the local population is also unknown.

More significantly, perhaps, because archaeology and geomorphology do not allow sufficient time-resolution, the timing of the lake reduction may post-date the decline and abandonment of Cival by one or two centuries. As far as we can tell from construction activity and reflooring of the plazas, Cival entered a period of rapid decline around AD 100. The last major construction project involved the building of the largest pyramid at the site yet, Group 1, a 20 meter-tall elevated plaza with temples towering up to 33 meters in total. The expenditure in manpower and material was significant. Not only were the platforms and pyramids raised by 5–7 meters of fill, but massive rectangular blocks lined the surfaces of temples and platforms alike. These were 1-meter-long finely cut tenoned blocks: that is, placed with the long side into the fill of the building rather than facing outward. This building strategy required three times more stone and labor than previous constructions. The technique was quite common at this time, almost a hallmark of the end of the Preclassic period. It appears not only at Cival, but in the Mundo Perdido at Tikal and in the largest of all Maya edifices, the Danta Complex. In their last stages, two other pyramids at Cival were finished in this expensive way. Richard Hansen has noted that not only the use of cut stone but the vast reflooring and lining

Figure 6.8 Tenoned blocks on Group 1 main stairway, Cival (circa AD 100)
Source: © F. Estrada-Belli

of buildings and plazas must have consumed immense resources, especially firewood to make lime plaster (Clark *et al.* 2000). However, in our Cival excavations, we observed that, while the use of stone in the final period showed great expenditure by the leadership, the thickness of plaster floors was actually greater in the Middle Preclassic and it progressively diminished in the Late Preclassic. This is evident at all other Preclassic sites in the Holmul region, too: Holmul K'o, Hamontun and T'ot. So it is unclear if the consumption of wood and stone—or, as Richard Hansen puts it, the conspicuous consumption of natural (and human) resources—led the environment and all settlements to the brink of collapse (Clark *et al.*, 2000).

At Cival, at least, we find other reasons to believe that neither the over-consumption of resources nor the diminished water in the lake was the primary cause of abandonment. Shortly after the AD 100 landmark renovations of most temples, the city apparently came under siege. On the main hill, the plaza, the main temples and elite palace platforms were encircled by a 2-meter-high stone wall (see Figure 4.2, above). On top of the stone base was probably a timber palisade reaching several meters in height. The wall ran on all sides of the hill except one, the northwest, for a length of 1.3 kilometers. This fortification left out many important elite platforms, especially those that were

131

outside the main hill. But the way the wall was laid out around the edges of the main hill is peculiar. Rather than being as close as possible to the edge of platforms and hilltop, it was placed a few meters from the edge. This layout may have been adopted because of an obscure military strategy. The other peculiar aspect of the wall is that, in some cases, it was built not flush with buildings but bisecting them. The apparent purpose was to use the stone from the buildings as construction material for the wall, while also using the remaining rubble to restrict attackers' movement. The well-known walls built in the Late Classic period by the besieged Dos Pilas elites are a very similar example of this technique. The stone was ripped from surrounding buildings and laid down without mortar, suggesting that the builders did not have sufficient time to build a proper foundation. Moreover, the fact that one side of the site was left unprotected suggests that the building project was never completed. In other words, the Civaleños may have been attacked while they were building their defenses.

Though the Cival wall was never completed, the site was not immediately abandoned. In the main plaza, the E-Group complex was rebuilt at least one more time. The renovations were not substantial, but this at least tells us that

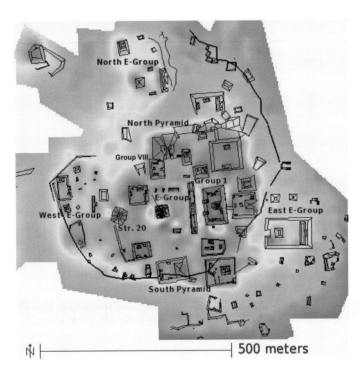

Figure 6.9 Map of Cival's main structures and topography (circa AD 100)

Source: © F. Estrada-Belli and Holmul Archaeological Project the elites of Cival were still there and continued to perform rituals for another century or so, during which time parts of the site were not maintained or renovated. In Group VIII, we have excavated elite residences, probably the ruling elite's, which were occupied through Terminal Preclassic times, probably as late as AD 300 (Estrada-Belli 2008). Large amounts of orange polychrome ceramics suggest that a small but active elite population lived in this compound. Other parts of the site were not left simply unoccupied. Some of the largest and most important buildings were ritually buried by depositing much rubble over them. A large labor force must have been involved. What today appears as collapsed buildings in reality is the rubble deposited by the latest occupants to bury and hide these remaining reminders of a bygone era. A small and dispersed population also continued to dwell in some of the hills around the main center, within easy walking distance. They were part of a small community that remained active through the beginning of the Classic period. In a wide area around Cival, one finds no further sign of occupation after about AD 300. Interestingly, while a handful of the hills on the outskirts of the Cival center were reoccupied centuries later during the Late Classic period, the center itself remained forever clear of signs of activity. Evidently, the forest quickly overtook the mounds and plazas, which were deliberately avoided through respect or because of stigma associated with them.

As Cival was reaching its final days, near AD 300, a much smaller ceremonial center to its south, Holmul, was gaining in importance. Between AD 150 and 300 a number of important individuals were buried in a small building in its main complex, Building B of Group II. From Middle Preclassic times (400 BC), the façade of this building was decorated by images of ancestors in rebirth (see Chapter 5, above). We do not know if it had originally been used as a temple or a seat of power. Possibly it was used for both purposes. But from around AD 150 it became the burial ground for a handful of high-status individuals (Estrada-Belli 2003a; Merwin and Vaillant 1932). It is important to recall that at most other Preclassic sites in which tombs have been found, they date from this final period and are located in buildings that originally did not contain burials—temples or palaces. The interment of individuals within

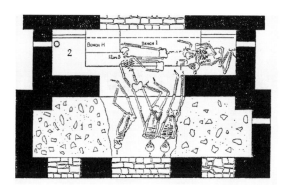

Figure 6.10 Holmul Building B-4th Room 1, burials from circa AD 350–400

Source: After Merwin and Vaillant 1932; courtesy of the Peabody Museum, Harvard University

the rooms implied a change in function and/or necessitated the building of a new structure above the old one.

We infer from the quality of the architecture of Building B that Holmul's elites were raising their profile while Cival's was on the decline. Other parts of the site, notably Group 1, the site's largest, remain unexcavated, but from sections exposed by looters it appears that more architecture dating to this period lies under later renovations.

We should not be quick to conclude from their prosperity that the Holmul elites were responsible for the decline of Cival. After all, many large and small centers throughout the Lowlands were meeting their end at the same time. So the army besieging Cival (and many other sites with late fortifications) could have come from a city outside of the Holmul region. It is also possible, as some have suggested, that no single attacker links El Mirador, Becan, Cival and other sites that were abandoned at this time, but that conflicts among all of these cities were sparked by a general crisis.

Another important series of events took place in the Holmul region around AD 300 as the Holmuleños built a small ceremonial center: a palace on a platform, a ritual plaza complete with ball-court, and a funerary pyramid-shrine, all only 1 kilometer outside the main ceremonial hill (Estrada-Belli 2001). This place is now known as La Sufricaya. Here the occupants carved inscriptions on stelae, some of the earliest in the Maya Lowlands. Their dates range from 376 to 422 and accurately reflect the occupation span of the place documented by archaeological excavations. The ritual space included a lower plaza for more public ceremonies, including the ball-game spectacle, an upper

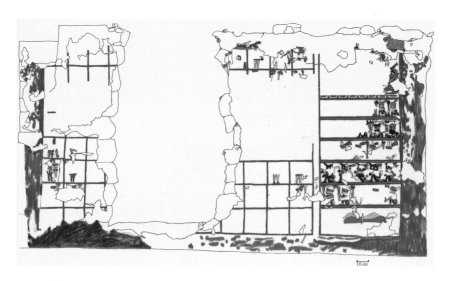

Figure 6.11 Mural 1, La Sufricaya palace, Holmul (circa AD 379)

Source: Drawing by J. deJulio; © Holmul Archaeological Project

Figure 6.12 Warrior figure from Mural 1, La Sufricaya palace (circa AD 379)

Source: Drawing by J. Ebersole; © Holmul Archaeological Project

terrace that was probably reserved for a more select audience of high-status individuals, and the palace itself, which housed the ruling elite.

But who were the new rulers who chose to build their seat of power away from the traditional ritual space of the Holmul hill? The inside and the outside of the palace were decorated with colorful murals. Painted on the walls of one of the rooms in the palace are scores of warriors dressed in Teotihuacan style and holding Teotihuacan-style weapons, such as trilobed-tipped darts and *atlatl* (Estrada-Belli 2003b; Estrada-Belli *et al.* 2009). They appear to be seated on the steps of a platform, perhaps that of the palace itself. Other individuals, wearing a mix of Maya and Teotihuacan garb, bring offerings or simply stand. We interpret these images as illustrations of a ceremony carried out at La Sufricaya.

The mural's main character is largely eroded, but enough remains to suggest that the warriors were attending a ceremony performed by a priest or a ruler. In another image, a Maya individual follows a path from one pyramid to another with a Teotihuacan-style façade. Here, he appears to receive something from a seated individual (see Figure 6.13). Other rooms were decorated with purely Maya images, such as one of the old god addressing his bird/human messenger, and another showing human sacrifice—a captive bound to a scaffold is about to be decapitated in re-enactment of a well-known ritual of royal accession (Estrada-Belli 2002b; Tomasic and Estrada-Belli 2003). The palace was therefore decorated with images suggestive of royal ceremonies and visiting dignitaries and it is possible that these events occurred locally. On another room's wall was an inscription recording the dedication of a stone, possibly the

Figure 6.13 Mural 6N, La Sufricaya palace (circa AD 379)

Source: Drawing by H. Hurst; © H. Hurst and Holmul Archaeological Project

inauguration of the palace or part of it (Three-Temple House). We are told it was done two years after the close of the 1 *ahaw katun*, and one year (364 days) after the *K'awiil* arrived at Mutal (Tikal), after *Siyaj K'ahk'* had arrived. The protagonist was identified by a long series of titles including, *chak tok wayaab* (cloud-red diviner; Estrada-Belli *et al.* 2009). This rare title is only known from another Holmul individual buried at roughly the same time in Building B. A stone stela found outside the palace (Stela 6) also may record the name

Figure 6.14 Mural 5, La Sufricaya palace, depicting a scaffold sacrifice ceremony (circa AD 400)

Source: Drawing J. Tomasic; © Holmul Archaeological Project

Siyaj K'ahk', but in an unclear context (Grube 2003). Another stela bears the image of a ruler raising a headdress similar to that worn by *Siyaj Chan K'awiil* on Tikal Stela 31 (dedicated in AD 435). All of these monuments link the small center of La Sufricaya/Holmul to Tikal in some way.

So here is evidence of a ruler erecting a new palace a short distance from a well-established, albeit minor, center of power. He is celebrated by a crowd of foreign warriors, he or someone like him has to travel to a foreign location to receive important ritual objects, and the final ceremony, as recorded, happens on the anniversary of the arrival of the great *Siyaj K'ahk'* at Tikal. At the same time (roughly—the archaeological dates leave 100-plus years margin of error), 18 individuals are buried in the main center of Holmul, where the former kings had ruled (see Figure 6.10, above).

It is easy to see the parallels between the series of events at Holmul and the arrival of foreigners at Tikal and Copan: the death of a former ruler upon arrival of a foreigner with Teotihuacan heritage, the building of new ceremonial spaces, and a new line of rulers establishing themselves. At Holmul, as at Tikal, the written dedication date for the palace should not be taken as the actual date of first occupation, since the archaeological evidence suggests the first building stones at La Sufricaya could have been laid a few decades before. The date should be taken figuratively, signaling the rising of a new ruler and the dedication of his palace as a royal seat. At Holmul, as at Tikal and Copan, it was necessary for the new ruler to journey to a distant location to receive the insignia of power, and to display the military support of Teotihuacan. In all iconographic references to Teotihuacan and textual references to *Siyaj K'ahk'* in the Early Classic we see the hand of Tikal rulers. At Holmul it is evident in the similarity of mixed Maya–Teo architectural and decoratives styles, and in the iconography of one of its monuments (La Sufricaya Stela 1 and Tikal Stela 31; see Figure 6.6, above). Tikal was the source of the Holmul incursion, in all likelihood to secure the east and northeast routes to ports on the Caribbean Coast.

This Tikal-backed coup established Holmul as a new center of power that quickly rose to prominence in the region, finally eclipsing Cival. As for the decline of Cival itself, following the raid, we lack evidence about the attackers. In contrast to El Mirador, we have found no signs of Teotihuacan-style weaponry at this site. More targeted excavations may rectify this. As we know now, the siege could pre-date the La Sufricaya palace by as much as 150 years. Unfortunately, our dating methods do not allow us sufficient resolution to determine if the two were close enough in time to establish causality. But all indicators point to these events being fairly close in time and possibly linked. It is likely that the same people who built La Sufricaya had previously attacked Cival. The attackers were a mix of locals backed by a powerful Tikal contingent and foreigners, a combination quite common in Mesoamerica. Or the Holmul elites could have simply taken over an area left void by a declining Cival.

At this point, it is a matter of choice which of these scenarios seems more likely. However, if we place these events in a wider context, we see the same pattern repeating itself. At El Mirador, there are signs of a last-ditch battle involving Teotihuacan weaponry. At Becan, a fortified center is largely abandoned but the last occupants are still sufficiently well connected to place elite ceramics with Teotihuacan-style decoration in ritual offerings. Further to the north, just inland from the coastal lagoon of Bacalar, is the city of Dzibanché, the Early Classic capital of the Snake Kingdom (Martin 2005; see Figure 6.3, above). Here, in the 5th century, the largest pyramid (the Cormoranes Pyramid) serves as the burial place of at least one important Snake king, Sky Witness, and is decorated with Teotihuacan *talud-tablero* and red-painted stucco friezes with Teotihuacan-style symbols (Nalda 2003). At Cerros, in Belize, the old seaport and ceremonial center is abandoned and a new neighboring port, Santa Rita Corozal, is established. There, too, ceramics and paintings indicate links with Teotihuacan. The other major Belizean coastal city, Altun Ha, while neither sacked nor abandoned, in AD 250 receives a hoard of Teotihuacan obsidian figurines, projectiles and vessels honoring one of its deceased rulers. In northern Yucatan, the old Preclassic center of

Figure 6.15
Cormoranes
Pyramid, Dzibanché,
containing the tomb
of King Sky Witness
(circa AD 500–600)

Source:
© F. Estrada-Belli

Komchen is largely abandoned and Teotihuacan-style architecture appears near by, in the Mirador Group at Dzibilchaltun (Andrews and Andrews 1980). Oxkintok and Chac are two of several northern sites with central Mexican links that also share architectural traits with Tikal (Smyth 2008; Varela Torrecilla and Braswell 2003; see Figure 6.3, above).

Until Teotihuacan began its own decline, Tikal remained the main hub of an immense network of political hegemony and trade connections within the southern Lowlands, for at least the first two centuries of the Classic period. Then, Tikal's rulers also began to run into trouble. In an intriguing twist of fate, the historical defeat of Tikal in AD 562, may have come at the hands of one of its former allies and, judging from the decoration of its funerary temple, a former participant in the Teotihuacan–Tikal connection: Sky Witness of Dzibanché (Martin and Grube 2008: 90).

7

CONCLUSION

Maya civilization is alive and well. Modern Maya men and women walk the streets of Mexican, Honduran and Guatemalan towns today (see Figure 1.17, above). Their culture has neither collapsed nor gone through anything like devolution. It has simply mutated into a new form incorporating western ideas and religion. It has done so not because of long-term laws of behavior or environmental forces. It has changed since the Spanish conquest because of and at the pace of changing historical, political and economic circumstances. In this book I have tried to move away from our own hitherto accepted assumptions about cultural change in general and about Maya civilization in particular. For too long these have caused us to misunderstand the Preclassic Maya, to devalue their achievements, to search in vain for the correlates of idealized social types in the archaeological record, chiefdom and state, so that at times we could fit the Maya into one or other category. And we are constantly playing catch-up from the expected correlates to institutions. Institutions are always believed to precede the correlate in development. Without the material correlate, the institution is invisible and unknowable to us. Therefore, by chasing institutions through their material correlates, we play a self-defeating game (Yoffee 2005; Pauketat 2007: 20). But the old assumptions of earlier generations of archaeologists are bending and breaking under the weight of an avalanche of new data.

In my view, what led to Maya civilization (as with any other civilization) was fundamentally a historical process, having little to do with universal causes of cultural evolution, laws of environmental adaptation, population growth, craft specialization or the invention of new forms of government. Rather, that process was mainly composed of such elements as community creation, place-making, formulating new identities, and co-opting existing symbols into a new discourse that gave meaning to life in the community. When we look at the life history of individual places like Cival, the crucial elements of this process appear in sharp focus.

It may seem surprising to speak of Maya civilization existing as early as 900 BC. In this book, I used the term "civilization" loosely to identify not a higher form of culture, a qualitative improvement on earlier conditions, but a historical process (Pauketat 2007: 17), one that has been ongoing since the onset of the first millennium BC in the Maya Lowlands. The Preclassic Maya should not be understood as constituting some evolutionary stage prior to a qualitative superior entity (the Classic Maya), but as a people who created new traditions, new communities and new narratives of identity. Within a short time, what were once distinct local groupings converged to form ever larger entities, eventually incorporating all the Maya Lowlands. The city of El Mirador may have been the culmination of this historical process, rather than its beginning.

A new beginning for Maya studies

This book proposes a perspective that challenges a number of old theories about the emergence of Maya civilization. This perspective can be described as "historical-processual," a term borrowed from Fernand Braudel's Annales School of historians (Braudel 1986; Peebles 1990; Knapp 1992a). It has the advantage of allowing for the analysis of historical detail made of events and short-term changes, interlaced with longer-term socio-economic and/or environmental processes drawn out over centuries or millennia. Long-term processes also provide the "big picture" context for historical action at the local level in which communities are made and remade. This approach departs from the linear perspective and ideal social categories of cultural evolutionism and the universal laws of behavior and ideal social types that have been part and parcel of the paradigm of the "New Archaeology" for the last 50 years. With a long-term perspective and with a wealth of localized data, we have examined the history of places like Cival not because this particular site had a more significant role than other locales in shaping Maya civilization, but because, through accidents of preservation, we have a very long and accessible record there of the relevant period—the first millennium BC. Other, perhaps more important sites have only partially accessible or truncated sequences.

With the support of our new data and perspective we confronted the old notions about the Preclassic Maya—that the Maya of the first millennium BC were 1) recent immigrants; 2) simple farmers; and 3) culturally stagnant— until a threshold point was reached in the first century BC. A corollary to all this was that the Lowland environment was unsuitable for generating a civilization, so everything significant about such a civilization had to come from other regions of Mesoamerica. In fact, these theories began to falter some time ago. Long-term excavations at sites such as Cuello, Cahal Pech, Kaxob, Colha, Cerros and even the much earlier Carnegie Institution's Uaxactun excavations had given us a feel for the complexity of the Preclassic Maya and the opportunities offered by Lowland soils. But because many studied sites were small, they also helped reinforce the notions that the Preclassic era was characterized by small-scale village farming lacking any monumentality until a very late date. It was when monumental Middle Preclassic architecture was excavated at Nakbe in the 1990s that we began to see things differently. But even so, a shift in perspective was necessary—one that abandons the search for correlates of our own abstractions and suppositions and focuses on what actually may have happened then and there.

One of the main points in our shift in perspective has involved the institution of kingship, a key ingredient of ancient state-level societies. The neo-evolutionary/processualist perspective that has dominated our field favors "universal" processes of change and denies the relevance of specific historical and ethnographic details almost as if they were undesired random "noise" (Wylie 1991; Yoffee 2005). Because the Maya of the Classic period had clearly inherited such institutions from the preceding phase, we were told it was crucial to find its antecedent, simpler forms. The difficulty of separating small-time kings from chiefs and, for that matter, of identifying either in the Maya archaeological record has been obvious to many. I have circumvented this problem here by looking at other manifestations of cultural change. I identified place-making as a crucial process. It involves the creation of a new sense of community wider then the village or town (Kolb and Snead 1997), a new identity, with a new narrative and new political and cultural practices. It is not about inventing new forms, but about elaborating or co-opting existing symbols in the service of new practices and meanings, in order to create new perceptions of world order. Not coincidentally, the narratives of Preclassic ceremonial centers are in most respects echoed by the royal narratives of the Classic period, thereby underscoring both the continuity and transformations of Maya civilization through time.

Long-term and life histories

Instead of feverishly looking for the correlates of early kings (tombs and palaces), I have identified important "moments" or, to use a Braudelian word, *conjunctures*, in the long-term history of the Lowlands. These are transitional phases, in which short-term social and economic changes occur, with far-reaching implications for other aspects of culture. In the first such moment, around 1000 BC, previously semi-itinerant farming populations clustered around dominant hilltops to form the original villages, at such places as Seibal, Holmul, Cival, Tikal, Cahal Pech, Yaxha and Komchen, among others. From such villages grew regional communities, using iconographic symbols that we can recognize as cosmological. The distribution of the Lowlands' earliest ceramic styles into distinct but somewhat similar groups underscores the existence of several "ethnic"[1] groups within the entire Yucatan Peninsula. The form and function of the ceramics, far from being evidence of foreign migrations or trade, are best understood as indicators of a new elite narrative, one that appropriated cosmic symbols and promoted feasting and reciprocity to reinforce communal belonging (and inequality). These are two common strategies in farming societies in many parts of the world. The goal was to establish cohesion and solidarity on a grander scale than the village permits. Here they stimulated a new level of integration for what may have been previously dispersed and autonomous hamlets.

The second, perhaps most crucial "moment" in the long history of Maya civilization can be dated within the 100–200 years following the appearance of the earliest ceramics. It involves the foundation of sacred ground, accompanied by the carving of elite narratives onto a man-made landscape. The center-building process happened on an unprecedented scale. It required the mastery of a huge labor force and served broad communities of sizes approximating those of Classic period kingdoms, drawing hundreds of laborers from a one-day walking distance, at least.

Within a few decades of the first foundation events, the elite narrative seen in the E-Groups of Nakbe, Tikal and Cival became the narrative of many other Middle Preclassic centers in the Lowlands. This was the first pan-Maya phenomenon. Maya civilization was blooming. It may have happened spontaneously at any number of places. Or we may soon find an older Lowland

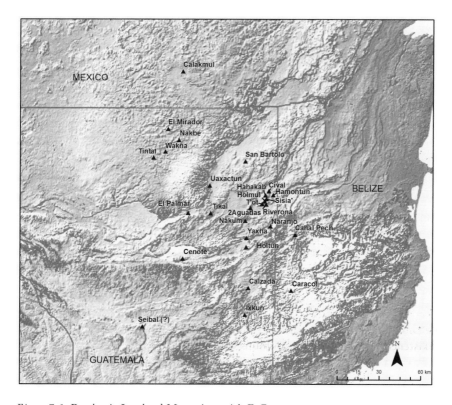

Figure 7.1 Preclassic Lowland Maya sites with E-Groups

Source: © F. Estrada-Belli, Topographic data courtesy of NASA SRTM mission

site that is the source of innovation, much as Cahokia was the source of Mississippian art and architecture in North America between AD 1050 and 1150. Whatever the case, this process of incorporating and homogenizing, like the process of Mississippianization in North America, brought together formerly independent communities under the umbrella of a new identity tied to sacred mounded places, ritual practices, and beliefs that mitigated both social inequality and ethnic diversity. All this was Maya civilization. It was not a form of government or a collection of social institutions, although kingship was part of it.

The underlying diversity in Maya civilization seen in the regionalism of the first millennium BC ceramic styles, however, was never completely suppressed and emerged every now and again as subtle local artistic variations. We see it gradually and superficially suppressed in ceramic styles with the advent of the Middle Preclassic Mamom style by 700 BC in the Mirador Basin, at Tikal, in Belize, and in northern Yucatan: its red and cream slips were made throughout the Lowlands but vessels came in diverse forms. By 600 BC Mamom ceramics were in use wherever there were people in the Lowlands.

In the Late Preclassic period, the Lowlands reached almost complete homogenization. We see this not only in the ubiquitous Chicanel-style waxy finish ceramics, but in architectural and sculptural styles. Distinct identities re-emerged after El Mirador had collapsed or elapsed. Even within inscriptions of the Classic period, epigraphers have noted a significant number of idiosyncrasies in each polity's or region's royal narratives. These testify to ethnic diversity[2] among Classic Maya kingdoms. The Maya may have conceived of the Lowlands as a patchwork of ethnic regions that cut across the individual kingdoms, with their own distinct histories and patron deities. For example, the area roughly corresponding to the central Peten was referred to as the "thirteen provinces," while the northeastern Peten was known as the "seven provinces" (Beliaev 2000).

Another conjuncture in Maya long-term history may have coincided with the creation of new architectural forms—the Triadic Group pyramids—and a new art form—sculpture in stone and stucco. This same moment marks the establishment of a new center, El Mirador, circa 300 BC, which may well have been the source of architectural innovations at this time. As noted earlier, this phase marks the greatest degree of cultural homogenization of art and ceramic styles in the Maya Lowlands. All indicators point to the rise of El Mirador as the greatest political power of its time in all of Mesoamerica, for this city with its 20-plus square kilometers of inhabited area, was several times larger and more populous than any other site in the Maya region. Kaminaljuyú, the largest center in the Maya Highlands, was only about half its size. Even in central Mexico, no site of this size existed at the time. If there was ever a time in which Maya civilization coincided with a single hegemonic political order, this might have been it. Size may not be the only indicator of power but it does matter, especially when seen together with stylistic similarities in

Figure 7.2 View of Danta pyramid at El Mirador, taken from El Tigre pyramid
Source: © F. Estrada-Belli

ceramics, art and architecture, and the radial distribution of the largest Maya cities around El Mirador.

But the history of Maya civilization cannot be the history of this one place, important as the "El Mirador phenomenon" might be. El Mirador went into decline as other sites rose in population and architectural splendor. Over the following 1500 years, until the Spanish conquest, this pattern repeated itself numerous times. Maya civilization was made through this process of appropriating an earlier tradition. It is a history of places, and El Mirador represents but one of its chapters.

Far from emerging in full form during one era, Maya civilization developed gradually after the foundation of ceremonial centers. The great plaza–pyramid complexes of Middle Preclassic centers like Cival and Nakbe were the incubators, not the results of the cultural process. The space created was of grandiose proportions for the size of the population of the site at the time, underscoring the imaginative foresight of the elite to attract and accommodate ever-greater crowds. It represented the cosmos and its *axis mundi* or center at once. It represented the mythical world of creation brought into the present. It was a place for elites and for commoners to engage in ritual. It was built of earth, stone and the collective memories that were the binding essence of the community's identity. Their narrative was a millenarian prophecy rooted in a distant past. With little modification, this ideological narrative continued through the Spanish conquest until the present day. We may now refer to it as Maya civilization.

Where do we go from here?

In previous chapters I have been able to suggest the contours of these processes only in broad brush strokes, adducing a minimum of detail from the architecture and art of those few places that are fairly well documented. We finally have the perspective to see these large-scale processes. We can now also see how we have made incredible progress since the publication of *Origins of Maya Civilization* in 1977. Then, the whole process of "origins" seemed obscure and unknowable, because the data were too fragmentary for scholars to connect the dots meaningfully. But today, with much more data, we have been able to push back the founding dates of ceremonial centers and the beginnings of Maya civilization, aligning it with the rest of early Mesoamerican history. And we also have better theoretical frameworks to contextualize the function and meaning of Preclassic Maya ritual centers.

Nevertheless, as great as recent discoveries at Cival, San Bartolo and El Mirador are, the most exciting new discoveries are surely still to come. Not only does the built mass of El Mirador remain almost completely unexplored, but hundreds of other cities and sites of every size lie around the Mirador Basin, still untouched by archaeologists. At our current pace, the job of fully documenting even the most salient of these sites is daunting, partly because the tropical forest keeps them out of reach, partly because of lack of resources for archaeology.

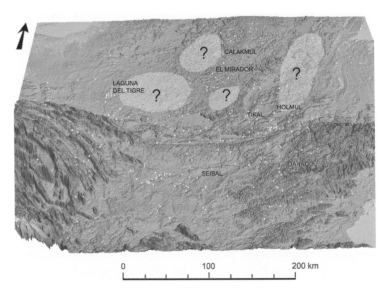

Figure 7.3 Map of southern Lowlands showing known sites and unexplored areas in northern Guatemala, southern Campeche and Quintana Roo

Source: © F. Estrada-Belli, Topographic data courtesy of NASA SRTM mission

Fortunately, new radar technology exists that can record ancient features below the forest canopy. If the promise of these techniques is realized, we will soon be able to produce meter-by-meter maps of Maya settlement for most of the northern Peten area, which at present remains largely uncharted. This will be an unprecedented data set that will generate a shockwave in Maya studies comparable only to that brought about by the decipherment of hieroglyphs. Places like Cival, Holmul, San Bartolo, Cuello, Cerros and Nakbe have been productive for our understanding of early Maya civilization, but giant sites like Tintal, Wakna, Xulnal and dozens more lying undocumented in northern Guatemala and neighboring Mexican states hold an untold number of secrets. We will finally be able to branch out to the periphery of these early sites to capture the life histories of the people who built them.

In short, we have only just begun to uncover ancient Maya civilization. Fortunately, for those who will study it, the best is yet to come.

NOTES

1 MAYA CIVILIZATION IN PERSPECTIVE

1 Estimates vary depending on how one defines language difference. But according to Guatemalan linguist Sergio Romero (personal communication 2010) there are between 31 and 35 Maya languages.
2 These occurred in the wake of the explorations by pioneers of Maya archaeology such as Alfred Maudslay (1889–1902), Teobert Maler (1911), the Comte de Perigney and Thomas Gann (1926) a few decades before.
3 Natural well.
4 The first elite burials in the North Acropolis (the preferred burial ground for Tikal kings) date to the Late Preclassic (circa 1st century AD) and the last stelae depicting the Tikal emblem glyph date to AD 889.
5 A *katun* is a 20-year period in the Maya Long Count.

4 PLANTING THE SEED OF CIVILIZATION

1 Beta-234440, Conventional radiocarbon age: 2670±40 BP, 2 Sigma calibrated result: (95% probability) Cal BC 900 to 790 (Cal BP 2850 to 2740), 1 Sigma calibrated result: (68% probability) Cal BC 840 to 800.
2 Beta-213528, Conventional radiocarbon age: 2520±40 BP, 2 Sigma calibrated result: (95% probability) Cal BC 800 to 520, 1 Sigma calibrated results: (68% probability) Cal BC 790 to 760 and Cal BC 680 to 550.
3 The comparison of volumetric maps was done in 3D GIS analytical environment using open-source software: http://www.osgeo.org.
4 Beta-213528, Conventional radiocarbon age: 2520±40 BP, 2 Sigma calibrated result: (95% probability) Cal BC 800 to 520, 1 Sigma calibrated results: (68% probability) Cal BC 790 to 760 and Cal BC 680 to 550. From a piece of charcoal recovered from the floor (CIV.T08.43).

5 EARTH–MOUNTAIN–CAVES AND SKY–SERPENT–BIRDS

1 Its wings are often represented as serpents' heads in profile, and are thus referred to as serpent-wings. Bardawil (1976) was the first to identify this composite being and named it the Principal Bird Deity.
2 See Thompson (1950) for the identification of God N with Mam, and Thompson (1970) for identification of the same god with the *bacabs*—the four directional gods supporting the sky. See also Taube (1992a) and Bassie-Sweet (2008) for a discussion of the phonetic reading of God N's name as *pawatun*. See Tozzer (1941:

137) for Mam and *bacabs* as aspects of *pawatun* in Colonial period Yucatan. For a discussion of present-day Maya myths of death and rebirth associated with ancestral gods, mountains and world trees, see also Carlsen and Prechtel (1991).

3 The turtle head interpretation is favored by this author based on direct observation.

4 The turtle as earth and turtle shells are associated with the PBD in the West Wall mural of the Pinturas Sub1A structure at San Bartolo (see Taube 2009), where an image of the maize god wearing the PBD headdress is seen through a quatrefoil-shaped opening in the shell of a turtle, symbol of the underworld, playing a turtle shell drum accompanied by the rain god and the god of standing water. Turtle shells are also an important attribute of the old god as *Itzamkanahk*. See Altar 4 at Tikal (Jones and Satterthwaite 1982: Figure 58) for a depiction of an old god with a turtle shell on his back emerging from a cave/*witz* monster; Stuart 2007a for a glyphic reading of the turtle shell as *ahk* as part of the old god's name; and the discussion of Holmul *witz* masks below.

5 Karl Taube and David Stuart suggest this motif means shining brilliance, and this character "shiner," therefore associated with sky and solar brilliance. Taube believes the Cival mask represents this same variant of the solar deity (personal communication 2010; Leonard and Taube 2007).

6 As *och b'ih*, smoke rising from censers or bowls (or ear spools) appears to be equated with the rising soul of ancestors when it is depicted as serpents passing through ear spools with ancestors emerging from their mouth (Taube 2005: 45–47). When deity symbols (heads, headdresses or glyphic symbols) rest on the body of the emerging serpent, they represent gods being conjured (Taube 2005: 42, Figure 18a).

7 See the Chalcatzingo "El Rey" Monument 1 rock carving for an even earlier (Middle Preclassic) example of the Mesoamerican notion of rain-clouds emanating from mountains/caves/quatrefoils and ancestors or gods (Grove 2000: Figure 2, frontispiece).

8 See Taube (1992a) and Bassie-Sweet (2008) for a discussion of the phonetic reading of the God N portrait glyphs (T1014, T64:548 T64:528) as *pawatun* (but see Stuart 2007a for a challenge to this reading).

9 See note 4 above.

10 God N's portrait glyph paired with the signs for *kan* (yellow) and *ahk* (turtle) may correspond to the name *Itzamkanahk*, known from Classic inscriptions and Yucatec colonial sources. See Stuart 2007a for a discussion of its phonetic reading and challenge to the *pawatun* reading.

11 Beta-1995-70, Conventional radiocarbon age: 2170±40, 2 Sigma calibrated result: (95% probability) Cal BC 360 to 90, 1 Sigma calibrated result: (68% probability) Cal BC 260 to 160. From a piece of charcol embedded in one of the masks' stucco lining (calibrated with Oxcal v. 2.0).

12 Tikal Stela 29 remains the earliest Long Count date inscription with an archaeologically documented provenience. Other unprovenienced sculptures of slightly earlier date exist in private collections.

6 THE PRECLASSIC–CLASSIC MAYA TRANSITION: A NEW BEGINNING?

1 *K'awiil* is the Maya god of lightning, also known as God K. A sceptre known as the God K sceptre or the manikin sceptre is an image of *K'awiil*. It has a human body, with one leg turning into a snake. The head is that a long-snouted animal wearing a mirror at the front. It emits smoke from a torch stuck in its mirror-like forehead. In Maya inscriptions the expression "he took the *K'awiil*" means the

king took office. "Eighteen are the snake heads" is a translation of the Maya name *Uxaclajuun Ubah Kan*. This is the name of the so-called "War Serpent" headdress often worn by Maya kings and it is perhaps an allusion to the serpents' heads on the Pyramid of the Feathered Serpent at Teotihuacan (Stuart 2000a: 493). *K'awiil* was to the Maya what Tlaloc was to Teotihuacaños: the god of rain and lightning and the symbol of absolute political power. While the "War Serpent" headdress adorned Teotihuacan's Pyramid of the Feathered Serpent, the upper temple was apparently decorated with Tlaloc imagery (Sugiyama 2005: 86).

2 Initially, he was thought to have been a Teotihuacan-born conqueror, based on the Teotihuacan iconography associated with him. Then Tikal was proposed because of the strong connection it had with Teotihuacan and because strontium isotope analysis of the bones of *Yax K'uk Mo'* indicated that, in his early years, he had lived in the limestone environment of the Lowlands but never at Teotihuacan (Buikstra *et al.* 2004). However, Caracol has a strontium signature that denotes a limestone-rich environment, so it is also a match for the sample of *Yax K'uk Mo'*.

7 CONCLUSION

1 "Ethnic" here is used in the sense of a community of more intense interaction of people within its boundaries, but which also shares much of its cultural background with neighboring groups. An example of this concept can be applied to the linguistically distinct but largely culturally homogeneous Maya groups of present-day Mexico and Guatemala.

2 Here, "ethnic diversity" among Maya Classic period kingdoms relates to local (regional or kingdom-specific) ideological narratives, including origin myths of dynasties, patron gods, certain rituals and sacred locations specific to the capital or landscape, not to linguistic differences.

REFERENCES

Adams, R. E. W. (1971) *The Ceramics of Altar de Sacrificios.* Cambridge, MA: Harvard University Press.

—— (ed.) (1977) *The Origins of Maya Civilization.* Albuquerque: University of New Mexico Press.

Adams, R. E. W. and Culbert, T. P. (1977) "The Origins of Civilization in the Maya Lowlands," in: Adams, R. E. W. (ed.) *The Origins of Maya Civilization.* Albuquerque: University of New Mexico, 3–24.

Andrews, A. P. (1981a) "'Guerrero' de Loltun: comentario analítico." *Boletín de la Escuela de Ciencias Antropológicas de la Universidad de Yucatán,* 8–9, 36–50.

Andrews, E. W. (1965) *Progress Report on the 1960–64 Field Seasons: National Geographic–Tulane University Dzibilchaltun Program.* New Orleans: Middle American Research Institute, Tulane University.

—— (1981b) "Komchen: An Early Maya Community in Northwest Yucatan." Paper presented at the Sociedad Mexicana de Antropología, San Cristobal, Chiapas, June 21–27.

—— (1990) *Early Ceramic History of the Lowland Maya.* Albuquerque: University of New Mexico Press.

Andrews, E. W. and Hammond, N. (1990) "Redefinition of the Swasey Phase at Cuello, Belize." *American Antiquity,* 55, 570–584.

Andrews, E. W. and Ringle, W. M. (1992) "Mayas tempranos en Yucatán: investigaciones arqueológicas en Komchén." *Mayab,* 8, 5–17.

Andrews, E. W. I. and Andrews, E. W. (1980) *Excavations at Dzibilchaltun, Yucatan, Mexico.* New Orleans: Middle American Research Institute, Tulane University.

Andrews, G. F. (1995) *Pyramids and Palaces, Monsters and Masks: The Golden Age of Maya Architecture: The Collected Works of George F. Andrews.* Lancaster, CA: Labyrinthos.

Ashmore, W. and Knapp, A. B. (1999) *Archaeologies of Landscape: Contemporary Perspectives.* Malden, MA: Blackwell.

Aveni, A. F., Dowd, A. S. and Vining, B. (2003) "Maya Calendar Reform? Evidence from Orientations of Specialized Architectural Assemblages." *Latin American Antiquity,* 14(2), 159–178.

Awe, J., 1992. *Dawn in the Land between the Rivers: Formative Occupation at Cahal Pech, Belize and its Implications for Preclassic Development in the Maya Lowlands.* Ph.D. Dissertation. University College, London.

Ball, J. W. (1977) "The Rise of the Northern Maya Chiefdoms: A Socioprocessual Analysis," in: Adams, R. E. W. (ed.) *The Origins of Maya Civilization*. Albuquerque: Univeristy of New Mexico, 101–132.

Bardawil, L. W. (1976) "The Principal Bird Deity in Maya Art: An Iconographic Study of Form and Meaning," in: Greene Robertson, M. (ed.) *Segunda Mesa Redonda de Palenque, 1974*. Peeble Beach, CA: Precolumbian Art Research Institute, 195–209.

Bassie, K. (2002) "Maya Creator Gods." *Mesoweb*. Online. Available from: <http://www.mesoweb.com/features/bassie/CreatorGods/CreatorGods.pdf> [accessed March 2008].

Bassie-Sweet, K. (2008) *Maya Sacred Geography and the Creator Deities*. Norman: University of Oklahoma Press.

Bauer, J. (2005) "El Pasado Preclásico y Monumental de Holmul: Resultados de las Temporadas de Excavación 2003 y 2004 en Cival, Petén," in: Laporte, J. P., Arroyo, B., Escobedo, H. L. and Mejia, H. E. (eds) *XVIII Simposio de Investigaciones Arqueológicas en Guatemala*. Guatemala: Ministerio de Cultura y Deporte, 201–214.

Beach, T., Dunning, N. P., Luzzadder-Beach, S. and Cook, D. E. (2006) "Impacts of the Ancient Maya on Soils and Soil Erosion in the Central Maya Lowlands." *Catena*, 65, 166–178.

Beach, T., Luzzadder-Beach, S., Dunning, N. and Cook, D. (2008) "Human and Natural Impacts on Fluvial and Karst Depressions of the Maya Lowlands." *Geomorphology*, 101(1–2), 308–331.

Beliaev, D. (2000) "Wuk Tsuk and Oxlahun Tsuk: Naranjo and Tikal in the Late Classic," in: Colas, P. R., Delvendahl, K., Kunhert, M. and Schubart, A. (eds) *The Sacred and the Profane: Architecture and Identity in the Southern Maya Lowlands. 3rd European Maya Conference, University of Hamburg, November 1998*. Markt Schwaben: Verlag Anton Saurwein, 63–81.

Bellwood, P. S. (2005) *First Farmers: The Origins of Agricultural Societies*. Malden, MA: Blackwell.

Bey, G. J., III, Bond, T. M., Ringle, W. M., Hanson, C. A., Houck, C. W. and Peraza Lope, C. (1998) "The Ceramic Chronology of Ek Balam, Yucatan, Mexico." *Ancient Mesoamerica*, 9(1), 101–120.

Blanton, R. E., Kowalewski, S. A., Peregrine, P. N. and Feinman, G. M. (1996) "Dual-Processual Theory for the Evolution of Mesoamerican Civilization." *Current Anthropology*, 37(1), 1–14.

Blom, F. (1924) "Report on the Preliminary Work at Uaxactun, Guatemala." *Carnegie Institution of Washington Year Book*, 23, 217–219.

Borhegyi, S. F. D. (1965) *Archaeological Synthesis of the Guatemalan Highlands*. Austin: University of Texas Press.

Brady, J. E., Ball, J. W., Bishop, R. L., Pring, D. C., Hammond, N. and Housley, R. A. (1998) "The Lowland Maya 'Protoclassic': A Reconsideration of its Nature and Significance." *Ancient Mesoamerica*, 9(1), 17–38.

Braudel, F. (1986) *La Méditerranée et le monde méditerranéen a l'époque de Philippe II*. Paris: A. Colin.

Buikstra, J. E., Price, D. T., Wright, L. E. and Burton, J. A. (2004) "Tombs from the Copan Acropolis: A Life-History Approach," in: Bell, E. E., Canuto, M. A. and Sharer, R. J. (eds) *Understanding Early Classic Copan*. Philadelphia: University of Pennsylvania Museum of Archaeology and Anthropology, 191–212.

Callaghan, M. G. (2006) "Cerámica del Proyecto Arqueológico Holmul, muestras de 2004 y 2005," in: Estrada-Belli, F. (ed.) *Investigaciones arqueológicas en la region de Holmul, Petén, Guatemala. Informe preliminar de la temporada 2005.* Boston, MA: Boston University, 225–328.

—— (2008) *Technologies of Power: Ritual Economy and Ceramic Production in the Terminal Preclassic Period Holmul Region, Guatemala.* Ph.D. Dissertation. Vanderbilt University.

Canuto, M. A. (2004) "The Rural Settlement of Copan: Changes through the Early Classic," in: Bell, E. E., Canuto, M. A. and Sharer, R. J. (eds) *Understanding Early Classic Copan.* Philadelphia: University of Pennsylvania Museum of Archaeology and Anthropology, 29–49.

Carlsen, R. S. and Prechtel, M. (1991) "The Flowering of the Dead: An Interpretation of Highland Maya Culture." *Man*, 26(1), 23–42.

Carr, R. F. and Hazard, J. E. (1961) *Map of the Ruins of Tikal, El Peten, Guatemala.* Philadelphia: University Museum, University of Pennsylvania.

Carrasco, R. (1996) "Calakmul." *Arqueología Mexicana*, 3(18), 46–51.

Carrasco, R. and Colon, M. (2005) "El Reino de Kaan y la antigua ciudad maya de Calakmul." *Arqueología Mexicana*, 13(75), 40–47.

Caso, A. (1947) *Calendario y escritura de las antiguas culturas de Monte Alban.* Mexico, D.F.: Talleres de la Nacion.

Chase, A. F. and Chase, D. Z. (1981) "Archaeological investigations at Nohmul and Santa Rita, Belize: 1979–1980." *Mexicon*, 3, 42–44.

—— (1998) "Scale and Intensity in Classic Period Maya Agriculture: Terracing and Settlement at the 'Garden City' of Caracol, Belize." *Culture and Agriculture*, 20(2–3), 60–77.

—— (1999) "External Impetus, Internal Synthesis, and Standardization: E-Group Assemblages and the Cristallization of Classic Maya Society in the Southern Lowlands," in: Grube, N. (ed.) *The Emergence of Lowland Maya Civilization.* Markt Schwaben: Verlag Anton Surwein, 87–102.

—— (2001) "Ancient Maya Causeways and Site Organization at Caracol, Belize." *Ancient Mesoamerica*, 12(2), 273–281.

Cheetham, D. (1998) *Interregional Interaction, Symbol Emulation, and the Emergence of Socio-Political Inequality in the Central Maya Lowlands.* MA Thesis. University of British Columbia.

—— (2005) "Cunil: A Pre-Mamom Horizon in the Southern Maya Lowlands," in: Powis, T. (ed.) *New Perspectives on Formative Mesoamerican Cultures.* Oxford: Archaeopress, 27–38.

Childe, V. G. (1929) *The Danube in Prehistory.* Oxford: Clarendon Press.

Christenson, A. J. (2000) *Popol Vuh: The Mythic Sections.* Provo, UT: Brigham Young University Press.

Clark, J. E. and Cheetham, D. (2002) "Mesoamerica"s Tribal Foundations," in: Parkinson, W. A. (ed.) *The Archaeology of Tribal Societies.* Ann Arbor: International Monographs in Prehistory, 278–339.

Clark, J. E. and Hansen, R. D. (2001) "The Architecture of Early Kingship: Comparative Perspective and the Origins of the Maya Royal Court," in: Inomata, T. and Houston, S. D. (eds) *Royal Courts of the Ancient Maya.* Boulder, CO: Westview Press, 1–45.

Clark, J. E., Hansen, R. D. and Perez Suarez, T. (2000) "La Zona Maya en el

Preclasico," in: Manzanilla, L. and Lopez Lujan, L. (eds) *Historia antigua de México: Volumen 1: El México antiguo, sus áreas culturales, los origenes, y el horizonte Preclásico*. Mexico, D.F.: Instituto de Antropología e Historia, 437–510.

Clark, J. E. and Pye, M. E. (2000) *Olmec Art and Archaeology in Mesoamerica*. Washington, D.C., and New Haven, CT: National Gallery of Art and Yale University Press.

Cobos, R. (2003) "Ancient Community Form and Social Complexity at Chichen Itza, Yucatan = Antiguas formas de comunidad y complejidad social en Chichen Itzá, Yucatán," in: Sanders, W. T., Mastache, A. G. and Cobean, R. H. (eds) *Urbanismo en Mesoamérica = Urbanism in Mesoamerica*. Mexico, D.F.: Instituto de Antropología e Historia, 451–472.

—— (2004) "Chichén Itzá: Settlement and Hegemony during the Terminal Classic Period," in: Demarest, A. A., Rice, P. M. and Rice, D. S. (eds) *The Terminal Classic in the Maya Lowlands: Collapse, Transition and Transformation*. Boulder: University Press of Colorado, 517–544.

Coe, M. D. (1966) *The Maya*. 1st edn. New York: Thames & Hudson.

—— (2005) *The Maya*. 7th edn. New York: Thames & Hudson.

Coe, W. R. (1965) "Tikal, Guatemala, and Emergent Maya Civilization." *Science*, 147(3664), 1401–1419.

—— (1990) *Excavations in the Great Plaza, North Terrace, and Acropolis of Tikal*. Philadelphia: University Museum, University of Pennsylvania.

Coggins, C. (1975) *Painting and Drawing Styles at Tikal: An Historical and Iconographical Reconstruction*. Ph.D. Dissertation. Harvard University.

—— (1980) "The Shape of Time: Some Political Implications of a Four-Part Figure." *American Antiquity*, 45(4), 727–739.

—— (in press) "The Measure of Man," in: Urton, G. and Ruggles, C. (eds) *Cultural Astronomy in New World Cosmologies*. Boulder: University Press of Colorado.

Colas, P. R., Helmke, C. G. B., Awe, J. J. and Powis, T. G. (2002) "Epigraphic and Ceramic Analyses of Two Early Classic Maya Vessels from Baking Pot, Belize." *Mexicon*, 2, 33–39.

Covarrubias, M. (1946) *Mexico South, the Isthmus of Tehuantepec*. 1st edn. New York: A. A. Knopf.

Cowgill, U. M., Hutchinson, G. E., Racek, A. A., Goulden, C. E., Patrick, R. and Tsukada, M. (1966) *The History of Laguna de Petenxil, a Small Lake in Northern Guatemala*. New Haven: Connecticut Academy of Arts and Sciences.

Culbert, P. T. (ed.) (1973) *The Classic Maya Collapse*. Albuquerque: University of New Mexico Press.

Culbert, T. P. (1977) "Early Maya Development at Tikal, Guatemala," in: Adams, R. E. W. (ed.) *The Origins of Maya Civilization*. Albuquerque: University of New Mexico Press, 27–43.

—— (1993) *The Ceramics of Tikal*. Philadelphia: University Museum, University of Pennsylvania.

Demarest, A. A. (1984) "The Harvard El Mirador Project, 1982–1983: Preclassic Ceramics of El Mirador: Preliminary Results and Ongoing Analysis." *Mesoamerica*, 5(7), 53–92.

—— (1993) "The Violent Saga of a Maya Kingdom." *National Geographic*, 183(2), 94–111.

—— (1997) "The Vanderbilt Petexbatun Regional Archaeological Project 1989–1994: Overview, History, and Major Results of a Multidisciplinary Study of the Classic Maya Collapse." *Ancient Mesoamerica*, 8(2), 209–227.

Demarest, A. A., Rice, P. M. and Rice, D. S. (2004) *The Terminal Classic in the Maya Lowlands: Collapse, Transition, and Transformation.* Boulder: University Press of Colorado.

Diehl, R. A. (2004) *The Olmecs: America's First Civilization.* New York: Thames & Hudson.

Dull, R. A., Southon, J. R. and Sheets, P. (2001) "Volcanism, Ecology and Culture: A Reassessment of the Volcan Ilopango TBJ Eruption in the Southern Maya Realm." *Latin American Antiquity*, 12(1), 25–44.

Estrada-Belli, F. (2001) "Maya Kingship at Holmul, Guatemala." *Antiquity*, 75(290), 685–686.

—— (2002a) "Anatomía de una ciudad Maya: Holmul. Resultados de investigaciones arqueológicas en 2000 y 2001." *Mexicon*, 24(5), 107–112.

—— (2002b) *Investigaciones arqueológicas en la region de Holmul, Petén, Guatemala. Informe preliminar de la temporada 2002.* Boston University. Online. Available from: <http://www.bu.edu/holmul/reports/>.

—— (2003a) "Anatomia de Holmul: Su ciudad y territorio," in: Laporte, J. P., Arroyo, B., Escobedo, H. and Mejía, H. (eds) *XVI Simposio de Investigaciones de Arqueología de Guatemala.* Guatemala: Museo Nacional de Arqueología y Etnología, 265–274.

—— (2003b) "La Pintura mural de la Sufricaya." *La Pintura Mural Prehispánica en Mexico. Buletín Informativo*, 9(18), 38–42.

—— (2004) *Investigaciones arqueológicas en la region de Holmul, Petén, Guatemala. Informe preliminar de la temporada 2004.* Boston University. Online. Available from: <http://www.bu.edu/holmul/reports/>.

—— (2006) *Investigaciones arqueológicas en la region de Holmul, Petén, Guatemala. Informe preliminar de la temporada 2005.* Boston University. Online. Available from: <http://www.bu.edu/holmul/reports/>.

—— (2008) *Investigaciones Arqueológicas en la region de Holmul, Peten, Guatemala. Informe preliminar de la temporada 2007.* Boston University. Online. Available from: <http://www.bu.edu/holmul/reports/>.

—— (2009) *Investigaciones Arqueológicas en la region de Holmul, Peten, Guatemala. Informe preliminar de la temporada 2008.* Boston University. Online. Available from: <http://www.bu.edu/holmul/reports/>.

Estrada-Belli, F., Grube, N., Wolf, M., Gardella, K. and Guerra-Librero, C. (2003a) "Preclassic Maya Monuments and Temples at Cival, Petén, Guatemala." *Antiquity*. Online. Available from: <http://antiquity.ac.uk/ ProjGall/belli/belli.html>.

Estrada-Belli, F., Bauer, J., Morgan, M. and Chavez, A. (2003b) "Symbols of Early Maya Kingship at Cival, Petén, Guatemala." *Antiquity*. Online. Available from: <http://antiquity.ac.uk/ProjGall/estrada_belli/ index.html>.

Estrada-Belli, F., Tokovinine, A., Foley, J., Heather, H., Ware, G., Stuart, D. and Grube, N. (2009) "A Maya Palace at Holmul, Peten, Guatemala and the Teotihuacan 'Entrada': Evidence from Murals 7 and 9." *Latin American Antiquity*, 20(2), 228–259.

Estrada-Belli, F. and Koch, M. (2007) "Remote Sensing and GIS Analysis of a Maya City and its Landscape: Holmul, Guatemala," in: Wiseman, J. R. and El-Baz, F. (eds) *Remote Sensing in Archaeology.* New York: Plenum Press.

Estrada-Belli, F., Neivens De Estrada, N. and Wahl, D. (2007) "Prehistoric Human–Environment Interactions in the Maya Lowlands: The Holmul Region's case." Paper presented at 73rd Annual Meeting of the Society for American Archaeology, Austin, TX.

Fahsen, F. (2001) "From Chiefdoms to Statehood in the Highlands of Guatemala," in: Grube, N. (ed.) *Maya: Divine Kings of the Rain Forest.* Cologne: Koenneman, 86–95.

Fash, W. L., Tokovinine, A. and Fash, B. W. (2009) "The House of New Fire at Teotihuacan and its Legacy in Mesoamerica," in: Fash, W. L. and Lopez Lujan, L. (eds) *The Art of Urbanism: How Mesoamerican Kingdoms Represented Themselves in Architecture and Imagery.* Washington, D.C.: Dumbarton Oaks Research Library and Collections, 201–229.

Fields, V. M. (1986) "Iconographic Heritage of the Maya Jester God," in: Fields, V. M. (ed.) *Sixth Palenque Round Table.* Norman: University of Oklahoma Press, 167–174.

Flannery, K. V. and Marcus, J. (1994) *Early Formative Pottery of the Valley of Oaxaca.* Ann Arbor: Museum of Anthropology, University of Michigan.

Folan, W. J., Fletcher, L. A., May Hau, J. and Florey Folan, L. (2001) *Las ruinas de Calakmul, Campeche, México: un lugar central y su paisaje cultural.* Campeche: Universidad Autónoma de Campeche, Centro de Investigaciones Históricas y Sociales.

Folan, W. J., Kintz, E. R. and Fletcher, L. A. (1983) *Cobá, a Classic Maya Metropolis.* New York: Academic Press.

Ford, A. (1986) *Population Growth and Social Complexity: An Examination of Settlement and Environment in the Central Maya Lowlands.* Tempe: Arizona State University.

Foster, L. and Wren, L. (1996) "World Creator and World Sustainer: God N at Chichen Itzá," in: Marcri, M. J. and Mchargue, J. (eds) *Eight Palenque Round Table, 1993.* San Francisco: The Pre-Columbian Art Research Institute.

Freidel, D. A. (1982) "The Maya City of Cerros." *Archaeology*, 35(4), 12–21.

—— (1985) "New Light on the Dark Age: A Summary of Major Themes," in: Chase, A. F. and Rice, P. M. (eds) *Lowland Maya Postclassic.* Austin: University of Texas Press, 285–310.

—— (1986) "The Monumental Architecture," in: Robertson, R. and Freidel, D. A. (eds) *Archaeology at Cerros, Belize. Central America. Volume I: An Interim Report.* Dallas, TX: Southern Methodist University Press, 1–22.

Freidel, D. A., Reese-Taylor, K. and Mora-Marín, D. (2002) "The Origins of Maya Civilization: The Old Shell Game, Commodity, Treasure and Kinship," in: Masson, M. A. and Freidel, D. A. (eds) *Ancient Maya Political Economies.* Walnut Cree, CA: Altamira Press, 41–87.

Freidel, D. A. and Schele, L. (1988) "Kingship in the Late Preclassic Maya Lowlands: The Instruments and Places of Ritual Power." *American Anthropologist*, 90(3), 547–567, ill.

Freidel, D. A., Schele, L. and Parker, J. (1993) *Maya Cosmos: Three Thousand Years on the Shaman's Path.* New York: Morrow and Co.

Fuentes Y Guzmán, F. A. D., Villacorta, C. J. A., Salazar, R. A. and Aguilar, S. (1932) *Recordación Florida. Discurso historial y demostración natural, material, militar y política del reyno de Guatemala.* Guatemala: Tipografía nacional.

Gann, T. W. F. (1926) *Ancient Cities and Modern tribes: Exploration and Adventure in Maya Lands.* New York: Charles Scribner's Sons.

Garber, J. F., Brown, K. M., Awe, J. and Hartman, C. (2004) "Middle Formative Prehistory of the Central Belize Valley: An Examination of Architecture, Material Culture, and Sociopolitical Change at Blackman Eddy," in: Garber, J. F. (ed.) *The Ancient Maya of the Belize Valley: Half a Century of Archaeological Research.* Gainsville: University Press of Florida, 25–47.

Gifford, J. (1965) "Ceramics," in: Willey, G. R., Bullard, W. R., Glass, J. B. and Gifford, J. (eds) *Prehistoric Maya Settlement Patterns in the Belize Valley.* Cambridge, MA: Peabody Museum of Archaeology and Ethnology, Harvard University.

Gill, R. B. (2000) *The Great Maya Droughts: Water, Life, and Death.* Albuquerque: University of New Mexico Press.

Girard, R. (1966) *Los Mayas: su civilizacion, su historia, sus vinculaciones continentales.* Mexico, D.F.: Libro Mex.

Golden, C., Scherer, A. K., Muñoz, A. R. and Vásquez, R. (2008) "Piedras Negras and Yaxchilan: Divergent Political Trajectories in Adjacent Maya Polities." *Latin American Antiquity*, 3, 249–274.

Graham, J. A., Heizer, R. F. and Shook, E. M. (1978) *Abaj Takalik 1976: Exploratory Investigations.* Berkeley: University of California Archaeological Research Facility.

Grove, D. C. (2000) "Faces of the Earth at Chalcatzingo, Mexico: Serpents, Caves, and Mountains in Middle Formative Period Iconography," in: Clark, J. E. (ed.) *Olmec Art and Archaeology.* Washington. D.C.: National Gallery of Art, 277–295.

Grube, N. (2003) "Monumentos jeroglíficos de Holmul, Petén, Guatemala," in: Laporte, J. P., Arroyo, B. Escobedo, H. and Mejía, H. (eds) *XVI Simposio de Investigaciones de Arqueología de Guatemala.* Guatemala: Museo Nacional de Arqueología y Etnología, 701–710.

—— (2004) "La Historia Dinastica de Naranjo, Peten." *Beitrage zur Allgemeinen und Vergleichenden Archaeologie*, 24, 197–213.

Grube, N. and Paap, I. (2008) "La exploración de Uxul, Petén Campechano: resultados de las investigaciones en el 2007," in: *Los investigadores de la cultura Maya.* Campeche: Universidad Autonoma de Campeche, 267–287.

Guernsey, J. (2006) *Ritual & Power in Stone: The Performance of Rulership in Mesoamerican Izapan Style Art.* Austin: University of Texas Press.

Guernsey Kappelman, J. and Reilly, K. F. (2001) "Paths to Heaven, Ropes to Earth: Birds, Jaguars and Cosmic Cords in Formative Mesoamerica." *Ancient America*, (2), 1–52.

Hammond, N. (1973) *British Museum–Cambridge University Corazal Project, 1973 Interim Report.* Cambridge: Cambridge University Centre of Latin American Studies.

—— (1974) "Preclassic to Postclassic in Northern Belize." *Antiquity*, 48, 177–189.

—— (ed.) (1977) *Social Process in Maya Prehistory: Studies in Honour of Sir Eric Thompson.* London: Academic Press.

—— (1980) "Early Maya Ceremonial at Cuello, Belize." *Antiquity*, 54(212), 176–190.

—— (1982) *Ancient Maya Civilization.* New Brunswick, NJ: Rutgers University Press.

—— (1985) *Nohmul, a Prehistoric Maya Community in Belize: Excavations, 1973–1983.* Oxford: BAR.

—— (1992) "Preclassic Maya Civilization," in: Danien, E. C. and Sharer, R. J. (eds) *New Theories on the Ancient Maya.* Philadelphia: University Museum of Archaeology and Anthropology, University of Pennsylvania, 137–144.

Hammond, N., Estrada-Belli, F. and Clarke, A. (1992) "Middle Preclassic Maya Buildings and Burials at Cuello, Belize." *Antiquity*, 66(253), 955–964.

Hammond, N., Pring, D., Berger, R., Switzer, V. R. and Ward, A. P. (1976) "Radiocarbon Chronology for Early Maya Occupation at Cuello, Belize." *Nature*, 44, 92–110.

Hansen, R. (1990) *Excavations in the Tigre Complex, El Mirador, Petén, Guatemala.* Provo, UT: New World Archaeological Foundation, Brigham Young University.

—— (1991) "Resultados preliminares de las investigaciones arqueológicas en el sitio Nakbé, Petén, Guatemala," in: Laporte, J. P. and Escobedo, H. L. (eds) *II Simposio de Investigaciones Arqueológicas en Guatemala: Museo Nacional de Arqueología y Etnología, 1988.* Guatemala: Ministerio de Cultura y Deportes, Asociación Tikal, IDAEH, 160–174.

—— (1992) *The Archaeology of Ideology: A Study of Maya Preclassic Architectural Sculpture at Nakbe, Peten, Guatemala.* Ph.D. Thesis. University of California.

—— (1998) "Continuity and Disjunction: The Preclassic Antecedents of Pre-Classic Maya Architecture," in: Houston, S. D. (ed.) *Function and Meaning in Classic Maya Architecture.* Washington, D.C.: Dumbarton Oaks.

—— (2001) "The First Cities—The Beginnings of Urbanization and State Formation in the Maya Lowlands," in: Grube, N. (ed.) *Maya: Divine Kings of the Rain Forest.* Cologne: Koenneman, 51–64.

—— (2005) "Perspectives on Olmec–Maya Interaction in the Middle Formative Period," in: Powis, T. (ed.) *New Perspectives on Formative Mesoamerican Cultures.* Oxford: Archaeopress, 51–72.

Hansen, R. and Guenter, S. P. (2005) "Early Social Complexity and Kingship in the Mirador Basin," in: Fields, V. M. and Reents-Budet, D. (eds) *Lords of Creation: The Origins of Sacred Maya Kinship.* Los Angeles: Los Angeles County Museum of Art, 60–61.

Hansen, R. D., Bozarth, S., Jacob, J., Wahl, D. and Schreiner, T. (2002) "Climatic and Environmental Variability in the Rise of Maya Civilization: A Preliminary Perspective from the Northern Peten." *Ancient Mesoamerica*, 13, 273–295.

Hansen, R. D., Fahsen, F. and Bishop, R. L. (1991) "Notes on Maya Codex-Style Ceramics from Nakbe, Peten, Guatemala." *Ancient Mesoamerica*, 2(2), 225–243.

Hansen, R. D., Howell, W. K. and Guenter, S. P. (2008a) "Forgotten Structures, Haunted Houses, and Occupied Hearts: Ancient Perspectives and Contemporary Interpretations of Abandoned Sites and Buildings in the Mirador Basin, Guatemala," in: Stanton, T. W. and Mignoni, A. (eds) *Ruins of the Past: The Use and Perception of Abandoned Structures in the Maya Lowlands.* Boulder: University Press of Colorado, 25–64.

Hansen, R. D., Suyuc, E. and Mejia, H. (2008b) *Mirador Basin 2008: A Field Report of the 2008 Season.* Palo Alto, CA: Global Heritage Fund.

Haug, G. H., Gunther, D., Petersen, L. C., Sigman, D. M., Hughen, K. A. and Aeschlimann, B. (2003) "Climate and the Collapse of Maya Civilization." *Science*, 299(5613), 1731–1735.

Healy, P. F., Cheetham, D., Powis, T. and Awe, J. (2004a) "Cahal Pech, Belize: The Middle Formative Period," in: Garber, J. F. (ed.) *The Ancient Maya of the Belize Valley: Half a Century of Archaeological Research.* Gainsville: University of Florida Press, 103–124.

Healy, P. F., Hohmann, B. and Powis, T. (2004b) "The Ancient Maya Center of

Pacbitun," in: Garber, J. F. (ed.) *The Ancient Maya of the Belize River Valley: Half a Century of Archaeological Research.* Gainsville: University Press of Florida, 207–228.

Hermes, B. (1993) "Dos reportes del laboratorio cerámico: vasijas miniatura y adiciones tipológicas para la Epoca Preclásica," in: Laporte, J. P. and Valdés, J. A. (eds) *Tikal y Uaxactun en el Preclásico.* Mexico, D.F.: Universidad Nacional Autonoma de Mexico, 47–52.

Hodell, D. A., Curtis, J. H. and Brenner, M. (1995) "Possible Role of Climate in the Collapse of Classic Maya Civilization." *Nature,* 375, 391–394.

Houston, S. (1993) *Hieroglyphs and History at Dos Pilas: Dynastic Politics of the Classic Maya.* Austin: University of Texas Press.

Hurst, H. (2005) "San Bartolo, Petén: Técnicas de pintura mural del Preclásico Tardío," in: Laporte, J. P., Arroyo, B. and Mejía, H. E. (eds) *XVIII Simposio de Investigaciones Arqueológicas en Guatemala, 2004.* Guatemala: Ministerio de Cultura y Deportes, Asociacion Tikal, IDAEH, FAMSI, 639–646.

Inomata, T., Triadan, D., Ponciano, E., Pinto, E., Terry, R. E. and Eberl, M. (2002) "Domestic and Political Lives of Classic Maya Elites: The Excavation of Rapidly Abandoned Structures at Aguateca, Guatemala." *Latin American Antiquity,* 3, 305–330.

Jacob, J. S. (1995) "Archaeological Pedology in the Maya Lowlands," in: Collins, M. E., Carter, B. J., Gladfelter, B. G. and Southard, R. J. (eds) *Pedological Perspectives in Archaeological Research.* Madison, WI: Soil Science Society of America, 51–80.

Jiménez Moreno, W. (1966) "Mesoamerica before the Toltecs," in: Paddock, J. (ed.) *Ancient Oaxaca.* Stanford, CA: Stanford University Press, 1–82.

Jones, C. (1991) "Cycles of Growth at Tikal," in: Culbert, T. P. (ed.) *Classic Maya Political History.* Cambridge: Cambridge University Press, 102–128.

Jones, C. and Satterthwaite, L. (1982) *The Monuments and Inscriptions of Tikal: The Carved Monuments.* Philadelphia: University of Pennsylvania Museum of Archaeology and Anthropology.

Jones, G. D. (1998) *The Conquest of the Last Maya Kingdom.* Stanford, CA: Stanford University Press.

Joralemon, P. D. (1971) *A Study of Olmec Iconography.* Washington, D.C.: Dumbarton Oaks Research Library and Collections.

Joyce, R. (1980) "Crossed Bands in Olmec, Maya and Izapa Art." Paper presented at Meeting of Midwestern Mesoamericanists, University of Iowa, Iowa City.

Justeson, J. S., Norman, W. M. and Hammond, N. (1988) "The Pomona Flare: A Preclassic Maya Hieroglyphic Text," in: Benson, E. and Griffin, G. (eds) *Maya Iconography.* Princeton, NJ: Princeton University Press, 94–151.

Kidder, A. V. (1950) "Introduction," in: Smith, A. L. (ed.) *Uaxactun, Guatemala: Excavations of 1931–1937.* Washington, D.C.: Carnegie Institution of Washington, 1–12.

Kidder, A. V., Jennings, J. D. and Shook, E. M. (1946) *Excavations at Kaminaljuyu.* Washington, D.C.: Carnegie Institution of Washington.

Knapp, A. B. (1992a) "Archaeology and Annales: Time, Space, and Change," in: Knapp, A. B. (ed.) *Archaeology, Annales, and Ethnohistory.* Cambridge: Cambridge University Press, 1–21.

—— (1992b) *Archaeology, Annales and Ethnohistory.* Cambridge: Cambridge University Press.

Kolb, M. J. and Snead, J. E. (1997) "It's a Small World after All: Comparative

Analyses of Community Organization in Archaeology." *American Antiquity*, 62(4), 609–628.

Kosakowsky, L. J. (1987) *Preclassic Maya Pottery at Cuello, Belize.* Tucson: University of Arizona Press.

Kosakowsky, L. J. and Pring, D. (1991) "Ceramic Chronology and Typology," in: Hammond, N. (ed.) *Cuello: An Early Maya Community in Belize.* Cambridge: Cambridge University Press, 60–69.

—— (1998) "The Ceramcis of Cuello, Belize: A New Evaluation." *Ancient Mesoamerica*, 9(1), 55–66.

Krejci, E. and Culbert, T. P. (1999) "Preclassic and Classic Burials and Caches in the Maya Lowlands," in: Grube, N. (ed.) *The Emergence of Lowland Maya Civilization.* Markt Schwaben: Verlag Anton Saurwein, 103–116.

Kunen, J. L., Culbert, T. P., Fialko, V. Mckee, B. R. and Grazioso, L. (2000) *"Bajo* Communities: A Case Study from the Central Peten." *Culture & Agriculture*, 22(3), 15–31.

Laporte, J. P., Hermes, B., Zea, L. D. and Iglesias, M. J. (1992) "Nuevos Entierros y Escondites de Tikal, Subfases Manik 3a y 3b," in: Kirkpatrick, M. and Gifford, C. A. (eds) *Ceramica de Cultura Maya et al.* Philadelphia: Laboratory of Anthropology, Temple University, 30–68.

Laporte, J. P. and Fialko, V. (1990) "New Perspectives on Old Problems: Dynastic References for the Early Classic Maya," in: Clancy, F. S. and Harrison, P. D. (eds) *Vision and Revision in Maya Studies.* Albuquerque: University of New Mexico Press, 33–66.

—— (1993) "El Preclásico de Mundo Perdido: Algunos aportes sobre los orígenes de Tikal," in: Laporte, J. P. and Valdés, J. A. (eds) *Tikal y Uaxactun en el Preclásico.* Mexico, D.F.: Universidad Nacional Autonoma de Mexico, 9–47.

Laporte, J. P. and Valdés, J. A. (1993) *Tikal y Uaxactun en el Preclasico.* Mexico, D.F.: Universidad Nacional Autonoma de Mexico.

Leonard, D. and Taube, K. A. (2007) "The God C Variant: A Reappraisal." Paper presented at the 72nd Annual Meeting for the Society for American Archaeology, Austin, TX, April 26.

Lohse, J. C., Awe, J., Griffith, C., Rosenwig, R. M. and Valdez, F. Jr (2006) "Preceramic Occupations in Belize: Updating the Paleoindian and Archaic Record." *Latin American Antiquity*, 17(2), 209–226.

Looper, M. G. (2003) *Lightning Warrior: Maya Art and Kingship at Quirigua.* 1st edn. Austin: University of Texas Press.

Loten, H. S. (2007) *Additions and Alterations: A Commentary on the Architecture of the North Acropolis, Tikal, Guatemala.* Philadelphia: University of Pennsylvania Museum of Archaeology and Anthropology.

Lowe, G. W. (1977) "The Mixe-Zoque as Competing Neighbors of the Early Lowland Maya," in: Adams, R. E. W. (ed.) *Origins of Maya Civilization.* Albuquerque: University of New Mexico Press, 197–248.

—— (1981) "Olmec Horizons Defined in Mound 20, San Isidro, Chiapas," in: Benson, E. (ed.) *Olmec and Their Neighbors.* Washington, D.C.: Dumbarton Oaks, 231–255.

—— (1989) "Algunas aclaraciones sobre la presencia olmeca y maya en el Preclásico de Chiapas," in: Macias, M. C. (ed.) *Preclásico o Formativo: Avances y Perspectivas.* Mexico, D.F.: Museo Nacional de Antropología, Instituto Nacional de Antroplogía e Historia, 363–383.

160

Maler, T. (1911) *Explorations in the Department of Peten, Guatemala, Tikal.* Cambridge, MA: Peabody Museum of Archaeology and Ethnology, Harvard University.

Manahan, T. K. (2004) "The Way Things Fall Apart: Social Organization and the Classic Maya Collapse of Copan." *Ancient Mesoamerica*, 1, 107–125.

Marcus, J. (1992) *Mesoamerican Writing Systems: Propaganda, Myth, and History in Four Ancient Civilizations.* Princeton, NJ: Princeton University Press.

—— (1993) "Ancient Maya Political Organization," in: Sabloff, J. and Henderson, J. (eds) *Lowland Maya Civilization in the Eighth Century AD.* Washington, D.C.: Dumbarton Oaks, 111–183.

Martin, S. (2003) "In Line of the Founder: A View of Dynastic Politics at Tikal," in: Sabloff, J. A. (ed.) *Tikal: Dynasties, Foreigners, and Affairs of State.* Santa Fe, NM: School of American Research Press.

—— (2005) "Of Snakes and Bats: Shifting Identities at Calakmul." *The PARI Journal.* Online. Available from: <http://www.mesoweb.com/pari/publications/journal/602/SnakesBats_e.pdf> [Accessed April 2009].

—— (2006) "The Great Sustainer: God N in Ancient Maya Religion." Paper presented at the Maya Weekend, University of Pennsylvania Museum of Archaeology and Anthropology.

Martin, S. and Grube, N. (2000) *Chronicle of the Maya Kings and Queens: Deciphering Dynasties of the Ancient Maya.* London: Thames & Hudson.

—— (2008) *Chronicle of the Maya Kings and Queens: Deciphering the Dynasties of the Ancient Maya.* 2nd edn. London: Thames & Hudson.

Matheny, R. T., Hansen, R. D., Gurr, D. L. and Matheny, R. T., (1980) *Preliminary Field Report, El Mirador, 1979 Season Update, Project El Mirador, Peten, Guatemala.* Provo, UT: New World Archaeological Foundation.

Maudslay, A. P. (1889–1902) *Biologia Centrali-Americana: Archaeology.* London: R. H. Porter and Dulau & Co.

McAnany, P. A. and Yoffee, N. (2008) *Questioning Collapse: Human Resilience, Ecological Vulnerability, and the Aftermath of Empire.* Cambridge: Cambridge University Press.

Merwin, R. E. and Vaillant, G. (1932) *The Ruins of Holmul.* Cambridge, MA: Peabody Museum of American Archaeology and Ethnology, Harvard University.

Mora-Marín, D. (2005) "Kaminljuyu Stela 1: Script Classification and Linguistic Affiliation." *Ancient Mesoamerica*, 16(1), 63–87.

Morley, S. G. (1920) *The Inscriptions at Copan.* Washington, D.C.: The Carnegie Institution of Washington.

—— (1943) "Archaeological Investigations of the Carnegie Institution of Washington in the Maya Area of Middle America, during the Past Twenty-Eight Years." *Proceedings of the American Philosophical Society*, 86(2), 205–219.

—— (1946) *The Ancient Maya.* Palo Alto, CA: Stanford University Press.

Nalda, E. (2003) "Prácticas funerarias en Dzibanché, Quintana Roo: los entierros en el Edificio de los Cormoranes." *Arqueología*, 31, 25–37.

Neff, H., Pearsall, D. M., Jones, J. G., Arroyo, B., Collins, S. K. and Freidel, D. E. (2006) "Early Maya Adaptive Patterns: Mid–Late Holocene Paleoenvironmental Evidence from Pacific Guatemala." *Latin American Antiquity*, 17(3), 287–315.

Norman, G. V. (1973) *Izapa Sculpture. Part I: Album.* Provo, UT: Brigham Young University Press.

Parsons, L. A. (1986) *The Origins of Maya Art: Monumental Sculpture of Kaminaljuyú,*

Guatemala and the Southern Pacific Coast. Washington, D.C.: Dumbarton Oaks Research Library and Collections.

Pauketat, T. R. (2007) *Chiefdoms and Other Archaeological Delusions.* Lanham, MD: AltaMira Press.

Pazstory, E. (1997) *Teotihuacan. An Experiment in Living.* Norman: University of Oklahoma Press.

Peebles, C. S. (1990) "From History to Hermeneutics: The Place of Theory in the Later Prehistory of the Southeast." *Southeastern Archaeology,* 9(1), 23–34.

Pellecer, M., (2006) "El Grupo Jabalí: un complejo arquitectónico de patrón triadico en San Bartolo, Peten," in: Laporte, J. P., Arroyo, B. and Mejía, H. E. (eds) *XIX Simposio de Investigaciones Arqueológicas en Guatemala, 2005.* Guatemala: Ministerio de Cultura y Deportes, Asociación Tikal, Fundación Reinhart, 937–948.

Pendergast, D. M. (1971) "Evidence of Early Teotihuacan Lowland Maya Contact at Altun Ha." *American Antiquity,* 36(4), 455–460.

—— (1981) "Lamanai, Belize: Summary of Excavation Results, 1974–1980." *Journal of Field Archaeology,* 8(1), 29–53, ill.

Pohl, M. D., Pope, K. O., Jones, J. G., Jacob, J. S., Piperno, D. R., Defrance, S. D., Lentz, D., Gifford, J. A., Denforth, M. E. and Josserand, K. J. (1996) "Early Agriculture in the Maya Lowlands." *Latin American Antiquity,* 7, 355–372.

Pohl, M. E. D., Pope, K. O. and Nagy, C. V. (2002) "Olmec Origins of Mesoamerican Writing." *Science,* 298(5600), 1984–1987.

Pollock, H. E. D., Roys, R. R., Proskouriakoff, T. and Smith, A. L. (1962) *Mayapan, Yucatan, Mexico.* Washington, D.C.: Carnegie Institution of Washington.

Popenoe de Hatch, M. (2002) "Evidencia de un observatorio astronomico en Abaj Takalik," in: Laporte, J. P., Arroyo, B. and Escobedo, H. L. (eds) *XV Simposio de Investigaciones Arqueológicas en Guatemala.* Guatemala: Museo Nacional de Arqueología y Etnología, 437–458.

Popenoe Hatch, M. (1997) *Kaminaljuyu/San Jorge. Evidencia Arqueologica de la Actividad Economica en el Valle de Guatemala 300 a.C. a 300 d.C.* Guatemala City: Universidad del Valle de Guatemala.

Pring, D. (1977) "Influence or Intrusion? The 'Protoclassic' in the Maya Lowlands," in: Hammond, N. (ed.) *Social Process in Maya Prehistory.* New York: Academic Press, 135–165.

—— (1979) "The Swasey Complex of Northern Belize: A Definition and Discussion," in: Graham, J. A. (ed.) *Studies in Ancient Mesoamerica.* Berkeley: University of California Press, 215–229.

—— (2000) *The Protoclassic in the Maya Lowlands.* Oxford: John and Erica Hedges Ltd.

Proskouriakoff, T. (1993) *Maya History.* Austin: University of Texas Press.

Puleston, D. E. (1973) *Ancient Maya Settlement and Environment at Tikal: Implications for Subsistence Models.* Ph.D. Thesis. University of Pennsylvania.

—— (1983) *The Settlement Survey of Tikal.* Philadelphia: University Museum, University of Pennsylvania.

Puleston, O. S. and Puleston, D. E. (1971) "A Processual Model for the Rise of Classic Maya Civilization in the Southern Lowlands," in: *Atti del XL Congresso Internazionale degli Americanisti,* Genoa: Tilger, 119–124.

Rathje, W. L. (1971) "The Origin and Development of Lowland Classic Maya Civilization." *American Antiquity,* 36(3), 275–285.

Reese-Taylor, K. (2002) "Ritual Circuits as Key Elements in Maya Civic Center

Design," in: Stone, A. (ed.) *Heart of Creation*. Tuscaloosa: University of Alabama Press, 143–165.

Reese-Taylor, K. and Walker, D. S. (2002) "The Passage of the Late Preclassic into the Early Classic," in: Masson, M. and Freidel, D. A. (eds) *Ancient Maya Political Economies*. New York: Altamira Press, 87–122.

Reilly, K. (1991) "Olmec Iconographic Influences on the Symbols of Maya Rulership: An Examination of Possible Sources," in: Greene Robertson, M. and Fields, V. (eds) *Sixth Palenque Round Table, 1986*. Norman: University of Oklahoma Press, 51–166.

Rice, D. S. (1976) *A Historical Ecology of Lakes Yaxha and Sacnab, El Peten, Guatemala*. Ph.D. Thesis. Pennsylvania State University.

—— (1979) "Introduction and the Middle Preclassic Ceramics of Lake Yaxha-Sacnab, Guatemala." *Ceramica de Cultura Maya*, 10, 1–36.

Ricketson, O. G. and Ricketson, E. B. (1937) *Uaxactun, Guatemala: Group E— 1926–1931*. Washington, D.C.: Carnegie Institution of Washington.

Rivera Dorado, M. (1987) "Proyecto Oxkintok: introducción." *Oxkintok*, 1, 8–17.

Robles Castellanos, F. and Andrews, A. P. (1986) "A Review and Synthesis of Recent Postclassic Archaeology in Northern Yucatan," in: Sabloff, J. A. and Andrews, E. W. (eds) *Late Lowland Maya Civilization*. Albuquerque: University of New Mexico Press, 53–98.

Roys, R. L. (1952) *Conquest Sites and the Subsequent Destruction of Maya Architecture in the Interior of Northern Yucatan*. Washington, D.C.: Carnegie Institution of Washington.

—— (1957) *The Political Geography of the Yucatan Maya*. Washington, D.C.: Carnegie Institution of Washington.

Ruppert, K. (1940) "A Special Assemblage of Maya Structures," in: Linton, R., Lothrop, S. K., Shapiro, H. and Vaillant, G. (eds) *The Maya and Their Neighbors*. New York: D. Appleton-Century, 222–231.

Ruz Lhuillier, A. (1955) "Exploraciones en Palenque," in: *30th International Congress of Americanists, Cambridge, England*. London: Royal Anthropological Institute, 5–22.

Sabloff, J. (1975) "Ceramics," in: Willey, G. R. (ed.) *Excavations at Seibal, Department of Peten, Guatemala*. Cambridge, MA: Harvard University Press.

Sanders, W. T. (1977) "Environmental Heterogeneity and the Evolution of Lowland Maya Civilization," in: Adams, R. E. W. (ed.) *The Origins of Maya Civilization*. Albuquerque: University of New Mexico Press, 287–298.

Sanders, W. T. and Michels, J. W. (1969) *The Pennsylvania State University Kaminaljuyu Project—1968 Season. Part I: The Excavations*. University Park: Department of Anthropology, Pennsylvania State University.

—— (1977) *Teotihuacan and Kaminaljuyu: A Study in Prehistoric Culture Contact*. University Park: Pennsylvania State University Press.

Sanders, W. T. and Price, B. J. (1968) *Mesoamerica: The Evolution of Civilization*. New York: Random House.

Saturno, W., Sever, T. L., Irwin, D. E., Howell, B. F. and Garrison, T. G. (2007) "Putting Us on the Map: Remote Sensing Investigation of the Ancient Maya Landscape," in: Wiseman, J. R. and El-Baz, F. (eds) *Remote Sensing in Archaeology*. New York: Springer, 137–160.

Saturno, W. A., Stuart, D. and Beltran, B. (2006) "Early Maya Writing at San Bartolo, Guatemala." *Science*, 311(5795), 1281–1283.

Saturno, W. A., Stuart, D. and Taube, K. (2005a) "La identificación de las figuras del Muro Oeste de Pinturas Sub-1, San Bartolo, Petén," in: Laporte, J. P., Arroyo, B. and Mejía, H. E. (eds) *XVIII Simposio de Investigaciones Arqueológicas en Guatemala, 2004*. Guatemala: Ministerio de Cultura y Deportes, Asociación Tikal, IDAEH, FAMSI, 647–656.

Saturno, W. A., Taube, K. and Stuart, D. (2005b) "The Murals of San Bartolo, El Petén, Guatemala. Part 1: The North Wall." *Ancient America*, 7, 1–56.

Schele, L. (1998) "The Iconography of Maya Architectural Façades during the Late Classic Period," in: Houston, S. (ed.) *Function and Meaning in Classic Maya Architecture*. Washington, D.C.: Dumbarton Oaks, 479–517.

Schele, L. and Freidel, D. A. (1990) *A Forest of Kings*. New York: William Morrow and Co.

Schele, L. and Mathews, P. (1998) *The Code of Kings: The Language of Seven Sacred Maya Temples and Tombs*. New York: Scribner.

Sedat, D. W. and Sharer, R. J. (1972) "Archaeological Investigations in the Northern Maya Highlands: New Data on the Maya Preclassic." *Contributions of the University of California Archaeological Research Facility*, 16, 23–35.

Sharer, R. J. (2003) "Founding Events and Teotihuacan Connections at Copán, Honduras," in: Braswell, G. E. (ed.) *The Maya and Teotihuacan: Reinterpreting Early Classic Interaction*. Austin: University of Texas Press, 143–166.

—— (2004) "External Interaction at Early Classic Copan," in: Bell, E. E., Canuto, M. A. and Sharer, R. J. (eds) *Understanding Early Classic Copan*. Philadelphia: University of Pennsylvania Museum of Archaeology and Anthropology, 297–318.

Sharer, R. J. and Gifford, J. (1970) "Preclassic Ceramics from Chalchuapa, El Salvador, and their Relationships with the Maya Lowlands." *American Antiquity*, 35(4), 441–462.

Sharer, R. J. and Sedat, D. (1973) "Monument 1, El Porton, Guatemala and the Development of Maya Calendrical and Writing Systems." Berkeley: University of California Press, 177–194.

Sharer, R. J. and Traxler, L. P. (2006) *The Ancient Maya*. 6th edn. Stanford, CA: Stanford University Press.

Sheets, P. D. (1971) "An Ancient Natural Disaster." *Expedition*, 14(1), 24–31.

Sheets, P. D. and Grayson, D. K. (1979) *Volcanic Activity and Human Ecology*. New York: Academic Press.

Shook, E. M. (1957) "The Tikal Project." *University Museum Bulletin*, 21, 36–52.

Shook, E. M. and Smith, R. E. (1950) "Descubrimientos arqueológicos en Poptún." *Antropología e Historia de Guatemala*, 2, 3–15.

Smith, L. A. (1950a) *Uaxactún, Guatemala: Excavations of 1931–1937*. Washington, D.C.: Carnegie Institution of Washington.

Smith, R. E. (1950b) *Ceramic Sequence at Uaxactun, Guatemala*. New Orleans, LA: Middle American Research Institute, Tulane University.

Smyth, M. P. (2008) "Beyond Economic Imperialism: The Teotihuacan Factor in Northern Yucatan." *Journal of Anthropological Research*, 3, 395–409.

Spinden, H. J. (1928) *Ancient Civilizations of Mexico and Central America*. New York: Anthropological Handbook Fund.

Sprajc, I. (2002) "Maya Sites and Monuments in SE Campeche, Mexico." *Journal of Field Archaeology*, 4, 385–407.

Stirling, M. W. (1940) *An Initial Series from Tres Zapotes, Vera Cruz, Mexico.* Washington, D.C.: National Geographic Society.

Strelow, D. and LeCount, L. (2001) "Regional Interaction in the Formative Southern Maya Lowlands: Evidence of Olmecoid Stylistic Motifs in a Cunil Ceramic Assemblage from Xunantunich, Belize." Paper presented at 66th Annual Meeting of the Society for American Archaeology, New Orleans, LA.

Stromsvik, G. (1946) *Actividades arqueológicas desarrolladas en Copán por el Gobierno de Honduras en cooperación con la Institución Carnegie de Washington.* Tegucigalpa: Secretaría de Educación Pública.

Stuart, D., (1988) "Blood Symbolism in Maya Iconography," in: Benson, E. and Griffin, G. G. (eds) *Maya Iconography.* Princeton, NJ: Princeton University Press, 175–221.

—— (1998) "'The Fire Enters His House': Architectural and Ritual in Classic Maya Texts," in: Houston, S. D. (ed.) *Function and Meaning in Maya Architecture.* Washington, D.C.: Dumbarton Oaks Research Library and Collections, 373–425.

—— (2000a) "The Arrival of Strangers: Teotihuacan and Tollan in Classic Maya History," in: Carrasco, D. S., Jones, L. and Sessions, S. (eds) *Mesoamerica's Classic Heritage: Teotihuacan to the Aztecs.* Boulder: University Press of Colorado, 465–513.

—— (2000b) "The Maya Hieroglyphs for Mam, 'Grandfather, Grandson, Ancestor.'" Online. Available from: <http://decipherment.files.wordpress.com/2007/09/mam-glyph.pdf> [Accessed March 2009].

—— (2004) "A Foreign Past: The Writing and Representation of History on a Royal Ancestral Shrine at Copan," in: Andrews, W. E. and Fash, W. L. (eds) *Copan: The History of an Ancient Maya Kingdom.* Santa Fe, NM: School of American Research Press, 373–394.

—— (2007a) "Old Notes on the Possible ITZAM Sign." Online. Available from: <http://decipherment.wordpress.com/2007/09/29/old-notes-on-the-possible-itzam-sign/> [Accessed September 2009].

—— (2007b) "The Origin of Copan's Founder." Online. Available from: <http://decipherment.wordpress.com/2007/06/25/the-origin-of-copans-founder/> [Accessed November 2009].

Sugiyama, S. (2005) *Human Sacrifice, Militarism, and Rulership: Materialization of State Ideology at the Feathered Serpent Pyramid, Teotihuacan.* Cambridge: Cambridge University Press.

Taube, K. (1992a) *The Major Gods of Ancient Yucatan.* Washington, D.C.: Dumbarton Oaks.

Taube, K. A. (1992b) "The Temple of Quetzalcoatl and the Cult of Sacred War at Teotihuacan." *RES*, 21, 53–87.

—— (1995) "The Rainmakers: The Olmec and Their Contribution to Mesoamerican Belief and Ritual," in: Benson, E. (ed.) *The Olmec World: Ritual and Rulership.* Princeton, NJ: The Art Museum, Princeton University, 83–103.

—— (2000) "Lightning Celts and Corn Fetishes: The Formative and the Development of Maize Symbolism in Mesoamerica and the American Southwest," in: Clark, J. E. and Pye, M. E. (eds) *Olmec Art and Archaeology in Mesoamerica.* Washington, D.C.: National Gallery of Art.

—— (2003) "Ancient and Contemporary Maya Conceptions about Field and Forest," in: Gómez-Pompa, A., Allen, M. F., Fedick, S. L. and Jimenez-Osornio, J. J. (eds) *The Lowland Maya: Three Millennia at the Human–Wildland Interface.* New York: Haworth Press, 461–492.

—— (2004) "Flower Mountain: Concepts of Life, Beauty and Paradise among the Classic Maya." *RES*, 45, 69–98.

—— (2005) "The Symbolism of Jade in Classic Maya Religion." *Ancient Mesoamerica*, 16(1), 23–50.

—— (2009) "The Maya Maize God and the Mythic Origins of Dance," in: Le Fort, G., Gardiol, R., Matteo, S. and Helmke, C. G. B. (eds) *The Maya and Their Sacred Narratives: Text and Context in Maya Mythologies*. Markt Schwaben: Verlag Anton Saurwein, 41–51.

Taube, K. A., Saturno, W. A. and Stuart, D. (2004) "Identificación mitológica de los personajes en el muro norte de la piramide de Las Pinturas sub-1, San Bartolo, Petén," in: Laporte, J. P., Arroyo, B., Escobedo, H. and Mejía, H. (eds) *XVII Simposio de Investigaciones Arqueológicas en Guatemala*. Guatemala: Museo Nacional de Arqueología y Etnología, Ministerio de Cultura y Deportes, Asociación Tikal, 871–880.

Tedlock, D. (1996) *Popol Vuh: The Maya Book of the Dawn of Life*. New York: Simon & Schuster.

Tedlock, B. and Tedlock, D. (1985) "Text and Textile: Language and Technology in the Arts of the Quiché Maya." *Journal of Anthropological Research*, 41, 121–146.

Thompson, J. E. S. (1950) *Maya Hieroglyphic Writing: An Introduction*. Washington, D.C.: Carnegie Institution of Washington.

—— (1954) *The Rise and Fall of Maya Civilization*. 1st edn. Norman: University of Oklahoma Press.

—— (1970) *Maya History and Religion*. Norman: University of Oklahoma Press.

Tomasic, J. and Estrada-Belli, F. (2003) "Nuevos datos sobre el Clasico Temprano en el area de Holmul: el caso de La Sufricaya," in: Laporte, J. P., Arroyo, B., Escobedo, H. and Mejía, H. (eds) *XVI Simposio de Investigaciones de Arqueología de Guatemala*. Guatemala: Museo Nacional de Arqueología y Etnología 275–280.

Tomasic, J. and Fahsen, F. (2004) "Exploracione preliminares en Tres Islas, Peten," in: Laporte, J. P., Arroyo, B., Escobedo, H. and Mejía, H. (eds) *XVII Simposio de Investigaciones Arqueológicas en Guatemala*. Guatemala: Museo Nacional de Arqueología y Etnología, 819–822.

Tourtellot, G., Estrada-Belli, F., Rose, J. and Hammond, N. (2003) "Late Classic Maya Heterarchy, Hierarchy, and Landscape at La Milpa, Belize," in: Scarborough, V. L., Valdez, J. F. and Dunning, N. (eds) *Heterarchy, Political Economy, and the Ancient Maya: The Three Rivers Region of the East–Central Yucatan Peninsula*. Tucson: Arizona University Press.

Tozzer, A. M. (1911) *A Preliminary Study of the Prehistoric Ruins of Tikal, Guatemala: A Report of the Peabody Museum Expedition, 1909–1910*. Cambridge, MA: Peabody Museum of American Archaeology and Ethnology, Harvard University.

——(1941) *Landa's Relacíon de las cosas de Yucatán: A Translation*. Cambridge, MA: Peabody Museum of Archaeology and Ethnology, Harvard University.

—— (1957) *Chichen Itza and its Cenote of Sacrifice: A Comparative Study of Contemporaneous Maya and Toltec*. Cambridge, MA: Peabody Museum.

Trik, A. S. (1963) "The Splendid Tomb of Temple I at Tikal, Guatemala." *Expedition*, 6(1), 2–18.

Uriarte, M. T. (1999) "The Painting of Cacaxtla," in: De La Fuente, B., Falcon, T., Ruiz Gallut, M. E., Solis, F., Staines Cicero, L. and Uriarte, M. T. (eds)

The Pre-Columbian Painting: Murals of the Mesoamerica. Mexico: Jaca Books/ CONACULTA Direccion General de Publicaciones, 71–134.

Vaillant, G. C. (1947) "Tiger Masks and Platyrrhine and Bearded Figures from Middle America," in: *Proceedings of the 27th International Congress of Americanists, Mexico City, 1939*, 131–135.

Valdés, J. A., Fahsen, F. and Escobedo, H. L. (1999) *Reyes Tumbas y Palacios: la historia Dinástica de Uaxactún*. Mexico, D.F.: Universidad Nacional Autonoma.

Varela Torrecilla, C. and Braswell, G. E. (2003) "Teotihuacan and Oxkintok: New Perpectives from Yucatan," in: Braswell, G. E. (ed.) *The Maya and Teotihuacan: Reinterpreting Early Classic Interaction*. Austin: University of Texas Press, 249–272.

Wahl, D., Schreiner, T., Hansen, R. D. and Starratt, S. (2006a) "Evidence of Holocene Environmental Change from Lago Paixban, a Maya Wetland in Northern Peten." Paper presented at the 102nd Annual Meeting of the Association of American Geographers, Chicago, IL.

Wahl, D., Byrne, R., Schreiner, T. and Hansen, R. (2006b) " Holocene Vegetation Change in the Northern Peten and its Implications for Maya Prehistory." *Quaternary Research*, 65, 380–389.

Wahl, D. and Estrada-Belli, F., (2009) "Human–Environment Interactions in the Holmul Region, Peten, Guatemala, from the Preclassic to Postclassic." Paper presented at the 74th Annual Meeting of the Society for American Archaeology, Atlanta, GA.

Webb, M. C. (1973) "The Peten Maya Decline Viewed in the Perspective of State Formation," in: Culbert, P. T. (ed.) *The Classic Maya Collapse*. Albuquerque: University of New Mexico Press, 367–404.

Webster, D. L. (1976) *Defensive earthworks at Becan, Campeche, Mexico: Implications for Maya Warfare*. New Orleans, LA: Middle American Research Institute, Tulane University.

—— (1977) "Warfare and the Evolution of Maya Civilization," in: Adams, R. E. W. (ed.) *The Origins of Maya Civilization*. Albuquerque: University of New Mexico Press, 335–372.

—— (2002) *The Fall of the Ancient Maya: Solving the Mystery of the Maya Collapse*. New York: Thames & Hudson.

—— (2004) *The Tikal Earthworks Revisited*. University Park: Department of Anthropology, Pennsylvania State University.

Willey, G. R. (1953) *Prehistoric Settlement Patterns in the Virú Valley, Perú*. Washington, D.C.: Smithsonian Institution.

—— (1970) *The Real Xe Ceramics of Seibal, Peten, Guatemala*. Cambridge, MA: Peabody Museum of Archaeology and Ethnology, Harvard University.

—— (1973) *The Altar de Sacrificios Excavations: General Summary and Conclusions*. Cambridge, MA: Peabody Museum of Archaeology and Ethnology, Harvard University.

—— (1977) "The Rise of Maya Civilization: A Summary View," in: Adams, R. E. W. (ed.) *The Origins of Maya Civilization*. Albuquerque: University of New Mexico Press, 383–423.

Willey, G. R., Coe, W. R. and Sharer, R. J. (1975) *Un proyecto para el desarrollo de investigación y preservación arqueológica en Copán (Honduras) y vecindad, 1976–81*. Tegucigalpa: Instituto Hondureño de Antropología e Historia.

Willey, G. R., Bullard, W. R., Glass, J. B. and Gifford, J. (1965) *Prehistoric Maya*

Settlements in the Belize Valley. Cambridge, MA: Peabody Museum Archaeology and Ethnology, Harvard University.

Willey, G. R. and Gifford, J. (1961) "Pottery of the Holmul I Style from Barton Ramie, British Honduras," in: Lothrop, S. K. (ed.) *Essays in Precolumbian Art and Archaeology.* Cambridge, MA: Harvard University Press, 151–170.

Willey, G. R. and Sabloff, J. A. (1974) *A History of American Archaeology.* San Francisco, CA: W. H. Freeman.

Willey, G. R., Smith, A. L. and Sabloff, J. A. (1982) *Excavations at Seibal, Department of Peten, Guatemala.* Cambridge, MA: Peabody Museum of Archaeology and Ethnology, Harvard University.

Winfield Capitaine, F. (1992) *La Estela 1 de La Mojarra.* Mexico, D.F.: Universidad Nacional Autonoma de Mexico.

Wylie, A. (1991) "Gender Theory and the Archaeological Record: Why Is There No Archaeology of Gender?" in: Gero, J. M. and Conkey, M. W. (eds) *Engendering Archaeology: Women and Prehistory.* Cambridge, MA: Blackwell, 31–54.

Yoffee, N. (2005) *Myths of the Archaic State: Evolution of the Earliest Cities, States and Civilizations.* Cambridge: Cambridge University Press.

INDEX

Page numbers in **bold** refer to illustrations